THE CHILDREN'S BIBLE

PREFACE

"The Children's Bible" provides, in simple English, a translation of selections from both the Old and the New Testament. These selections have been made as a result of more than twenty-five years of observation and study. The text is that of the Bible itself, but in the language of the child, so that it may easily be read to the younger children and by those who are older. It is not in words of one syllable, for while the child is reading the Bible he should gradually learn the meaning of new words and idioms.

The Bible contains the foundations on which the religious life of the child must be built. The immortal stories and songs of the Old and New Testaments are his richest inheritance from the past. To give him this heritage in language and form that he can understand and enjoy is the duty and privilege of his parents and teachers.

It is hoped that "The Children's Bible" will meet the need and the demand, which parents and educators alike have long felt and often expressed, for a simple translation of selections from the Bible most suited to the needs and the interests of the child. It is also believed that after the child has learned to appreciate and love these stories and songs, he will be eager and able to read the Bible as a whole with genuine interest and understanding.

* * * * *

CONTENTS

THE OLD TESTAMENT

PSALMS

THE SAYINGS OF THE WISE

THE NEW TESTAMENT

LIST OF ILLUSTRATIONS

THE OLD TESTAMENT

THE STORY OF CREATION

In the beginning God made the heavens and the earth, and while the earth was still unformed, God said, "Let there be light," and there was light. And God saw that the light was good. Then God separated the light from the darkness. And God called the light Day and the darkness Night. And there was an evening and a morning, making the first day.

And God said, "Let there be a sky and let it divide the waters that are below from the waters that are above the sky." And it was done. And God called the sky the Heavens. And there was an evening and a morning, making the second day.

And God said, "Let the waters under the heavens be brought together, and let the dry land appear." And it was done. And God called the dry land Earth and the waters that were brought together Seas. And God saw that it was good.

And God said, "Let plants and trees grow from the earth." And it was done. And plants and trees grew from the earth, each plant bringing forth its own kind of seed and each tree its own kind of fruit, and God saw that it was good. And there was an evening and a morning, making the third day.

And God said, "Let there be lights in the heavens to separate the night from the day. Let them be signs to mark the seasons, the days, and the years. Let them be lights in the heavens to light the earth." And it was done. So God made the two great lights (the sun and the moon): the greater to rule the day and the lesser to rule the night. God made the stars also and placed them in the heavens to throw light upon the earth. And God saw that it was good. And there was an evening and a morning, making the fourth day.

And God said, "Let the waters bring forth many living creatures and let birds fly above the earth and in the sky." And God made large sea-monsters and all kinds of living creatures with which the waters abound, and all kinds of birds. And God saw that it was good. And he blessed them, saying, "Increase and fill the waters in the seas, and let the birds increase on the earth." And there was an evening and a morning, making the fifth day.

And God said, "Let the earth bring forth all kinds of living creatures, cattle and creeping things and wild beasts." And it was done. So God made all the different kinds of wild beasts, and the cattle, and everything that crawls upon the ground. And God saw that it was good.

And God said, "Let us make man like ourselves. Let him rule over the fish in the sea, the birds of the sky, the cattle, the wild beasts and all the living things that crawl upon the ground." And God made man like himself, like God he made him. He made them male and female.

And God blessed them, and said to them, "Have children, increase, live all over the earth, and conquer it; rule over the fish of the sea, the birds of the sky, and over every living thing that crawls upon the ground."

And God said, "See, to you I give every plant which grows on all the earth, and every tree which bears fruit with its own kind of seed. It shall be food for you. And to every wild beast and to every bird of the sky and to every thing that crawls on the earth and is alive, I give every green herb for food." And it was done.

And when God saw everything that he had made, he saw that it was very good. And there was an evening and a morning, making the sixth day.

And the heavens and the earth were finished and all that there was in them. And on the seventh day when God had finished the work which he had done, he rested from all his work. And God blessed the seventh day and made it holy, for in it he rested from all the work which he had done.

GOD'S GOOD GIFTS TO MAN

At the time when Jehovah made earth and heaven, no trees or plants grew on the earth, for Jehovah had not yet sent the rain; and there was no man to till the soil; but a mist rose from the earth and watered the ground.

Then Jehovah made man out of dust taken from the ground and breathed into him the breath of life; and man became a living being. And Jehovah planted a garden in Eden, far in the East; and out of the ground he made grow all kinds of trees that are pleasant to look at and good for food, also the tree of life and the tree that gives the knowledge of good and evil.

Then Jehovah took the man and put him in the garden of Eden to till it and to care for it. And Jehovah gave the man this command: "You may eat all you wish from every tree of the garden, except from the tree that gives the knowledge of good and evil; from this you shall not eat, for if you eat from it you shall surely die."

Then Jehovah said, "It is not good for the man to be alone; I will make a companion for him." So out of the ground Jehovah made all the wild beasts and birds, and brought them to the man to see what he would name them; and whatever he called each living thing that became its name. But for the man himself there was found no companion suited to him.

Then Jehovah made the man fall into a deep sleep; and while he slept, he took one of his ribs and closed up its place with flesh. The rib which he had taken from the man, Jehovah made into a woman and brought her to the man. Then the man said, "Because she was made from my body, she shall be called Woman."

THE FIRST DISOBEDIENCE

Now the serpent was more deceitful than any other animal that Jehovah had made; and it said to the woman, "Has God really said, 'You shall not eat from any tree of the garden'?" The woman answered, "We may eat of the fruit of all the trees of the garden except the fruit of the tree which is in the middle of the garden, for God has said, 'You shall not eat from it, nor shall you touch it; for if you do, you shall die.'" Then the serpent said to the woman, "You shall not surely die; for God knows that as soon as you eat of it your eyes will be opened, and you will know what is good and what is evil."

When the woman saw that the tree was good for food, beautiful to look at and that it would make her wise, she took some of its fruit and ate it. Then she gave some to her husband who was with her, and he ate.

Then the eyes of both of them were opened, so that they knew that they were naked; and they sewed fig-leaves together and made girdles for themselves. When they heard the sound of the footsteps of Jehovah, as he was walking in the garden in the cool of the day, the man and his wife hid from him among the trees of the garden.

And Jehovah called to the man and said to him, "Where are you?" and he answered, "I heard the sound of thy footsteps in the garden and I was afraid, because I was naked; so I hid myself." Jehovah said, "Who told you that you were naked? Have you eaten from the tree from which I forbade you to eat?" The man answered, "The woman whom thou didst give to me—she gave me fruit from the tree and I ate." Jehovah said to the woman, "What is this that you have done?" The woman replied, "The serpent deceived me, and I ate."

Then Jehovah said to the serpent, "Because you have done this, you shall be hated more than all beasts. You shall crawl on your belly and eat dust all your life, and men and serpents shall always be enemies. They shall bruise your head, and you shall wound them on the heel."

To the woman he said, "I will greatly increase your trouble and your pain, and you shall be subject to your husband, and he shall rule over you."

But to the man he said, "Because you have listened to your wife and have eaten of the tree from which I forbade you to eat, as long as you live you shall earn a living only by hard work. By hard work shall you raise food to eat. And you shall die and your body go back to the ground, for from dust you were made, and to dust you shall return!"

And Jehovah made garments of skins for the man and his wife, and clothed them. And he sent them out of the garden of Eden to till the ground.

CAIN AND HIS BROTHER ABEL

Adam named his wife Eve, because she was the mother of all living beings. She had two sons, Cain and Abel. Abel was a shepherd, but Cain was a farmer.

One day Cain brought, as an offering to Jehovah, some fruit and grain that he had grown. Abel, too, brought some of the best animals of his flock and sacrificed their fat pieces to Jehovah. Jehovah was pleased with Abel and his offering, but Cain and his offering did not please him.

This made Cain very angry and his face showed it. So Jehovah said to Cain, "Why are you angry and why do you scowl? If you do what is right and good, will not your offering be accepted? But if you do wrong, sin crouches like a wild beast at the door and the desire to sin will overcome you; but you should master it."

Cain said to his brother Abel, "Let us go into the field." And while they were in the field, Cain struck his brother Abel and killed him.

When Jehovah said to Cain, "Where is your brother Abel?" Cain answered, "I do not know; am I my brother's keeper?" Jehovah said, "What have you done? Hark! your brother's blood is crying to me from the ground. Even now you are condemned by the very ground that has opened to receive your brother's blood from your hand. Whenever you till the ground, it shall no longer yield to you its strength; you shall be a tramp and a wanderer on the earth."

Then Cain said to Jehovah, "My punishment is more than I can bear. See, thou hast driven me out to-day from this land, and I shall no longer be able to worship thee; I shall become a tramp and a wanderer on the earth, and whoever finds me will kill me."

But Jehovah said to him, "If any one kills you, he shall be punished sevenfold." So Jehovah placed a mark on Cain, to keep any one who found him from killing him. And Cain went out from Jehovah's presence and lived as a wanderer, away from Eden.

NOAH AND THE GREAT FLOOD

When Jehovah saw that men were growing more wicked in the world and that their thoughts were always evil, he was greatly grieved and regretted that he had made man. Therefore, Jehovah said, "I will completely destroy all living beings from off the earth, for I regret that I have made them."

But Noah had won Jehovah's favor. So Jehovah said to Noah, "I have decided to put an end to all living beings, for the earth is filled with their wicked acts. I am going to destroy them from the earth. Make yourself an ark of cypress wood. Build rooms in the ark, and cover it within and without with pitch. This is how you shall build it: the ark shall be five hundred feet long, eighty feet wide, and fifty feet high. Make a roof for it and place the door on the side. Build it with lower, second, and third stories. For I am about to bring floods of water upon the earth to destroy every living creature in which is the breath of life. Every creature that is on the earth shall die."

Then Jehovah said to Noah, "Enter with all your household into the ark, for I see that of all the people who are now alive you alone are upright. Of all the beasts that are fit for food and sacrifice you shall take with you seven, the male and the female; but of the beasts that are not fit for food and sacrifice two, the male and the female; and of the wild birds that are fit for food and sacrifice seven, to keep each kind alive on all the earth. After seven days I will send rain on the earth for forty days and forty nights; and I will destroy every living thing that I have made."

Then Noah did all that Jehovah commanded him. When the waters of the flood came upon the earth, he, his sons, his wife, and his sons' wives, together with the beasts that were fit for food and sacrifice and the beasts that were not fit, and the birds, and everything that creeps upon the ground, entered the ark because of the waters of the flood.

The rain fell upon the earth forty days and forty nights, and Jehovah shut Noah in the ark. And the waters rose higher and higher and raised up the ark, and it was lifted high above the earth. All creatures living on the land died. Noah only was left and they who were with him in the ark.

Then God remembered Noah and all the beasts and all the animals that were with him in the ark. And God caused a wind to blow over the earth, and the flood went down, the rain from heaven ceased, and the waters withdrew more and more from the land.

After forty days Noah opened the window of the ark and sent out a raven; and it kept going to and fro until the waters were dried up on the earth. He also sent out a dove to see if the waters had gone from the surface of the earth. But the dove found no rest for her foot, and so returned to him to the ark, for the waters covered the whole earth. Therefore, Noah reached out his hand and took her and brought her back into the ark.

Then he waited seven days longer and again sent out the dove from the ark. And the dove came in to him at dusk; and in her mouth was a freshly plucked olive-leaf. So Noah knew that the waters had gone from the earth. And he waited seven days more and again sent out the dove, but it did not return to him.

So Noah took off the covering of the ark and looked and saw that the surface of the ground was dry. Then he, with his sons, his wife, and his sons' wives, went out of the ark.

And Noah built an altar to Jehovah and took one of every beast and bird that was fit for sacrifice and offered burnt-offerings on the altar. And Jehovah said to himself, "I will never again condemn the ground because of man, nor will I again destroy every living creature, as I have done. While the earth remains, seedtime and harvest, cold and heat, summer and winter, day and night, shall not cease."

And God said, "This is the sign of the solemn agreement that I make for all time between me and you and every living creature that is with you: I have placed my rainbow in the cloud and it shall be the sign of the solemn agreement between me and the people who live on the earth. Whenever I bring a cloud over the earth and the rainbow is seen in the cloud, I will remember the agreement which is between me and you and every living creature; and the waters shall never again become a flood to destroy them."

THE STORY OF THE TOWER OF BABEL

All the people of the earth spoke one language; and as they travelled westward, they found a broad valley in the land of Babylonia, and made their home there.

Then they said one to another, "Come, let us make bricks and thoroughly bake them." So they had bricks for stone and asphalt for mortar. And they said, "Come, let us build us a city, and a tower whose top will touch the heavens, and thus make a landmark, that we may not be scattered over all the earth."

But when Jehovah came down to see the city and the tower men had built, he said, "See, they are one people and all have one language. This is but the beginning, and now nothing which they plan to do will seem too difficult for them. Come, let us go down and confuse their language, that they may not understand one another."

So Jehovah scattered them from there over all the earth; and they stopped building the city. Therefore they named it Babel, which means Confusion, for there Jehovah confused the language of all the people on the earth and scattered them over the whole world.

Building the Tower of Babel
Painted by J. James Tissot

ABRAHAM, THE FRIEND OF GOD AND MAN

The sons of Noah who came out of the ark were Shem, Ham and Japheth. Terah, a descendant of Shem, was the father of Abraham, Nahor and Haran; and Haran was the father of Lot.

Jehovah said to Abraham, "Go from your country, your relatives, and your father's house to the land that I will show you. And I will make of you a great nation; and I will surely bless you and make your name famous, so that you shall be a blessing. And all the families of the earth shall ask for themselves a blessing like your own."

So Abraham set out, as Jehovah had commanded him; and Lot went with him. Abraham was seventy-five years old when he left Haran. He took Sarah his wife and Lot his brother's son and everything that they had, and started for the land of Canaan.

Abraham passed through the land to a place called Shechem, to the oak of Moreh. There Jehovah appeared to Abraham and said, "To your children will I give this land." There Abraham built an altar to Jehovah who had appeared to him. From there he removed to the hill near Bethel and pitched his tent with Bethel on one side and Ai on the other, and there too he built an altar to Jehovah and prayed to him.

Now Abraham was very rich in cattle, in silver, and in gold; Lot also, who went with Abraham, had so many flocks and herds and tents that the land was not rich enough to support them both. So when there was a quarrel between Lot's herdsmen and Abraham's herdsmen, Abraham said to Lot, "I beg of you, let there be no quarrel between me and you, nor between my herdsmen and yours, for we are relatives. Is not the whole land before you? I beg of you, separate yourself from me. If you go to the left, then I will go to the right; or if you go to the right, then I will go to the left."

So Lot looked about and saw that all the plain of the Jordan, as far as Zoar, was well watered everywhere, like a garden of Jehovah. So Lot chose for himself all the valley of the Jordan, and lived in the cities of the plain and moved his tent as far as Sodom. But the men of Sodom were very wicked and sinned against Jehovah.

Jehovah said to Abraham, after Lot had gone away from him, "Lift up your eyes and look from the place where you are northward, southward, eastward and westward, for all the land that you see I will give to you and to your children forever. I will make them as many as the dust of the earth, so that if a man can count the dust of the earth, then your children may also be counted. Rise, walk through the length and breadth of the land, for I will give it to you."

Then Abraham moved his tent and lived in the oak grove of Mamre, which is in Hebron, and built there an altar to Jehovah.

Jehovah also appeared to Abraham by the oaks of Mamre, as he was sitting at the entrance of his tent in the heat of the day; and, as he looked up, three men stood there before him. As soon as he saw them, he ran from the entrance of his tent to meet them and bowed to the ground and said, "Sirs, if you are willing to do me a favor, do not, I beg of you, pass by your servant. Since you have come to your servant, let a little water be brought, that you may wash your feet, and lie down under the tree. And let me bring some food, that you may refresh yourselves; afterward you may go on your way." They replied, "Do as you have said."

So Abraham hastened to Sarah's tent and said, "Make ready quickly four measures of fine meal, knead it, and make cakes." Abraham also ran to the herd, and took a calf that was tender and good, and gave it to the servant, and he prepared it quickly. Then Abraham took curd and milk, with the calf which he had prepared, and served them; and he waited on them under the tree, while they ate.

Then they said to him, "Where is your wife?" He said, "There, within the tent." One of them said, "I will surely return to you about nine months from now, and then, Sarah your wife shall have a son."

LOT'S ESCAPE FROM A WICKED CITY

And Abraham went along with them to start them on their way. Jehovah said, "The complaint has come that the people of Sodom and Gomorrah have committed great and terrible sins. I will go down and see whether they have done exactly as the complaint comes to me; and if they have not, I will know."

Then the men turned from there and looked off in the direction of Sodom.

Then Abraham drew near to Jehovah and said, "Wilt thou sweep away the righteous with the wicked? Suppose there are within the city fifty people who are righteous. Wilt thou sweep away and not spare the place for the fifty righteous who are in it? Far be it from thee to do this: to slay the righteous with the wicked! And that the righteous should be treated as the wicked, far be it from thee! Shall not the Judge of all the earth do what is just?" Jehovah said, "If I find in the city of Sodom fifty who are righteous, I will spare the whole place for their sake." Abraham answered, "I have dared to speak to Jehovah, even though I am but dust and ashes. Suppose there be five lacking of the fifty righteous. Wilt thou sweep away all the city for lack of five?" Jehovah said, "I will not sweep it away, if I find forty-five there."

Then Abraham spoke to him again, and said, "Suppose forty are found there?" He replied, "For the sake of forty I will not do it." Then Abraham said, "Oh, let not Jehovah be angry, but let me speak. Suppose thirty are found there?" He answered, "I will not do it, if I find thirty there." Then Abraham said, "Thou seest that I have dared to speak to Jehovah. Suppose twenty are found there?" He replied, "For the sake of twenty I will not destroy it." Then Abraham said, "Oh, let not Jehovah be angry, but let me speak just once more. Suppose ten are found there?" And he said, "For the sake of the ten I will not destroy it." Then Jehovah went his way, and Abraham returned home.

Two angels in human form came to Sodom in the evening, as Lot was sitting at the gate of Sodom. When Lot saw them, he rose up to meet them, and he bowed with his face to the earth and said, "Sirs, turn aside, I beg of you, into your servant's house and spend the night and wash your feet; then you can rise up early and go on your way." They said, "No, we will spend the night in the street." But he urged them so strongly that they went with him and entered his house. And he made a feast for them and baked bread made without yeast, and they ate.

But before they had lain down, the people of Sodom, both young and old, all the people from every quarter, surrounded the house. And they called out to Lot, "Where are the men who came in to you to-night? Bring them out to us that we may do to them what we desire."

Then Lot went out to them at the entrance of his house, but he shut the door after him. And he said, "I beg of you, my friends, do not do what is wrong. Do nothing to these men, for they have come under the shadow of my roof." But they replied, "Stand back, or we will treat you worse than them." And they pressed hard against Lot and advanced to break the door. But the men reached out and drew Lot to them into the house and shut the door. Then they smote the men who were at the door of the house, both small and great, with blindness, so that they grew tired of searching for the door.

Then the men said to Lot, "Have you any one else here? Bring your sons-in-law, your sons, and daughters, and whoever you have in the city out of this place, for we are about to destroy it, because great complaint concerning the people has come to Jehovah and he has sent us to destroy it." So Lot went out and said to his sons-in-law, "Up, go out of this place, for Jehovah will destroy the city." But his sons-in-law thought he was only jesting.

When the dawn appeared, the angels urged Lot, saying, "Get up, take your wife and your two daughters that you may not be swept away in the punishment of the city." When he hesitated, the men took him by the hand and led him and his wife and his two daughters outside the city, for Jehovah was merciful to him.

When they had brought them outside, they said, "Run for your life; do not look behind you nor stay anywhere in the plain. Escape to the heights, that you may not be swept away!" But Lot said to them, "Oh, sirs, not so! See, your servant has found favor with you, and you have shown great mercy to me in saving my life. I cannot escape to the heights, lest some evil overtake me, and I die. See now, this village is near enough to run to, and it is small. Oh, let me escape there, and my life will be saved." Jehovah said to him, "I have also granted you this favor, in that I will not destroy the village of which you have spoken. Make haste, escape to it, for I can do nothing until you arrive there."

The sun had risen when Lot came to Zoar. Then Jehovah caused brimstone and fire from heaven to rain upon Sodom and Gomorrah, and he destroyed those cities and all the plain, with all the people who lived in it and all that grew on the ground. But Lot's wife, who was following him, looked back, and she became a pillar of salt.

Early in the morning Abraham rose and went to the place where he had stood before Jehovah; and as he looked toward Sodom and Gomorrah and all the plain, he saw the smoke of the land going up as the smoke of a smelting-furnace.

GOD'S CARE FOR THE BOY ISHMAEL

Hagar and Ishmael in the Wilderness
Painted by W. L. Taylor

Jehovah remembered what he had told Sarah, and he did as he had promised. So Sarah had a son, and when the child grew up, Abraham made a great feast on the day that he was weaned. But Sarah saw the son of Hagar the Egyptian and of Abraham playing with her son Isaac. And she said to Abraham, "Drive out this slave girl and her son, for the son of this slave girl shall not be heir with my son Isaac." This request was very displeasing to Abraham because the boy was his son. But Jehovah said to Abraham, "Do not be displeased because of the boy and because of your slave girl. Listen to all that Sarah says to you, for Isaac only and his children shall bear your name. But I will also make of the son of the slave girl a great nation, because he is your son."

Then Abraham rose early in the morning and took bread and a skin of water and gave it to Hagar; and he put the boy upon her shoulder and sent her away. So she set out and wandered in the desert of Beersheba. When the water in the skin was gone, she left the child under one of the desert shrubs and went a short distance away and sat down opposite him, for she said, "Let me not see the child die."

While she sat there, the boy began to cry; and Jehovah heard the cry of the boy, and said, "What troubles you, Hagar? Fear not, for Jehovah has heard the cry of the boy. Rise, lift him up, and hold him fast by the hand, for I will make him a great nation." And Jehovah opened her eyes and she saw a well of water. Then she went and filled the skin with water and gave the boy a drink.

And Jehovah cared for the boy; and when he grew up, he lived in the wilderness of Paran and became a bowman. And his mother secured a wife for him from Egypt.

ABRAHAM'S LOYALTY TO GOD

Later Jehovah tested Abraham, saying to him, "Abraham"; and he answered, "Here am I." Jehovah said, "Take your son, your only son

Isaac, whom you love, and go to the land of Moriah, and offer him there as a burnt-offering on one of the mountains of which I shall tell you."

So Abraham rose early in the morning and saddled his ass and took two of his servants with him, and his son Isaac. When he had split the wood for the burnt-offering, he set out for the place of which God had told him. On the third day, when Abraham looked up and saw the place in the distance, he said to his servants, "Stay here with the ass, while I and the lad go over there. When we have worshipped, we will come back to you."

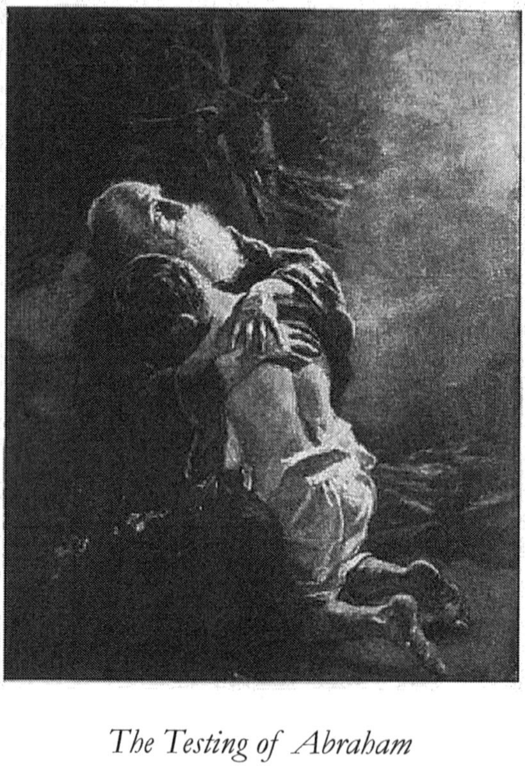

The Testing of Abraham
Painted by Fritz von Uhde

Then Abraham took the wood for the burnt-offering and laid it on Isaac, his son. And he took the fire and the knife, and they both went on together. And Isaac spoke to Abraham his father and said, "My father!" and Abraham answered, "Yes, my son." Isaac said, "Here is the fire and the wood, but where is the lamb for a burnt-offering?" Abraham answered, "My son, God will himself provide a lamb for a burnt-offering." So the two went on together.

When they came to the place of which God had told him, Abraham built the altar there and laid the wood on it and bound Isaac his son and laid him on the altar upon the wood. Then Abraham reached out his hand, and took the knife to kill his son. But the angel of Jehovah called to him from heaven, saying, "Abraham, Abraham!" and he answered, "Here am I." And he said, "Do not put your hand upon the boy, nor do anything to him, for now I know that you love God, for you have not refused to give your son, your only son, to him."

Then Abraham looked up, and he saw a ram caught in the thicket by his horns. So Abraham took the ram and offered him up as a burnt-offering instead of his son. And he named the place Jehovah-jireh, which means, "Jehovah will Provide."

The angel of Jehovah again called to Abraham and said, "Jehovah declares, 'Because you have done this thing and have not kept back your son, your only son, I will surely bless you, and I will make your children as many as the stars of the heavens and as the sand, which is on the seashore, so that they shall conquer their enemies, and all the nations of the earth shall ask for themselves a blessing like theirs, because you have obeyed my command.'"

HOW REBEKAH BECAME THE WIFE OF ISAAC

When Abraham was very old and Jehovah had blessed him in every way, Abraham said to the eldest of his household servants, who had charge of all his affairs, "Put your hand under my hip, while I make you promise by Jehovah, the God of heaven and earth, that you will not let my son marry one of the daughters of the Canaanites, among whom

I live, but that you will go to my own country and to my relatives and there get a wife for my son Isaac." The servant said to him, "Perhaps the woman will not be willing to follow me to this land. Must I then take your son back to the land from which you came?" Abraham said to him, "See to it that you do not take my son back there. Jehovah, the God of heaven, who took me from my father's house and from my native land and who solemnly promised me, 'To your children I will give this land,' will send his angel before you and there you will get a wife for my son. But if the woman is not willing to come with you, then you will be free from this promise to me; only never take my son back there." So the servant put his hand under Abraham's hip and made the promise.

Then the servant took ten of his master's camels and set out with precious gifts from his master. So he went to the town of Nahor. And he made the camels kneel down outside the town by the well in the evening, at the time when women go out to draw water. Then he said, "O Jehovah, the God of my master Abraham, give me, I pray thee, success to-day, and show kindness to my master Abraham. Here I am standing by the spring of water, and the daughters of the men of the town are coming out to draw water. May that young woman to whom I shall say, 'Please let down your water-jar that I may drink'; and who answers, 'Drink and I will also water your camels,' may she be the one thou hast chosen for thy servant Isaac. By this I shall know that thou hast shown kindness to my master."

Then even before he was through speaking, Rebekah, who was the grand-daughter of Nahor, Abraham's brother, came out with her water-jar upon her shoulder. She was very beautiful and unmarried. She went down to the spring, filled her jar, and came up. Then the servant ran to meet her and said, "Please let me drink a little water from your jar." She answered, "Drink, sir," and quickly let down her water-jar from her shoulder upon her hand and gave him a drink.

When she had finished giving him a drink she said, "I will draw water for your camels also, until they have finished drinking." So she quickly emptied her jar into the trough and ran again to the well to draw water, and drew for all his camels. Meanwhile the man was silently gazing at her in order to find out whether Jehovah had made his journey successful or not.

As soon as the camels had finished drinking, the man took a gold ring, five ounces in weight, and put it in her nose, and put on her arms two golden bracelets weighing five ounces, and said, "Whose daughter are you? Tell me, I beg of you. Is there room in your father's house for us to spend the night?" She answered, "I am the grand-daughter of Milcah and Nahor. We have plenty of straw and feed, and there is a place for you to spend the night."

Then the man bowed his head and worshipped Jehovah, saying, "Blessed be Jehovah, the God of my master Abraham, who has continued to show his mercy and his faithfulness toward my master. As for me, Jehovah has led me on the way to the house of my master's relatives."

Then the young woman ran and told these things to her mother's family. Now Rebekah had a brother named Laban; and Laban ran out to the man at the spring. And when he saw the bracelets on his sister's hands and the ring, and when he heard Rebekah say, "This is what the man said to me," he went to the man, who was still standing by the camels at the spring, and said, "Come in, you who are blessed by Jehovah! Why do you stand outside? For I have cleared the house and have room for the camels." So he brought the man into the house and took the packs off the camels and furnished straw and feed for them, and water to wash his feet and the feet of the men who were with him.

But when food was set before him to eat, he said, "I will not eat until I have made known my errand." They answered, "Speak." He said, "I am Abraham's servant; and Jehovah has blessed my master greatly, so that he has become very rich. He has given him flocks and herds, silver and gold, servants, and camels and asses. Now Sarah, my master's wife, had a son when she was old, and my master has given him all that he has. My master also made me promise, saying, 'Do not let my son marry one of the daughters of the Canaanites, in whose land I live, but go to my father's home and to my relatives and there find a wife for my son.'

Rebekah Comes to Isaac
Painted by W. L. Taylor

"When I said to my master, 'What if the woman will not follow me?' he said to me, 'Jehovah, whom I love and serve, will send his angel with you and make you successful, and you will find for my son a wife from among my relatives and my father's family. Then you shall be free from your promise to me. But if you go to my family and they do not give her to you, you shall also be free from your promise to me.' So I came to-day to the spring and said, 'O Jehovah, the God of my master Abraham, see, I am standing by the spring of water, if thou wilt make the errand on which I am going successful, then let the young woman who comes to draw, to whom I say, Please give me a little water from your jar to drink, and who shall say to me, Drink, and I will also draw for your camels, let that one be the woman whom Jehovah has chosen for my master's son.'

"Even before I was through speaking, Rebekah came out with her water-jar on her shoulder and went down to the spring and drew water. And when I said to her, 'Please let me drink,' she quickly let down her water-jar from her shoulder and answered, 'Drink, and I will also water your camels.' So I drank, and she also watered the camels. Then I asked her, 'Whose daughter are you?' And she said, 'The grand-daughter of Nahor and Milcah.' So I put the ring in her nose and the bracelets on her arms. And I bowed my head and worshipped and blessed Jehovah the God of my master Abraham who had led me on the right way to find the daughter of my master's brother for his son. Tell me whether or not you will deal kindly and truly with my master, so that I shall know what to do!"

Then Laban and his family answered, "The matter is in the hands of Jehovah. We cannot say either 'yes' or 'no.' See, Rebekah is before you; take her and go and let her be the wife of your master's son, as Jehovah has said."

When Abraham's servant heard their words, he bowed to the ground before Jehovah. Then he brought out gold and silver ornaments and clothing and gave them to Rebekah. He also gave costly gifts to her brother and to her mother. And he and the men who were with him ate and drank and spent the night there.

When they rose in the morning, the servant said, "Send me away to my master." But Rebekah's brother and mother answered, "Let the young woman stay with us a month or at least ten days; after that she may go." But he said to them, "Do not delay me, for Jehovah has given me success. Send me away that I may go to my master."

Then they said, "We will call the young woman and ask her." So they called Rebekah and said to her, "Will you go with this man?" She answered, "I will go." So they sent away their sister Rebekah and her nurse with Abraham's servant and his men.

They also blessed Rebekah, saying to her, "Our sister! may your children and their children become thousands and thousands!" Then Rebekah set out with her maids and, riding upon the camels, they followed the man. So the servant took Rebekah and went away.

Now Abraham had given all that he had to Isaac and had breathed his last, dying in a good old age, satisfied with living. In the evening, when Isaac had gone out in the field to meditate, he looked up and saw camels coming. Rebekah too looked up, and when she saw Isaac, she quickly alighted from the camel and said to the servant, "Who is this man walking in the field to meet us?" When the servant said, "It is my master," she took her veil and covered her face. Then the servant told Isaac all that he had done. And Isaac brought Rebekah to the tent of Sarah his mother, and she became his wife; and he loved her.

HOW JACOB DECEIVED HIS FATHER

Now Isaac prayed to Jehovah for his wife, because she had no children; and Jehovah heard his prayer, and Rebekah became the mother of twin boys. They named one Esau and the other Jacob.

As they grew up, Esau became a skilful hunter, a man who lived out in the fields; but Jacob was a quiet man who stayed about the tents. Isaac loved Esau, for he was fond of game; but Rebekah loved Jacob.

Once when Jacob was preparing a stew, Esau came in from the fields, and he was very hungry; so he said to Jacob, "Let me swallow some of that red stew, for I am very hungry." But Jacob said, "Sell me first of all your right as the eldest." Esau replied, "See, I am nearly dead now! So of what use is this birthright to me?" Jacob said, "First solemnly promise to give it to me." So Esau solemnly promised and sold his birthright to Jacob. Then Jacob gave Esau bread and stewed lentils, and when he had

had something to eat and drink, he got up and went away. In this way Esau gave away his birthright.

When Isaac was so old and so nearly blind that he could not see, he called Esau his oldest son and said to him, "My son." Esau answered, "Here am I." Then Isaac said, "See, I am old and do not know how soon I may die. Now, therefore, take your quiver and your bow and go out into the fields and hunt game for me and prepare for me savory food, such as I love, and bring it to me that I may eat and that I may bless you before I die."

Rebekah was listening when Isaac spoke to his son Esau. So when Esau went into the fields to hunt game, Rebekah said to her son Jacob, "I just now heard your father say to your brother Esau, 'Bring me game and prepare for me savory food that I may eat it and bless you before I die.' Now, my son, do as I tell you: Go to the flock and bring me from there two good kids, and I will make of them savory food for your father, such as he loves. Then take it to him, that he may eat, so that he may bless you before he dies." But Jacob said to Rebekah his mother, "You know that my brother Esau is a hairy man, while I am smooth. Perhaps my father will feel of me; then I shall appear to him as a deceiver, and I shall bring blame upon me and not a blessing." But his mother said to him, "Upon me be the blame, my son; only obey me and go, bring the kids to me." So he went and brought them to his mother, and his mother made savory food such as his father loved.

Rebekah also took the fine clothes of her older son Esau, which she had with her in the tent, and put them on her younger son Jacob. Then she put the skins of the kids upon his hands and upon the smooth part of his neck, and she placed the savory food and the bread which she had prepared in his hand, and he went to his father and said, "My father." Isaac answered, "Here am I; who are you, my son?" Jacob said, "I am Esau your oldest son. I have done as you commanded me. Sit up and eat of my game, that you may bless me." Isaac said to his son, "How very quickly you have found it, my son." He answered, "Yes, because Jehovah your God gave me success."

Then Isaac said to Jacob, "Come here, my son, that I may feel of you to find out whether you are really my son Esau or not." So Jacob went near to Isaac his father, and he felt of him and said, "The voice is the voice of Jacob, but the hands are the hands of Esau. Are you really my son Esau?" Jacob answered, "I am." And Isaac did not recognize him, for his hands were hairy like his brother Esau's. So he blessed him. Then Isaac said, "Bring the food to me, that I may eat of my son's game and bless you." So he brought it to him, and he ate. Jacob also brought him wine, and he drank.

Then his father Isaac said to him, "Come near now and kiss me, my son." As he came near and kissed him, he smelled the smell of his garment, and blessed him.

As soon as Isaac had given Jacob his blessing, and Jacob was about to leave his father, Esau his brother came in from his hunting. He also had made savory food and was bringing it to his father. So he said to him, "Father, rise and eat of your son's game, that you may bless me." But Isaac his father said to him, "Who are you?" He answered, "I am your son, your oldest, Esau." Then Isaac trembled and said, "Who then is he that has hunted game and brought it to me, so that I ate plentifully before you came, and blessed him? Also blessed shall he be!"

When Esau heard the words of his father, he uttered a loud and bitter cry and said to his father, "Bless me, even me also, O my father."

But Isaac said, "Your brother came with deceit and has taken away your blessing." Esau said, "Is it not because he was named Jacob, which means Supplanter, that he has supplanted me these two times: he took my birthright, and now he has taken my blessing!" Then he said, "Have you kept a blessing for me?" Isaac answered Esau, "See, I have made him your master and I have given to him all his relatives as servants and grain and wine as his food. What then can I do for you, my son?" Esau said to his father, "Is that the only blessing you have, my father?" and Esau began to weep aloud. Then Isaac his father answered him:

> "You shall live far from earth's fertile places,
> And away from the dew of heaven.
> By your sword you shall live,
> And your brother you shall serve."

JACOB'S DREAM

Esau hated Jacob because of the blessing which his father had given him. And Esau said to himself, "My father will soon die; then I will kill Jacob, my brother."

When the words of her older son Esau were told to Rebekah, she sent for her younger son Jacob and said to him, "Your brother, Esau, is going to kill you. Now therefore, my son, listen to me: run away to my brother Laban at Haran and stay with him for a time until your brother is no longer angry and he forgets what you have done to him. Then I will send and bring you back. Why should I lose both of you in one day?"

Then Jacob set out from Beersheba and went toward Haran. And when he arrived at a certain place, he passed the night there, because the sun had set. And he took one of the stones from its place and put it under his head and lay down to sleep. Then he dreamed and saw a ladder set up on the earth, and its top reached to heaven; and the angels of God were going up and down on it.

Jehovah also stood beside him and said, "I am Jehovah, the God of Abraham and the God of Isaac. The land on which you lie I will give to you and to your children. See, I am with you, and will keep you wherever you go and will bring you again to this land; for I will not leave you until I have done what I have promised you."

When Jacob awoke from his sleep, he said, "Surely Jehovah is in this place, and I did not know it." And he was filled with awe and said, "This place is the house of God, and this is the gate of heaven."

So Jacob rose early in the morning and took the stone that he had put under his head and set it up as a pillar and poured oil upon the top of it. And he named that place Bethel, which means House of God. Jacob also made this promise, "If God will be with me and protect me on this journey which I am making and give me bread to eat and clothing to put on, and if I return safe and sound to my father's house, then Jehovah shall be my God, and this stone which I have set up as a pillar shall be a house of God. And of all that thou shalt give me I will surely give a tenth to thee."

THE DECEIVER DECEIVED

Then Jacob went on his journey and arrived at the land of the children of the East. And he looked and saw a well in the field, and there were three flocks of sheep lying down by it; for from that well they watered the flocks; but there was a large stone over the well. When all the flocks were gathered there, they used to roll away the stone and water the sheep and then put the stone back in its place over the well.

Jacob said to the men, "My friends, from where do you come?" They said, "We are from Haran." Then he said to them, "Do you know Laban the son of Nahor?" And they said, "We know him." And he said to them, "Is all well with him?" And they said, "All is well; indeed, this is Rachel his daughter coming with the sheep." And he said, "See, the sun is still high! It is not time for the cattle to be gathered together. Water the sheep and feed them." But they said, "We cannot until all the flocks are gathered together, and they roll away the stone from the well; then we will water the sheep."

While he was still speaking with them, Rachel came with her father's sheep; for she was a shepherdess. When Jacob saw Rachel the daughter of Laban, his mother's brother, and Laban's sheep, he went up and rolled the stone from the well and watered the flock of Laban his mother's brother. Then Jacob kissed Rachel and wept aloud. And when Jacob told Rachel that he was a relative of her father and that he was Rebekah's son, she ran and told her father.

As soon as Laban heard about Jacob, his sister's son, he ran to meet him, put his arms around him, kissed him many times, and brought him to his home. When Jacob told Laban all about these things, Laban said to him, "Surely you are my bone and my flesh." So he remained with him a whole month.

Then Laban said to Jacob, "Should you serve me for nothing simply because you are related to me? Tell me what shall be your wages?" Now Laban had two daughters: the name of the older was Leah, and the name of the younger was Rachel. Leah's eyes were weak, but Rachel was beautiful. Jacob loved Rachel, and so he said, "I will serve you seven years for Rachel your younger daughter." And Laban said, "It is better for me to give her to you than to give her to any other man. Stay with me." So Jacob served seven years for Rachel, and they seemed to him but a few days, because he loved her so.

Then Jacob said to Laban, "Give me my wife, for my time is up, and let me marry her." So Laban gathered all the men of the place and made a feast. In the evening he took Leah his daughter and brought her to him, and Jacob received her as his wife.

When in the morning Jacob found it was Leah, he said to Laban, "What is this you have done to me? Did I not serve you for Rachel? Why then have you deceived me?" Laban said, "It is not the custom among us to give the younger in marriage before the older. Remain with this one during the marriage week, then we will give you the other also for the service which you shall give me during seven more years." Jacob did so: he remained with Leah during the marriage week. Then Laban gave him Rachel his daughter to be his wife, but Jacob loved Rachel more than Leah. So he had to serve Laban seven years more.

MEETING A BROTHER WHO HAD BEEN WRONGED

In time Jacob became very wealthy, and he had large flocks, slaves, and asses. But he heard Laban's sons say, "Jacob has taken all that was our father's, and from that which was our father's he has gotten all this wealth." He also saw that Laban did not act toward him the same as before. So Jacob rose and put his sons and his wives upon the camels and drove away all his cattle. He deceived Laban, for he did not tell him that he was fleeing away. So he fled across the river Euphrates, with all that he had, and set out on his way toward Mount Gilead.

Then Jacob sent messengers before him to his brother Esau. And he gave them this command, "Say to my lord Esau: 'Your servant Jacob declares, I have lived with Laban and have stayed until now. I have oxen and asses, flocks and slaves, and I have sent to tell my lord, in order that I may win your favor.'" The messengers returned to Jacob with the report, "We came to your brother Esau, even as he was coming to meet you with four hundred men."

Then Jacob was greatly alarmed and worried. So he divided the people that were with him and the flocks and the herds and the camels into two parts and said, "If Esau comes to the one and attacks and destroys it, then the other which is left can escape."

Jacob also prayed, "O God of my father Abraham and God of my father Isaac, deliver me, I pray thee, from the hand of my brother, from the hand of Esau, for I fear that he will come and attack me and kill the mothers and the children."

Then Jacob took as a present for his brother Esau, two hundred female goats and twenty male goats, two hundred ewes and twenty rams, thirty milch camels and their young, forty cows and ten bulls, twenty female asses and ten young asses. These he put, each drove by itself, in the care of his servants and said to them, "Go on before me and leave a space between the droves."

He gave those in front this command: "When my brother Esau meets you and asks you, 'To whom do you belong? and where are you going? and whose are these before you?' then you shall say, 'To your servant Jacob; it is a present sent by him to my lord Esau; and Jacob himself is just behind us.'" Jacob also commanded the second, and the third, and all that followed the droves, to make the same answer, and to say, "Jacob himself is just behind us." For he said to himself, "I will please him with the present that goes before me, and then, when I meet him, perhaps he will welcome me." So he sent the present over before him; but he himself spent that night in the camp.

Later that night he rose up and took his two wives, his two maid servants, and his eleven children, and sent them over the river Jabbok.

Jacob was left alone, and one wrestled with him until daybreak. When he saw that he did not win against Jacob, he struck the socket of his hip, and the socket of Jacob's hip was strained, as he wrestled with him. Then he said, "Let me go, for the dawn is breaking." But Jacob replied, "I will not let thee go unless you bless me." So he said to him, "What is your name?" He answered, "Jacob." Then he said, "Your name shall be no longer Jacob, but Israel, which means Struggler with God; for you have struggled with God and with men and have won." So he blessed him there. And Jacob called the place Penuel, which means Face of God, for he said, "I have seen God face to face, and my life has been saved."

When Jacob looked up, he saw Esau coming with four hundred men. And he put the maid servants and their children in front, Leah and her children next, and Rachel and her son Joseph in the rear. Then Jacob himself went in front of them, and he bowed down to the ground seven times, as he drew near to his brother. Esau ran to meet him, threw his arms about his neck, and kissed him, and they wept.

When Esau looked up and saw the women and the children, he said, "Who are these with you?" Jacob answered, "The children whom God has so kindly given me." Then the maid servants with their children came up and bowed down to the ground. Leah and her children also came and bowed down, and afterward Joseph and Rachel came up and bowed down before Esau.

Esau asked, "What do you mean by all this company which I met?" Jacob answered, "To win your friendship, my lord." Esau said, "I have enough, my brother; keep what you have." But Jacob replied, "No, if now I have won your favor, receive this present from me to show that you are my friend. Take, I beg of you, the gift that I bring to you, for God has been generous to me, and I have enough." So he urged Esau until he took it.

Then Esau said, "Let me at least leave with you some of the people who are with me." But Jacob replied, "What need is there? Let me only enjoy your friendship, my Lord." So Esau turned back that day on his way to Seir.

JOSEPH SOLD AS A SLAVE BY HIS BROTHERS

When Joseph was seventeen years old, he and his brothers were shepherds, but he made them angry, for he brought a bad report about them to their father. Now Jacob loved his son Joseph, who was born in his old age; and he made him a long coat with sleeves. When his brothers saw that their father loved him more than all his other sons, they hated Joseph and would not speak to him in a friendly way.

Joseph had a dream which he told to his brothers; and they hated him still more. This is what he said to them, "I dreamed that, as we were binding sheaves in the field, my sheaf rose up and remained standing, while your sheaves came around and bowed down to my sheaf." His brothers said to him, "Will you really be king over us? Will you indeed rule over us?" So they hated him still more because of his dreams and his words.

Then he had another dream and told it to his brothers, saying, "I have had another dream, and it seemed to me that the sun and the moon and eleven stars bowed down to me." But when he told it to his father and his brothers, his father reproved him and said, "What is this dream that you have dreamed? Shall I and your mother and your brothers indeed come and bow down to the earth before you?" Therefore his brothers were jealous of him; but his father remembered the dream.

When his brothers went to pasture his father's flocks in Shechem, Jacob said to Joseph, "Go, see whether all goes well with your brothers and with the flock, and bring me back word." So he sent him out, and a certain man found him, as he was wandering in the field, and the man asked him, "What are you looking for?" He said, "I am looking for my brothers; tell me, I beg of you, where they are pasturing the flock." The man said, "They have gone away, for I heard them say, 'Let us go to Dothan.'" So Joseph went after his brothers and found them in Dothan.

When they saw him in the distance, before he came to them, they planned together to kill him. And they said one to another, "See, here comes that great dreamer! Come, let us kill him and throw him into one of the pits, and we will say, 'A fierce beast has devoured him.' Then we shall see what will become of his dreams!"

Judah, however, when he heard it, saved Joseph's life by saying, "Let us not take his life." Reuben also said to them, "Do not shed blood; throw him into this pit, here in the wilderness; but do not harm him." Reuben said this to save Joseph from their hands so that he could bring him back to his father. So when Joseph came to his brothers, they took off his long coat with sleeves and threw him into the pit. But the pit was empty, there being no water in it.

Then they sat down to eat and, when they looked up, they saw a band of Ishmaelites coming from Gilead; and their camels were loaded with spices, gum, and ladanum on their way to carry it down to Egypt. And Judah said to his brothers, "What do we gain if we kill our brother and hide his blood? Come, let us sell him to the Ishmaelites, and let us do him no harm, for he is our brother, our own flesh and blood." So his brothers listened to him; and, drawing up Joseph, they sold him for twenty pieces of silver to the Ishmaelites, who brought him to Egypt.

Then his brothers took Joseph's long coat, killed a he-goat, dipped the coat in the blood, and brought it to their father, and said, "We found this; see whether it is your son's coat or not." He recognized it and said, "It is my son's coat! A wild beast has devoured him! Joseph surely is torn in pieces." Then Jacob tore his clothes, put sackcloth about his waist, and mourned for his son many days. All his sons and his daughters tried to comfort him, but he refused to be comforted, saying, "I shall go down to the grave mourning for my son." Thus Joseph's father mourned for him.

JOSEPH'S EAGERNESS TO HELP OTHERS

Joseph was taken down to Egypt, and Potiphar, an Egyptian, one of Pharaoh's officers, the captain of the guard, bought him from the Ishmaelites.

Now Jehovah was with Joseph, so that he prospered; and he was in the house of his master, the Egyptian. When his master saw that Jehovah was with him and made everything succeed that he undertook, he trusted him and made him his own servant. He also made him overseer of his household and placed all that he had in his care. From the time that he made him overseer in his house and over all that he had, Jehovah blessed the Egyptian's household for Joseph's sake, and the blessing of Jehovah was upon all that he had in the house and in the field. Potiphar left all that he had in Joseph's charge, and he knew nothing about his affairs except about the food which he ate. And Joseph was handsome and attractive.

After these honors had come to Joseph, his master's wife tried to tempt him to be unfaithful to his trust. But he refused, saying to her, "See, my master knows nothing about what I do in the house, and he has put all that he has in my charge. How then can I do this great wrong and sin against God?" Day after day she tempted Joseph, but he did not listen to her. One day, however, when he went into the house to do his work and when none of the men of the household were at home, she caught hold of his garment and again tried to tempt him, but he left his garment in her hand and fled out of the house.

She kept his garment by her until his master came home; then she said to him, "The Hebrew slave whom you have brought to us came to me to insult me; and when I cried aloud, he left his garment with me and fled."

When Joseph's master heard what his wife said to him, he was very angry; and he took Joseph and put him into the prison, in the place where the king's prisoners were kept. So he was left there in prison. But Jehovah was with Joseph and showed kindness to him and helped him to win the friendship of the keeper of the prison, so that he placed all the prisoners in Joseph's charge and made him responsible for whatever they did there.

After these things the butler of the king of Egypt and his baker offended their master the king of Egypt, and Pharaoh was so angry with these two officers that he put them in the same prison where Joseph was. And the captain of the guard appointed Joseph to wait on them; and they stayed in prison for some time.

And the butler and the baker of the king of Egypt, who were in the prison, both had dreams the same night, each with a different meaning. When Joseph came in to them in the morning, he saw plainly that they were sad. So he asked Pharaoh's officers, "Why do you look so sad to-day?" They answered, "We have had a dream, and there is no one who can tell what it means." Then Joseph said to them, "Is not God the one who knows what dreams mean? Tell them to me, if you will."

Then the chief butler told his dream to Joseph and said to him, "In my dream I saw a vine before me, and on the vine were three branches, and the buds put out blossoms, and its clusters brought forth ripe grapes. Pharaoh's cup was in my hand, and I took the grapes and squeezed the juice into his cup and gave the cup to Pharaoh."

Then Joseph said to him, "This is what it means: the three branches are three days. Within three days Pharaoh will let you out of prison and restore you to your office, and you will give Pharaoh's cup into his hand as you used to do when you were his butler. But when all goes well with you, remember me, show kindness to me and speak for me to Pharaoh and bring me out of this prison; for I was unjustly stolen from the land of the Hebrews, and here also I have done nothing that they should put me in the dungeon."

When the chief baker saw that the meaning of the butler's dream was good, he said to Joseph, "I also saw something in my dream: there were three baskets of white bread on my head, and in the upper basket there were all kinds of baked food for Pharaoh, and the birds were eating them out of the basket on my head." Joseph answered, "This is what it means: the three baskets are three days; within three days Pharaoh will take off your head and hang you on a tree, and the birds shall eat your flesh."

Now on the third day, which was Pharaoh's birthday, he made a feast for all his servants. Then he set free the chief butler and the chief baker. He restored the chief butler to his office, so that he again gave the cup to Pharaoh; but the chief baker he hanged, as Joseph had told them. Yet the chief butler did not remember Joseph, but forgot him.

A PRISONER WHO BECAME A MIGHTY RULER

Two years later Pharaoh had a dream: as he stood by the river Nile, he saw coming up from the water seven cows, well fed and fat, for they had been feeding in the river grass. Then seven other cows came up after them out of the Nile, poorly fed and thin, and they stood by the other cows on the bank of the Nile. The poorly fed, lean cows ate up the seven well-fed, fat cows. Then Pharaoh awoke.

Afterward he slept and had a second dream and saw seven ears, plump and good, growing up on one stalk. Also seven ears, thin and withered by the east wind, grew up after them. The thin ears swallowed up the seven plump, full ears. Then Pharaoh awoke, and knew that it was only a dream.

In the morning Pharaoh was worried. So he sent for all the magicians and wise men of Egypt and told them his dreams; but no one could tell him what they meant.

Then the chief butler said to Pharaoh, "I now remember my sins: Pharaoh was very angry with his servants and put me and the chief baker in prison in the house of the captain of the guard. We both had dreams the same night, each with a different meaning. There was also with us a young Hebrew, a servant of the captain of the guard. We told him our dreams and he told each of us what our dreams meant. And our dreams came true just as he said they would: I was restored to my office, but the chief baker was hanged."

Then Pharaoh sent for Joseph, and they quickly brought him out of the dungeon; and he shaved his face, changed his clothes, and came to Pharaoh. Pharaoh said to Joseph, "I have had a dream, and there is no one who can tell what it means. Now I have heard that when you hear a dream, you can tell what it means." Joseph answered Pharaoh, "Not I; God alone can give Pharaoh a true answer."

Then Pharaoh said to Joseph, "In my dream as I stood on the bank of the Nile, I saw seven cows, fat and well fed, which had been feeding in the river grass. There came up after them seven more cows, poorly fed and thin, worse than I ever saw in all the land of Egypt; and the lean and poorly fed cows ate up the first seven fat cows. When they had eaten them up, one could not tell that they had eaten them, for they were still as thin as at the beginning. Then I awoke.

"Again I dreamed and saw seven ears, plump and good, grow up on one stalk; then seven thin ears, withered with the east wind, sprang up after them; and the thin ears swallowed up the seven good ears. I have told the dream to the magicians, but there is no one who can tell me what it means."

Then Joseph said to Pharaoh, "Pharaoh's two dreams mean the same thing; God has made known to Pharaoh what he is about to do. The seven good cows are seven years, and the seven good ears are seven years. It is one dream. The seven lean and poorly fed cows that came up after them are seven years, and the seven empty ears withered with the east wind mean seven years of famine. That is why I said to Pharaoh, 'God has shown to Pharaoh what he is about to do.' Seven years of great plenty all through the land of Egypt are coming. They shall be followed by seven years of famine, so that all the plenty will be forgotten in the land of Egypt. The famine will use up all that the land produces; and plenty will not be known in the land because of that famine which follows, for it will be very severe.

"The dream came twice to Pharaoh to show that the famine will surely come, and that God will soon make the dream come true. Now therefore let Pharaoh pick out a man who is sensible and wise and place him in charge of the land of Egypt. Let Pharaoh act quickly and put overseers over the land and collect one-fifth of all that grows in the land of Egypt in the seven years of plenty. Let them gather all the food of these good years that are coming and store up grain under the authority of Pharaoh, and let them hold it in the cities for food. The food will supply the land during the seven years of famine which shall be in the land of Egypt, so that the people of the land may not die because of the famine."

The plan pleased Pharaoh and all his people; and he said to his people, "Can we find one like this, a man in whom is the spirit of God?" So Pharaoh said to Joseph, "As God has shown you all this, there is no one so sensible and wise as you. You shall be at the head of my country, and all my people shall be ruled as you command. Only on the throne I will be above you."

So Pharaoh said to Joseph, "See, I have placed you over all the land of Egypt." And Pharaoh took off his signet-ring from his finger and put it upon Joseph's finger and clothed him in garments of fine linen and put a golden collar about his neck. He also made him ride in the second chariot which he had; and they cried before him, "Attention!" So he placed him over all the land of Egypt. Pharaoh also said to Joseph, "I am Pharaoh, but without your consent no man shall lift up his hand or his foot in all the land of Egypt." Pharaoh gave him as a wife Asenath, the daughter of Potiphera. And Joseph was thirty years old when he was made the ruler of the land of Egypt.

In the seven years of plenty there were large harvests, and Joseph gathered up all the food of the seven years of plenty, which were in the land of Egypt, and stored the food in the cities, putting in each city the food that grew in the fields about it. Joseph stored up grain as the sand of the sea, in great quantities, until he no longer kept account, because it could not be measured.

When the seven years of plenty in the land of Egypt were over, the seven years of famine began, as Joseph had said. There was famine in all lands, but all through the land of Egypt there was food, for when all the land of Egypt was hungry, the people cried to Pharaoh for bread, and Pharaoh said to all the Egyptians, "Go to Joseph and do what he tells you." So when the famine was over all the country, Joseph opened all the storehouses and sold food to the Egyptians: but the famine was severe in the land of Egypt. The peoples of all lands came to Joseph in Egypt to buy grain, for everywhere the famine was severe.

THE TESTING OF JOSEPH'S BROTHERS

When Jacob learned that there was grain for sale in Egypt, he said to his sons, "Why do you stand looking at each other? I have heard that there is grain for sale in Egypt; go down there and buy some for us, that we may live and not die." So Joseph's ten brothers went down to buy grain from Egypt. But Jacob did not send Benjamin, Joseph's own brother, with his brothers, for he feared that some harm might come to him. So the sons of Jacob went with others to buy grain, for the famine was in the land of Canaan.

Now Joseph was the governor over Egypt; it was he who sold grain to all the people of the land. So Joseph's brothers came and bowed before him with their faces to the earth. When Joseph saw his brothers, he knew them; but he acted as a stranger toward them and spoke harshly to them and said, "Where do you come from?" They said, "From the land of Canaan to buy food." So Joseph knew his brothers, but they did not know him.

Joseph also remembered the dreams which he had had about them and said to them, "You spies! you have come to see how defenseless the land is." But they said to him, "No, my lord; your servants have come to buy food. We are all sons of one man; we are honest men; your servants are not spies." But he again said to them, "No, you have come to see how defenseless the land is." They answered, "We, your servants, are twelve brothers, the sons of one father in the land of Canaan. The youngest is to-day with our father, and one is dead." Joseph said to them, "It is just as I said to you, 'You are spies.' By this you shall be tested: as sure as Pharaoh lives you shall not go away unless your youngest brother comes here. Send one of you, and let him bring your brother, while you remain in prison, that it may be proved whether you are telling the truth or not. Or else, as sure as Pharaoh lives, you are indeed spies." So he put them all into prison for three days.

Then Joseph said to them on the third day, "Do this and live, for I fear God: if you are honest men, let one of your brothers stay in prison, but you go, carry grain for the needs of your households and bring your youngest brother to me. So you will prove that you have told the truth and you shall not die."

They did as Joseph commanded, but they said to one another, "We are indeed guilty because of the way we treated our brother, for when we saw his trouble and when he pleaded with us, we would not listen. That is why this trouble has come upon us." Reuben added, "Did I not say to you, 'Do not sin against the boy,' but you would not listen?"

They did not know, however, that Joseph understood them, for he had spoken to them through an interpreter. But he turned away from them and wept. Then he came back and spoke to them, and taking Simeon from among them, bound him before their eyes. Then Joseph gave orders to fill their vessels with grain and to put every man's money back in his sack and to give them food for the journey; and thus it was done to them. So they loaded their asses with their grain and went away.

When they came to Jacob their father in the land of Canaan, they told him all that had happened, saying, "The man who is master in that land spoke harshly to us and put us in prison as spies. We said to him, 'We are honest men; we are not spies; we are twelve brothers, sons of the same father; one is no longer living, and the youngest is to-day with our father in the land of Canaan.' But the man who is master in that land said to us, 'This is how I shall know that you are honest men: leave one of your brothers with me and take the grain to supply the needs of your households and go. Bring your youngest brother to me; then I shall know that you are not spies, but that you are honest men; and I will give your brother back to you and you shall be free to go about in the land.'"

As they were emptying their sacks, they found that each man's purse with his money was in his sack; and when they and their father saw their purses and the money, they were afraid and they turned trembling to one another with the question, "What is this that God has done to us?" Jacob their father said to them, "You have robbed me of my children: Joseph is no longer living and Simeon is no longer here, and now you would take Benjamin also! All this trouble has come to me!" But Reuben said to his father, "You may put my two sons to death, if I do not bring him to you. Put him in my charge and I will bring him back to you." Then Jacob said, "My son shall not go down with you, for his brother is dead and he only is left. If harm should come to him on the way by which you go, then you will bring down my gray hairs with sorrow to the grave."

The famine was severe in the land; and when Joseph's brothers had eaten up the grain which they had brought from Egypt, their father said to them, "Go again, buy us a little food." But Judah said to him, "The man plainly said to us: 'You shall not see me again unless your brother is with you.' If you will send our brother with us, we will go down and buy you food, but if you will not send him, we will not go down; for the man said to us, 'You shall not see me unless your brother is with you.'" Jacob said, "Why did you bring trouble upon me by telling the man you had another brother?" They replied, "The man asked all about us and our family, saying, 'Is your father still alive? Have you another brother?' So we answered his questions as he asked them. How were we to know that he would say, 'Bring your brother down'?"

Then Judah said to Jacob, his father, "Send the lad with me, and we will go at once, that both we and you and our little ones may live and not die. I will be responsible for him; from me you may demand him. If I do not bring him to you and set him before you, let me bear the blame forever; for if we had not waited so long, surely we would by this time have come back the second time." So their father said to them, "If it must be so, then do this: take some of the fruits of the land in your jars and carry a present to the man, a little balsam, a little syrup, spices, ladanum, pistachio nuts, and almonds. Take twice as much money with you, carrying back the money that was put in your sacks. Perhaps it was a mistake. Take also your brother and go again to the man. May God Almighty grant that the man may be merciful to you and free Benjamin and your other brother. But if I am robbed of my sons, I am bereaved indeed!" So the men took the present and twice as much money and Benjamin, and went down to Egypt and stood before Joseph.

When Joseph saw Benjamin with them, he said to the steward of his house, "Bring the men into the house, kill animals, and prepare the meal, for these men will dine with me at noon." The steward did as Joseph ordered, and brought the men into Joseph's house. But the men were afraid, because they were brought into Joseph's house, and they said, "We are being brought in on account of the money that was put in our grain sacks at our first visit, that he may accuse us and fall upon us and take us as slaves, together with our asses."

So when they came near to Joseph's steward, they spoke to him at the door of the house and said, "Oh, my lord, we came down the first time only to buy food; but when we reached home, we opened our sacks and found that each man's money was in the mouth of his sack, our money in its full weight; and we have brought it back with us. We have brought down with us more money with which to buy food. We do not know who put our money into our sacks." He replied, "Peace be to you, fear not; your God and the God of your father has given you the treasure in your sacks; your money came to me."

Then he brought Simeon out to them. The steward also took the men to Joseph's house and gave them water with which to wash their feet, and he gave their asses fodder. Then they made ready the present for Joseph, when he should come at noon, for they had heard that they were to eat there.

When Joseph came into the house, they gave him the present which they had brought and bowed down low before him. He asked them about their welfare and said, "Is your father well, the old man of whom you spoke? Is he still living?" They replied, "Your servant, our father, is well; he is still alive." Then they bowed their heads and knelt down before him.

When Joseph looked up and saw Benjamin his brother, his own mother's son, he said, "Is this your youngest brother of whom you spoke to me?" And he added, "God be gracious to you, my son." Then because of his longing for his brother he sought a place in which to weep. So he went into his room and wept there.

Then he bathed his face and came out and said, "Bring on the food." So they brought food for him by himself and for them by themselves and for the Egyptians who ate with him by themselves, because the Egyptians would not eat with the Hebrews, for to do so was hateful to them. Joseph's brothers were seated before him, the eldest first, as was his right as the oldest, and the youngest last, and the men looked at each other in astonishment. Then Joseph had portions served to them from the food before him. But Benjamin's portions were five times as much as any of theirs. So they drank and were merry with him.

Joseph Converses with Judah, his Brother
Painted by J. James Tissot

Then he gave this command to the steward of his household: "Fill the men's grain sacks with food, as much as they can carry, and put my cup, the silver cup, in the mouth of the sack of the youngest and the money too that he paid for his grain." And the steward did as Joseph commanded.

As soon as the morning light appeared, the men were sent away with their asses. When they had gone out of the city, but were not yet far away, Joseph commanded his steward, "Follow after the men and when you overtake them, say to them, 'Why have you returned evil for good? Why have you stolen my silver cup, that from which my master drinks? You have done wrong in so doing.'"

So the steward overtook them and said these words to them. They said to him, "Why does my lord speak such words as these? Far be it from your servants to do such a thing! Remember that we brought back to you from the land of Canaan the money which we found in our sacks. Why then should we steal silver or gold from your master's house? Let that one of your servants with whom it is found die, and we will be my lord's slaves." He said, "Let it now be as you have said: he with whom it is found shall be my slave; but you shall be innocent." Then each one quickly took down his sack and opened it. The steward searched, beginning with the oldest and ending with the youngest; and the cup was found in Benjamin's sack. Then they tore their clothes, and every man loaded his ass and returned to the city.

JOSEPH'S FORGIVENESS OF HIS BROTHERS

When Judah and his brothers came back to Joseph's house, Joseph was still there; and they threw themselves before him on the ground. Joseph said to them, "What deed is this that you have done? Do you not know that a man like me can always tell where things are?" Judah replied, "What shall we say to my lord? What shall we speak or how shall we clear ourselves? God has found out the guilt of your servants. See, both we and he also with whom the cup was found are my lord's slaves." But Joseph said, "Far be it from me that I should do so! The man with whom the cup was found shall be my slave; but you yourselves go up in peace to your father."

Then Judah came close to him and said, "Oh, my lord, let your servant, I beg of you, speak a word in my lord's ears, and let not your anger be aroused against your servant, for you are even as Pharaoh. My lord asked his servants, saying, 'Have you a father or a brother?' And we said to my lord, 'We have a father, an old man, and a child of his old age, a little one.

As his brother is dead, he is the only son of his mother who is left; and his father loves him.' You said to your servants, 'Bring him down to me, that I may see him.' But we said to my lord, 'The boy cannot leave his father; for if he should leave his father, his father would die.' Then you said to your servants, 'Unless your youngest brother comes down with you, you shall not see me again.'

"When we went up to your servant, my father, we told him the words of my lord; and our father said, 'Go again, buy us a little food.' But we said, 'We cannot go down. If our youngest brother is with us, then we will go; for we cannot see the man again unless our youngest brother is with us.' Your servant, my father, said to us, 'You know that my wife had two sons; and one went from me,' and I said, 'Surely he is torn in pieces; and I have not seen him since. If you take this one also from me, and harm come to him, you will bring down my gray hairs with sorrow to the grave.' Now if I return to your servant, my father, and Benjamin with whose life his heart is bound up is not with us, and he sees that there is no boy, he will die, and your servants will bring down the gray hairs of your servant our father with sorrow to the grave. For your servant became responsible for the boy to my father, when I said, 'If I do not bring him to you, then I will bear the blame before my father forever.' Now, therefore, let me, instead of the boy, remain as a slave to my lord, I beg of you; but let the boy go back with his brothers. For how can I go back to my father, if the boy is not with me, lest I should see the sorrow that would come upon my father?"

Then Joseph could not control himself before all those who were standing by him; so he cried out, "Let every man leave me." So no Egyptian was present while Joseph made himself known to his brothers. But he wept so loudly that the Egyptians and Pharaoh's court heard.

And Joseph said to his brothers, "I am Joseph. Is my father still alive?" But his brothers could not answer him, for they were too ashamed to look him in the face. Then Joseph said to his brothers, "Come near to me, I beg of you." So they came near. He said, "I am Joseph, your brother, whom you sold into Egypt. Do not be troubled nor angry with yourselves that you sold me here, for God sent me before you to save your lives. For the famine has already been two years in the land, and there are still five years in which there shall be neither ploughing nor harvest. God sent me before you to save your lives through a great deliverance and thus give you children on the earth. So now it is not you who sent me here, but God. He has made me like a father to Pharaoh and master of all his household and ruler over all the land of Egypt.

"Go up quickly to my father and say to him, 'Your son Joseph says: God has made me master of all Egypt. Come down to me without delay. You shall live in the land of Goshen, and you shall be near me with your children and your grandchildren, with your flocks and your herds and all that you have, so that you, with your household and all that you have, may never want. There I will provide for you, for there will be five more years of famine.' Now you and my brother Benjamin see that it is I who am speaking to you. Tell my father all about my honor in Egypt and what you have seen; and you must quickly bring him down here."

Then he fell upon his brother Benjamin's neck and wept, and Benjamin wept upon his neck. He also kissed all his brothers and wept upon them. After that his brothers talked with him.

JOSEPH'S LOYALTY TO HIS FAMILY

The news that Joseph's brothers had arrived became known in Pharaoh's palace; and it pleased Pharaoh and his servants greatly. Pharaoh said to Joseph, "Say to your brothers, 'Do this: load your beasts, go to the land of Canaan, and take your father and your families and come to me, and I will give you the best there is in the land of Egypt, and you shall eat the best that the land can give. Now you are commanded to do this: take wagons from the land of Egypt for your little ones and for your wives, and bring your father and come. Also do not pay any attention to your household goods, for the best of all there is in the land of Egypt is yours.'" And the sons of Jacob did as they were commanded.

So Joseph gave them wagons, as Pharaoh ordered, and what was needed for the journey. To each of them he gave a change of clothing, but to Benjamin he gave three hundred pieces of silver and five changes of clothing. To his father he sent this gift: ten asses loaded with the best products of Egypt and ten asses loaded with grain and bread and provisions for his father on the journey.

So he sent his brothers away, and, as they went, he said to them, "See that you do not quarrel on the journey!" So they went up out of Egypt and came into the land of Canaan to Jacob their father, and told him, "Joseph is still alive, and he is ruler over all the land of Egypt!" Then Jacob's heart stood still, for he could not believe them. But when they told him all that Joseph had said to them and when he saw the wagons which Joseph had sent to carry him, the spirit of Jacob their father revived, and he said, "It is enough; Joseph my son is still alive. I will go and see him before I die."

Then Jacob set out on his journey with all that he had. He first went to Beersheba and offered sacrifices to the God of his father Isaac. God spoke to him in a vision by night and said, "Jacob, Jacob." He answered, "Here am I." God said, "I am God, the God of your father. Do not fear to go down into Egypt, for there I will make of you a great nation. I myself will go down with you into Egypt; I will surely bring you back again; and Joseph shall close your dying eyes."

When Jacob left Beersheba, his sons carried him and their little ones and their wives in the wagons that Pharaoh had sent. Jacob also sent Judah before him to Joseph, that he might show him the way to Goshen.

When they came into the land of Goshen, Joseph made ready his chariot, and went up to Goshen to meet Jacob his father. When he met him, Jacob fell on his neck and wept there a long time.

Then Jacob said to Joseph, "Now let me die, for I have seen your face and know that you are still alive." But Joseph said to his brothers and to his father's household, "I will go up and tell Pharaoh and will say to him, 'My brothers and my father's family who were in the land of Canaan have come to me. Now the men are shepherds, for they have been keepers of cattle; and they have brought their flocks and cattle and all that they have.' When Pharaoh calls you, and asks, 'What is your business?' you shall say, 'Your servants have been keepers of cattle from our youth even until now, both we and our fathers.' Say this that you may live in the land of Goshen, for every shepherd is looked down upon by the Egyptians."

Then Joseph went in and told Pharaoh and said, "My father and my brothers with their sheep and cattle and all that they possess have come from the land of Canaan; and now they are in the province of Goshen." And he took five of his brothers and presented them to Pharaoh. Pharaoh said to them, "What is your business?" They answered, "Your servants are shepherds, both we and our fathers." They also said to Pharaoh, "We have come to live in your country; because the famine is severe in the land of Canaan, and there is no pasture for your servants' flocks. Now, therefore, we beg of you, let your servants stay in the land of Goshen." Then Pharaoh said to Joseph, "Let them stay in the land of Goshen; and if you know any able men among them, put them in charge of my cattle."

Joseph also brought in Jacob his father and presented him to Pharaoh; and Jacob blessed Pharaoh. Then Pharaoh said to Jacob, "How many years have you lived?" Jacob answered, "I have lived a hundred and thirty years; few and evil have been the years of my life, and they have not been as many as those that my forefathers lived on earth." After Jacob had blessed Pharaoh, he went out from Pharaoh's presence. So Joseph gave his father and his brothers a place to live in and a home in the land of Goshen, in the best part of the land of Egypt, as Pharaoh had commanded.

Joseph also provided food for his father and his brothers and all his father's family according to the number of the little children. So the

Israelites lived in Egypt, in the land of Goshen, and there they grew wealthy and had many children.

THE BOYHOOD AND TRAINING OF MOSES

After the death of Joseph and his brothers, the Israelites increased so rapidly and became so many and powerful that the land was filled with them. But a new king who did not know Joseph ruled over Egypt. He said to his people, "See, the Israelites are becoming too many and powerful for us. Come, let us deal wisely with them, for fear that they become so many that, if war is begun against us, they will join our enemies and fight against us and leave the land."

So the Egyptians set taskmasters over them to put burdens upon them. And they built for Pharaoh the store-cities, Pithom and Rameses. But the more the Egyptians afflicted them, the more numerous they became and the more they spread everywhere, so that the Egyptians dreaded what they might do. And the Egyptians were cruel and made slaves of them, making their lives bitter with hard labor in mortar and brick, and by all kinds of hard work in the field.

Pharaoh also gave this command to all his people, "You shall throw into the river every son that is born to the Hebrews, but every daughter you shall save alive."

Now a man of the tribe of Levi married a woman of the same tribe, and she had a son. When she saw that he was a beautiful child, she hid him for three months. But when she could no longer hide him, she took a basket made of papyrus reeds, daubed it with mortar and pitch, and put the child in it. Then she placed it in the reeds by the bank of the river Nile, while his sister stayed near by to see what would happen to him.

The daughter of Pharaoh came down to bathe in the Nile, and while her maids were walking along the river's bank, she saw the basket among the reeds and sent her waiting-maid to bring it. When she opened it and saw the child, the boy was crying; and she felt sorry for him and said, "This is one of the Hebrew children."

The Finding of Moses
Painted by Juliaan de Vriendt

Then his sister said to Pharaoh's daughter, "Shall I go and call one of the Hebrew women to nurse the child for you?" Pharaoh's daughter said to her, "Go." So the maiden went and called the child's mother, and Pharaoh's daughter said to her, "Take this child away and nurse it for me, and I will pay you your wages." Then the woman took the child and nursed it. When the child had grown up, she brought him to Pharaoh's daughter, and he became her son; and she named him Moses, for she said, "I drew him out of the water."

One time, after Moses had grown up, he went out to his own people; and as he was watching them at their hard labor, he saw an Egyptian beating a Hebrew, one of his own race. He looked around and seeing that there was no one in sight, he killed the Egyptian and hid him in the sand.

On the next day Moses went out, and saw two Hebrews struggling together; and he said to the one who was in the wrong, "Why do you strike your fellow workman?" The man replied, "Who made you a ruler and a judge over us? Do you intend to kill me as you killed the Egyptian?" Then Moses was afraid and said, "What I have done is known!" When Pharaoh heard what had taken place, he tried to put Moses to death; but Moses left the country and made his home in the land of Midian.

As he was sitting by a well, the seven daughters of the priest of Midian came and drew water and filled the troughs to water their father's flock, but the shepherds came and drove them away. Then Moses stood up and protected the women and watered their flock.

When they came to their father, he said, "How is it that you have come back so early to-day?" They replied, "An Egyptian protected us from the shepherds, and besides, he drew water for us and watered the flock." Then he said to his daughters, "Where is he? Why have you left the man? Ask him to eat with us." So Moses made his home with the man; and he gave Moses his daughter Zipporah to be his wife. She had a son, and Moses named him Gershom.

THE VOICE FROM THE BUSH

After a long time the king of Egypt died. Moses was taking care of the flock of Jethro his wife's father. Once he led the flock to the other side of the pasture and came to Horeb, the mountain of God. There the angel of Jehovah appeared to him in a flame of fire from the midst of a thorn bush. As he looked, the bush flamed up without being burned.

Moses said, "I will stop here and see this wonderful sight, why the bush is not burned up."

When Jehovah saw that Moses stopped to look, he called to him from the midst of the bush, "Moses, Moses." Moses answered, "Here am I." Then God said, "Do not come near; take your shoes off your feet, for the place where you are standing is holy ground." He also said, "I am the God of your forefathers, the God of Abraham, the God of Isaac, and the God of Jacob." Then Moses covered his face; for he was afraid to look upon God.

But Jehovah said, "I have certainly seen the suffering of my people who are in Egypt and have heard their cry of distress because of their taskmasters, for I know their sorrows. I have come down to rescue them from the power of the Egyptians and to bring them out of that land into a land that is beautiful and wide, to a land with plenty of milk and honey. I have heard the cry of the Israelites and I have seen how they suffer at the hands of the Egyptians. Come now, I will send you to Pharaoh that you may bring my people, the Israelites, out of Egypt."

But Moses said to God, "Who am I, that I should go to Pharaoh and should bring the Israelites out of Egypt?" He answered, "I will surely be with you; and this shall be the sign to you that I have sent you: when you have brought the people out of Egypt, you shall worship God upon this mountain."

Then Moses said to God, "If I go to the Israelites and say to them, 'The God of your forefathers has sent me to you,' and they ask me, 'What is his name?' what shall I answer them?" God said to Moses, "I AM WHAT I AM"; and he said, "Declare to the Israelites: 'I AM has sent me to you.' Go and gather the leaders of Israel together and say to them, 'Jehovah the God of your forefathers, the God of Abraham, Isaac, and Jacob, has appeared to me and said, I have surely remembered you and have seen what is being done to you in Egypt, and I have declared that I will bring you up out of the suffering in Egypt to a land with plenty of milk and honey.' They will listen to your voice; and you, together with the leaders of Israel, shall go to the king of Egypt and say to him, 'Jehovah, the God of the Hebrews, has appeared to us. Now let us go three days' journey into the wilderness, that we may offer a sacrifice to Jehovah our God.' But I know that the king of Egypt will not let you go unless he is made to do so by a mighty power. Therefore I will use my power and overwhelm Egypt with all the marvellous deeds that I will do there. After that he will let you go."

Moses said to Jehovah, "O, Lord I am not able to speak well; for I am slow to speak and slow in saying what I think." Jehovah said to him, "Who has given man a mouth? Or who makes one deaf or dumb, or blind or able to see? Is it not I, Jehovah? Now go, and I will be with you and teach you what you shall say; and your brother Aaron shall speak for you to the people."

Then Moses went back to Jethro, his wife's father, and said to him, "Let me go again to my people in Egypt to see whether they are still alive." Jethro answered Moses, "Go, with my blessing."

PHARAOH THE STUBBORN RULER

Then Jehovah said to Aaron, "Go into the wilderness to meet Moses." So he went and met him on the mountain of God and kissed him. And Moses told Aaron all that Jehovah had sent him to declare. So Moses and Aaron gathered all the leaders of the Israelites, and Aaron repeated all the words which Jehovah had spoken to Moses. The people believed; and when they heard that Jehovah had remembered the Israelites and that he had seen their suffering, they bowed their heads and worshipped.

Then Moses and Aaron went to Pharaoh and said to him, "Jehovah, the God of Israel commands, 'Let my people go that they may hold a feast in my honor in the wilderness.'" But Pharaoh said, "Who is Jehovah that I should obey his command to let Israel go? I do not know Jehovah, and I will not let Israel go." They said, "The God of the Hebrews has appeared to us; let us go three days' journey into the wilderness that we may offer a sacrifice to Jehovah our God, that he may not attack us with pestilence or with the sword." But the king of Egypt replied, "Moses and Aaron, why do you try to turn the people from their work? Go to your tasks!"

The same day Pharaoh gave this command to the taskmasters who were over the people: "You shall no longer give the people straw for making bricks as before. Let them go and gather straw for themselves. But you shall demand of them the same number of bricks that they have been making before; you shall not lessen the number at all, for they are lazy; that is why they cry out, 'Let us go and offer a sacrifice to our God.' Let heavier work be laid upon the men, that they may be kept so busy that they will not pay attention to lying words."

So the taskmasters who were over the people went out and said to them, "This is Pharaoh's order, 'I will no longer give you straw. Go yourselves, get straw wherever you can find it; but your work shall not be made less.'" So the people were scattered over all the land of Egypt to gather stubble for straw. The taskmasters urged them on, saying, "You must finish your daily task just as when there was straw." The overseers of the Israelites, whom Pharaoh's taskmasters had put over them, were also beaten and asked, "Why have you not finished to-day as many bricks as yesterday?"

Then the overseers of the Israelites went to Pharaoh and said, "Why do you deal in this way with your servants? No straw is given to your servants, and yet they say to us, 'Make bricks.' See how your servants are beaten and how you wrong your people." But he said, "You are lazy, you are lazy; therefore you say, 'Let us go and offer a sacrifice to Jehovah.' Now go and work, for no straw shall be given you; yet you must make the same number of bricks."

Then Moses turned again to Jehovah and said, "Jehovah, why hast thou brought misfortune upon this people? Why is it that thou has sent me? For since I came to Pharaoh to speak in thy name he has wronged this people, and thou hast done nothing at all to rescue thy people."

Jehovah answered Moses, "Now you shall see what I will do to Pharaoh; for compelled by a mighty power he shall surely let them go, and compelled by a mighty power he shall drive them out of his land."

THE COST OF BEING CRUEL AND STUBBORN

Then Jehovah said to Moses, "Pharaoh is stubborn; he will not let the people go. Go to Pharaoh early in the morning, as he is going out on the water, and stand by the bank of the Nile to meet him. Say to him, 'Jehovah, the God of the Hebrews, has sent me to you with this command: Let my people go that they may worship me in the wilderness, but so far you have not listened. Jehovah declares, By this you shall know that I am Jehovah: See, I will strike the waters which are in the river with the rod that is in my hand and they shall be changed into blood. The fish, too, that are in the Nile shall die, and the Nile shall become foul, so that the Egyptians will hate to drink its water.'"

Then Moses lifted up the staff and in the presence of Pharaoh and his servants struck the waters that were in the river Nile; and all its waters were changed into blood. The fish, too, that were in the Nile died, and the river became so foul that the Egyptians could not drink its water, but dug round about the Nile for water to drink.

Seven days later Jehovah gave this command to Moses, "Go in to Pharaoh and say to him, 'Jehovah commands: Let my people go that they may worship me. If you refuse to let them go, then I will afflict all your land with frogs; and the Nile shall swarm with frogs which shall go up and come into your house, into your sleeping chamber, upon your bed, into the houses of your servants, upon your people, and into your ovens and kneading-troughs; and the frogs shall come up even upon you and your people and all your servants.'"

Then Jehovah said to Moses, "Say to Aaron: 'Stretch out your hand with your staff over the rivers, over the canals, and over the pools, and cause frogs to come up over the land of Egypt.'" So Aaron stretched out his hand over the waters of Egypt; and the frogs came up and covered the land of Egypt.

Then Pharaoh called for Moses and Aaron and said, "Pray to Jehovah to take away the frogs from me and my people; then I will let the people go, that they may offer a sacrifice to Jehovah." Moses said to Pharaoh, "Will you do yourself the honor of telling me at what time I shall pray to Jehovah in your behalf and in behalf of your servants and people, that the frogs be destroyed from your palaces and be left only in the Nile?" Pharaoh answered, "To-morrow." Then Moses said, "Let it be as you say; that you may know that there is none like Jehovah our God, the frogs shall depart from you, from your palaces, and from your servants and people; they shall be left only in the Nile."

When Moses and Aaron had gone out from Pharaoh, Moses prayed to Jehovah to remove the frogs which he had brought upon Pharaoh; and Jehovah did as Moses asked. The frogs died in the houses, in the courts, and in the fields, and the people gathered them together in many heaps; and the land was filled with a vile odor. But when Pharaoh saw that relief had come, he was stubborn and, as Jehovah had said, did not listen to Moses and Aaron.

Then Jehovah said to Moses, "Get up early in the morning and stand before Pharaoh, just as he goes out to the water, and say to him, 'Jehovah commands: Let my people go that they may worship me. If you will not let my people go, I will send swarms of flies upon you, upon your servants, and upon your people and into your palaces, so that the houses of the Egyptians shall be full of swarms of flies, as well as the ground upon which they stand. But at that time I will set apart the land of Goshen in which my people live, and no swarms of flies shall be there, so that you may know that I, Jehovah, am in the midst of the earth.'"

And Jehovah did so: a vast swarm of flies came upon Pharaoh's palace and into the homes of his servants; and all the land of Egypt was ruined by the swarms of flies.

Then Pharaoh called for Moses and Aaron and said, "I will let you go that you may offer a sacrifice to Jehovah your God in the wilderness; only you must not go far away. Pray for me." Moses replied, "I will go out and will pray to Jehovah that the swarms of flies may depart from Pharaoh, from his servants and from his people to-morrow; only let not Pharaoh again act deceitfully by refusing to let the people go to offer a sacrifice to Jehovah."

So Moses went out from Pharaoh and prayed to Jehovah. And Jehovah did as Moses asked; but this time also Pharaoh was stubborn and would not let the people go.

Then Jehovah said to Moses, "Go to Pharaoh and tell him, 'Jehovah the God of the Hebrews commands: Let my people go that they may worship me. For if you refuse to let them go and still hold them, then the power of Jehovah will bring a very severe pest upon your cattle which are in the field, upon the horses, the asses, the camels, the herds, and the flocks. But Jehovah will make a difference between the cattle of Israel and the cattle of Egypt, and not one that belongs to the Israelites shall die.'"

So Jehovah set a fixed time, saying, "To-morrow Jehovah will do this in the land." Jehovah did this on the next day, and all the cattle of the Egyptians died; but none of the cattle of the Israelites. Then Pharaoh sent and found that not even one of the cattle of the Israelites was dead; but Pharaoh was stubborn and would not let the people go.

Then Jehovah said to Moses, "Get up early in the morning and stand before Pharaoh, and say to him,'Jehovah, the God of the Hebrews, commands: Let my people go, that they may worship me. Do you still set yourself against my people, so that you will not let them go? To-morrow about this time I will send down a very heavy fall of hail, such as has not been in Egypt from the day that it became a nation until now.'"

So Jehovah sent down hail upon the land of Egypt, and the lightning flashing in the midst of the hail was very severe, such as had not been before in all Egypt since it became a nation. Through the whole land of

Egypt the hail struck down everything that was in the field, both man and beast. The hail also struck down all the growing plants and broke all the trees in the fields. Only in the land of Goshen, where the Israelites were, there was no hail.

Again Pharaoh sent and called for Moses and Aaron and said to them, "I have sinned this time; Jehovah is right and I and my people are wrong. Pray to Jehovah, for there has been enough of these mighty thunderings and hail, and I will let you go, and you shall stay no longer." Moses said to him, "As soon as I have gone out of the city, I will spread out my hands in prayer to Jehovah; the thunders shall stop, and there shall be no more hail, that you may know that the earth is Jehovah's. But as for you and your servants, I know that even then you will not fear Jehovah."

So Moses went out of the city from Pharaoh and spread out his hands to Jehovah; and the thunders and hail stopped, and the rain was no longer poured upon the earth. But when Pharaoh saw that the rain and the hail and the thunders had stopped, he sinned again, and he and his servants became stubborn, and he would not let the Israelites go.

So Moses and Aaron went to Pharaoh, and said to him, "Jehovah, the God of the Hebrews, commands: 'How long will you refuse to obey me? Let my people go that they may worship me. For if you refuse to let my people go, then to-morrow I will bring locusts into your land, and they will cover the surface of the earth, so that no one will be able to see the ground, and they shall eat the rest of that which is left to you from the hail, and they shall eat all your trees which grow in the field.'"

Then Moses and Aaron were driven out from Pharaoh's presence, but Moses stretched out his staff over the land of Egypt, and Jehovah caused an east wind to blow over the land all that day and night. In the morning the east wind brought the locusts, and they went over all the land of Egypt and settled down in all the land of Egypt, a very large swarm, more locusts than there ever were before or ever will be again. For they covered the surface of the whole land, so that the land was darkened and nothing green was left, neither tree nor growing plants, anywhere in all the land of Egypt.

Then Pharaoh called for Moses in haste and said, "I have sinned against Jehovah your God and against you. Now therefore forgive my sin only this once, and pray to Jehovah your God to take away from me this deadly plague." So Moses went out from Pharaoh and prayed to Jehovah, and Jehovah made a very strong west wind to blow which took up the locusts and drove them into the Red Sea; not a single locust was left in all the land of Egypt. But Jehovah let Pharaoh's heart remain stubborn, so that he would not let the Israelites go.

Then Jehovah said to Moses, "Stretch out your hand toward heaven, that there may be darkness over the land of Egypt, so dark that it may be felt." So Moses stretched out his hand toward heaven; and there was complete darkness in all the land of Egypt for three days; no one could see another, nor did any one move about for three days. But the Israelites had light in their homes.

Then Pharaoh called Moses and said, "Go, worship Jehovah; only let your flocks and your herds stay behind; let your little ones go with you." But Moses said, "You must also give us animals for sacrifices and burnt-offerings, that we may offer a sacrifice to Jehovah our God. Our cattle too must go with us; not a hoof shall be left behind, for we must take these to offer to Jehovah our God, and we do not know what we must offer to Jehovah until we arrive there."

But Jehovah let Pharaoh's heart remain stubborn, and he would not let them go. And Pharaoh said to him, "Go away from me; take care that you never come to me again; for on the day that you come to me you shall die." Moses replied, "You have spoken truly, I shall never see you again."

Moses said to Pharaoh, "Jehovah declares: 'About midnight I will go through all of Egypt. All the eldest sons in the land of Egypt shall die, from the eldest son of Pharaoh who sits upon his throne, even to the eldest son of the slave girl who is behind the mill, and all the first-born of the cattle. There shall be a great cry of sorrow all over the land of Egypt, such as has never been before and never shall be again.' But not a single dog shall bark at any of the Israelites nor their animals, that you may know that Jehovah does make a difference between the Egyptians and Israelites. All these your servants shall come to me and bow down before me, saying, 'Go away, together with all the people that follow you.' After that I will go away." And Moses went from Pharaoh in great anger.

THE ESCAPE FROM EGYPT

Moses called together all the leaders of Israel, and said to them, "Take lambs from the herds according to your families and kill the passover lamb. You shall also take a bunch of hyssop and dip it in the blood that is in the basin and strike the lintel and the two door posts with the blood that is in the basin. And not one of you shall go out of the door of his house until morning, for Jehovah will pass through to kill the Egyptians, and when he sees the blood upon the lintel and on the two door posts, he will pass over the door and will not let the destroyer come into your houses to destroy you. You and your children shall observe this event as a custom forever.

"When your children shall say to you, 'What do you mean by this service?' you shall say, 'It is the sacrifice of the passover of Jehovah, for he passed over the houses of the Israelites in Egypt, when he destroyed the Egyptians and released our people.'"

Then the people bowed their heads and worshipped; and the Israelites went and did as Jehovah had commanded Moses and Aaron.

At midnight Jehovah destroyed all the eldest sons in the land of Egypt, from the eldest son of Pharaoh who sat on his throne to the eldest son of the captive who was in prison. Then Pharaoh arose in the night, together with all his servants and all the Egyptians, and there was a great cry of sorrow, for there was not a house in Egypt in which there was not one dead. Pharaoh called Moses and Aaron at night and said, "Go away from among my people, both you and the Israelites; go, worship Jehovah as you have asked. Also take with you your sheep and your cattle, as you have asked, go and ask a blessing for me also." The Egyptians also told the people to hasten out of the land, for they said, "We shall all perish." So the people took their dough before the yeast had worked, and their kneading-troughs were bound up in their clothes upon their shoulders.

The Israelites went on foot from Rameses to Succoth; and a mixed multitude went with them, and they had a great many flocks and herds. They baked unraised cakes of the dough which they had brought with them from Egypt, for there was no yeast in it, because they had been driven out of Egypt and could not wait, neither had they prepared for themselves any food for the journey.

And they went from Succoth and camped at Etham on the border of the wilderness. Jehovah went before them by day in a pillar of cloud, to show them the way, and at night in a pillar of fire, to give them light, that they might march both by day and by night; the pillar of cloud by day and the pillar of fire at night stayed in front of the people.

When the king of Egypt was told that the people had fled, the feeling of Pharaoh and his servants toward them was changed, and they said, "Why have we done this and let the Israelites escape from serving us?" So he made ready his chariot and took his people with him. He also took six hundred chosen chariots and the rest of the chariots of Egypt with captains over all of them; and Jehovah let the heart of Pharaoh, king of Egypt, remain stubborn, so that he followed the Israelites, because they had defied him.

When Pharaoh drew near to them the Israelites looked up and saw the Egyptians marching after them; and they were very much afraid and cried to Jehovah. And they said to Moses, "Why have you misled us by bringing us out of Egypt? Is not this what we told you in Egypt, when we said, 'Let us alone, that we may serve the Egyptians? For it is better for us to serve the Egyptians than to die in the wilderness.'" But Moses said to the people, "Do not be frightened, remain quiet and you will see how Jehovah will save you to-day; for as surely as you now see the Egyptians you shall never see them again. Jehovah will fight for you, and you are to keep still."

Then the angel of God who went before the army of Israel changed his position and went behind them. The pillar of cloud also changed its position from in front of them and stood behind them, coming between the army of the Egyptians and the army of the Israelites. On the one side the cloud was dark and on the other side it lighted up the night, so that throughout all the night neither army came near the other.

Then Moses stretched out his hand over the sea, and Jehovah by means of a strong east wind caused the sea to go back all that night and made the bed of the sea dry. And the Israelites crossed over on the dry bed of the sea. The Egyptians followed and all of Pharaoh's horses, his chariots, and his horsemen went after them into the sea. In the morning before sunrise, Jehovah looked out through the pillar of fire and of cloud upon the army of the Egyptians and threw them into confusion. He also bound their chariot wheels, so that they dragged heavily. Therefore the Egyptians said, "Let us flee from the Israelites, for Jehovah fights for them against us."

Then Jehovah said to Moses, "Stretch out your hand over the sea, that the waters may come back upon the Egyptians, upon their chariots, and upon their horsemen." So Moses stretched out his hand over the sea, and toward morning the sea returned to its ordinary level while the Egyptians were flying before it. So Jehovah overthrew the Egyptians in the midst of the sea, and the waters returned and covered the chariots and the horsemen, and all the army of Pharaoh that went after them into the sea, so that not one of them was left. Thus Jehovah saved the Israelites that day from the power of the Egyptians; and they saw the Egyptians dead upon the seashore. When the Israelites saw the great work which Jehovah did to the Egyptians, the people feared Jehovah and believed in him and in his servant Moses.

And Miriam the prophetess, the sister of Aaron, took a tambourine in her hand; and as all the women followed her with tambourines and with dancing, she sang with them:

> "Sing to Jehovah, for he has triumphed gloriously:
> Both horse and rider has he hurled into the sea."

Then Moses and the Israelites sang this song to Jehovah:

"I will sing to Jehovah, for he has triumphed gloriously:
Both horse and rider he has hurled into the sea.
Jehovah is my strength and song, he has delivered me;
He is my God, I will praise him; my father's God whom I honor."

GOD'S COMMANDS TO THE PEOPLE

Moses led the Israelites forward from the Red Sea until they came to the wilderness of Sinai, and there the Israelites camped before the mountain.

Moses went up into the presence of God, and Jehovah called to him from the mountain and said, "Tell the Israelites: 'You have seen what I did to the Egyptians and how I bore you on eagles' wings and brought you to myself. Now therefore, if you will listen to my voice and keep your solemn agreement with me, you shall be my own treasure taken from among all peoples, for all the earth is mine. You shall be a nation of priests, a people devoted to my service.'"

So Moses called together the leaders of the people and told them all these words, as Jehovah had commanded him. And all the people answered together, "We will do all that Jehovah has commanded."

When Moses told Jehovah the answer of the people, Jehovah said to him, "See, I come to you in a thick cloud, that the people may hear when

I speak and may always believe in you." And Jehovah said to Moses, "Go to the people and keep them pure to-day and to-morrow, and let them wash their garments and be ready on the third day, for on the third day I will come down on Mount Sinai within sight of all the people."

On the third day, when morning came, there were thunderings and lightnings and a thick cloud rested upon the mountain, and a very loud trumpet blast sounded, so that all the people who were in the camp trembled. Then Moses brought the people out of the camp to meet God; and they stood at the foot of the mountain. Mount Sinai was entirely covered with smoke, because Jehovah came down upon it in fire. And from it smoke went up like the smoke of a furnace, and the entire mountain shook violently.

Then God spoke all these words: "I am Jehovah your God who brought you out of the land of Egypt, from a place where you were slaves.

"Thou Shalt Have no other Gods except Me.

"Thou Shalt Not Make for Thyself a Graven Image, nor any image of anything that is in the heavens above, on the earth beneath, or in the waters that are under the earth. Thou shalt not bow down before them, nor serve them, for I Jehovah thy God am a jealous God visiting the sins of the fathers upon the children to the third and fourth generation, but showing acts of kindness to the thousandth generation of those who love me and keep my commands.

"Thou Shalt Not Take the Name of Jehovah Thy God in Vain, for Jehovah will not leave him unpunished who takes his name in vain.

"Remember the Sabbath Day to Keep It Holy. Six days shalt thou labor and do all thy work; but the seventh day is the Sabbath of Jehovah thy God. In it thou shalt not do any work, neither thou, nor thy son, nor thy daughter, nor thy male servant, nor thy female servant, nor thy cattle, nor the guest who is with thee, for in six days Jehovah made the heavens and the earth, the sea and all that in them is, and rested on the seventh day. Therefore Jehovah blessed the Sabbath day and made it holy.

"Honor Thy Father and Thy Mother, that thou mayest live long on the land which Jehovah thy God giveth thee.

"Thou Shalt Not Murder.

"Thou Shalt Not Commit Adultery.

"Thou Shalt Not Steal.

"Thou Shalt Not Bear False Witness Against Thy Neighbor.

"Thou Shalt Not Covet Thy Neighbor's House; thou shalt not covet thy neighbor's wife, nor his male servant, nor his female servant, nor his ox, nor his ass, nor anything that belongs to thy neighbor."

Then Jehovah said to Moses, "Write down these words, for in accord with these words I have made a solemn agreement with you and with Israel."

OUR DUTIES TO GOD AND MAN

Hear O Israel: Jehovah our God is the one Lord. You shall love Jehovah your God with all your heart, with all your soul, and with all your strength.

Behold, the heavens, the highest heavens, the earth and all that is on it belong to Jehovah your God. Jehovah showed his love to your fathers more than to any other people, and he has chosen their children after them and you out of all the nations. Therefore, open your heart to him and no longer refuse to be guided by him. For Jehovah your God is God of gods and Lord of lords, the great, the mighty, the wonderful God, who shows no favors and takes no bribes, who sees that what is right is done to the orphan and widow, who loves the foreigner and gives him food and clothing. Love Jehovah your God and always keep his laws and his commands.

You shall not deceive one another.

You shall not lie to one another.

You shall not swear falsely in my name.

You shall not wrong nor rob your neighbor.

You shall not curse the deaf.

You shall not put a stumbling-block before the blind.

You shall not tell stories about one another.

You shall not hate any one.

You shall not take vengeance nor bear a grudge against any one.

You shall love your neighbor as yourself.

You shall rise before the hoary head and honor an old man.

If a foreigner lives in your land, you shall do him no wrong. You shall treat him as one of your own people and you shall love him as yourself.

THE REPORT OF THE HEBREW SPIES

Moses sent certain men to explore the land of Canaan and said to them, "Go up into the South Country and on into the highlands, and see what the land is and whether the people who live there are strong or weak, whether they are few or many, and whether the land in which they live is good or bad, and what kinds of cities they live in, whether in camps or in strongholds. See whether the land is fertile or barren, whether there is wood in it or not. Be courageous and bring some of the fruit of the land," for it was the time when the grapes first begin to ripen.

So they went up to the South Country and came to Hebron. When they came to the valley of Eshcol, they cut down from there a branch with one cluster of grapes and brought it away on a pole carried by two men. They also took some pomegranates and figs. That place was called the valley of the Grape Cluster because of the cluster which the Israelites cut down there.

Then they returned to Moses and Aaron and all the Israelites at Kadesh and brought back word to them and showed them the fruit of the land. They reported to Moses, "We went to the land to which you sent us; and it indeed is full of milk and honey; and this is some of its fruit. But the people who live in the land are strong, and the cities are very large and have high walls about them."

Then Caleb quieted the people and said, "Let us go up at once and take it, for we are well able to conquer it." But the men who had gone up with him said, "We are not able to conquer the people, for they are stronger than we, and all the people whom we saw there are very tall and large. There we saw the giants; we were as grasshoppers in our own sight, and so we seemed to them."

All the people wept that night and cried out, "Why did Jehovah bring us to this land to fall by the sword? Our wives and our little ones will be taken captive. Would it not be better for us to return to Egypt?" So they said to one another, "Let us choose a leader and return to Egypt."

Then Moses and Aaron bowed low before all the Israelites who were gathered there, and Joshua and Caleb, who were among those who explored the land, tore their clothes and said to them, "The land which we went to explore is a very good land. If Jehovah is pleased with us, he will bring us into this land and give it to us, a land which is full of milk and honey. Only do not rebel against Jehovah. Fear not the people of the land, for they will supply us with food. Their defense is taken away from over them, and Jehovah is with us; fear them not." But the people would not trust Jehovah.

Then Jehovah said to Moses, "How long will this people despise me? How long will they refuse to trust me in spite of all of the wonders which I have performed before their eyes? I will send sickness upon them and destroy them, and I will make you and your family a nation greater and mightier than theirs."

But Moses said to Jehovah, "When the Egyptians hear it, they will say, 'Jehovah has killed them in the wilderness because he was not able to bring this people into the land which he solemnly promised to them.' Forgive, I pray thee, the guilt of this people, because thy love is great, even as thou hast forgiven them from the time they left Egypt even until now."

Jehovah said, "I have forgiven as you have asked; but as surely as I live and as surely as the whole earth shall be filled with the glory of Jehovah, none of the men who have seen my glory and my wonders which I performed in Egypt and in the wilderness, and yet have tested me these ten times and have not listened to my voice, shall see the land which I have solemnly promised to their fathers, neither shall any of those who despise me see it. But I will bring my servant Caleb to the land to which he went, for he has shown a different spirit and has faithfully followed me, and his children shall possess it. But your little ones, who, you said, would be captives of war, I will bring in, and they shall possess the land which you have refused. Your dead bodies shall fall in this wilderness, and your children shall be wanderers there forty years and shall suffer for your unfaithfulness until your bodies have all decayed in the wilderness."

THE LAST WORDS OF MOSES

When Moses was old, he said to all the Israelites, "I am a hundred and twenty years old this day. I can no longer go out and come in, and Jehovah has said to me, 'You shall not go over this river Jordan.' Jehovah your God is going over before you. He will destroy these nations before you, and you shall drive them out; and Joshua is going over to lead you as Jehovah has commanded. Be brave and strong, do not be afraid of them, for Jehovah your God is leading you; he will not fail you nor forsake you."

Moses also called Joshua and said to him in the presence of all Israel, "Be brave and strong, for you shall bring this people into the land which Jehovah has promised to their fathers to give them; and you shall give it to them. Jehovah is going before you; he will be with you, he will not fail nor forsake you; fear not, nor be frightened."

Then Moses went up on the plains of Moab to Mount Nebo to the summit of Pisgah opposite Jericho. And Jehovah showed him all the land, and said to him, "This is the land which I have solemnly promised to Abraham, to Isaac, and to Jacob, saying, 'I will give it to your children.' I have let you see it with your own eyes, but you shall not go over there."

So Moses, the servant of Jehovah, died there in the land of Moab as Jehovah had said. And Jehovah buried him in the deep valley in the land of Moab; but to this day no man knows the place where he was buried. Moses was a hundred and twenty years old when he died, but his eye was not dim nor had he lost his strength. The Israelites wept for Moses on the plain of Moab thirty days, and then the days of weeping and mourning for Moses were ended.

Joshua the son of Nun was filled with the spirit of wisdom, for Moses had laid his hands upon him; and the Israelites listened to him and did as Jehovah commanded Moses. But in Israel no prophet had yet arisen whom Jehovah knew as well as he did Moses.

CROSSING THE RIVER JORDAN

After the death of Moses, Jehovah said to Joshua, Moses' helper, "Moses my servant is dead: Now arise, go over the Jordan with all this people to the land which I am about to give to the Israelites. As long as you live no one will be able to stand against you. As I was with Moses, so I shall be with you: I will not fail you nor forsake you. Be brave and strong, for you shall give this people the land which I solemnly promised their fathers I would give them. Only be brave and strong to keep faithfully all the law, as Moses my servant commanded you. Turn not from it to the right nor to the left, and you shall have success wherever you go. Have I not commanded you? Be brave and strong; fear not nor be afraid, for Jehovah your God is with you wherever you go."

Then Joshua gave this order to the officers who were over the people: "Go through all the camp and give this command: 'Prepare food for yourselves, for within three days you are to cross this Jordan, to go in and take the land which Jehovah your God has given you as your own.'"

While Joshua was at Shittim, he secretly sent two men as spies, with the command: "Go, explore the land and especially Jericho." So they went and entered the house of a woman named Rahab, and stayed there.

It was reported to the king of Jericho, "Some men came here to-night from the Israelites to explore the land." Therefore the king of Jericho sent to Rahab and said, "Bring out the men who entered your house, for they have come to explore all the land."

Now the woman had taken the two men and hidden them; so she said, "It is true, some men came to me, but I did not know where they came from. When the time came to shut the gate at night, the men went out and I do not know where they have gone. Follow after them quickly, for you may overtake them." She, however, had brought them up to the roof and hidden them with the stalks of flax which she had spread out there. So the men of Jericho followed after them in the direction of the fords of the Jordan; and as soon as the men of Jericho had gone out, the gate was closed.

The spies had hardly lain down when Rahab came up to them on the roof and said, "I know that Jehovah has given you the land and that fear of you has seized us and that because of you all who live in the land are losing heart. Now therefore swear to me by Jehovah, since I have treated you with kindness, that you will also treat my family kindly, and promise me that you will save the lives of my father, my mother, my brothers, and my sisters, together with all that they have, and will not put us to death." The men said to her, "We are ready to give our lives for you, if you do not tell what we are doing; and when Jehovah gives us the land, we will treat you kindly and faithfully."

Then she let them down by a rope through the window, for the house in which she lived was built into the city wall. She said to them, "Go into the hills, that the men who are looking for you may not find you, and hide yourselves there three days until they have returned. Then you may go on your way."

The men said to her, "We shall be free from our solemn promise to you, unless, when we come into the land, you bind this cord of scarlet thread in the window through which you let us down and gather your father, your mother, your brothers, and all your family into your house.

If any one goes out of the doors of your house into the street, he shall be responsible for his death and we shall be innocent. If any one stays with you in the house, we will be responsible for his death if any one lays hands on him. But if you tell what we are doing, we shall be free from our solemn promise to you." She replied, "It shall be as you say." So she sent them away. And when they were gone, she bound the scarlet cord in the window.

So they left and went into the hills and stayed there three days until those who were looking for them had returned. They sought for them in every direction but did not find them. Then the two men came down from the hills, crossed the river, and came to Joshua and told him all that had happened to them.

Joshua rose up early in the morning and set out from Shittim. And he and all the Israelites came to the Jordan and spent the night there before crossing. And Joshua said to the people, "Consecrate yourselves, for to-morrow Jehovah will do wonders among you. Come and hear the words of Jehovah your God. By this you shall know that a living God is with you: the ark of the Lord of all the earth is about to pass over before you into the Jordan. When the priests who bear the ark of the Lord of all the earth step into the waters of the Jordan, its waters shall be cut off, so that the waters that come down from above will stand still in a heap."

So when the people left their tents to pass over the Jordan, the priests, who were carrying the ark were in front of them. And when the bearers of the ark came to the Jordan, and the feet of the priests who were carrying the ark dipped in the brink of the water—for the Jordan overflows all its banks during the harvest time—the waters that came down from above stood still and its waters rose in a heap a long distance up the river at Adam, the city that is near Zarethan. The waters that went down toward the Dead Sea were wholly cut off, while the people crossed over opposite Jericho. The priests who were carrying the ark of Jehovah stood firm on dry ground in the middle of the Jordan, while all the Israelites passed over on dry ground, until the whole nation had completed the crossing of the Jordan.

When they had all crossed, Jehovah said to Joshua, "Command them to take from the middle of the Jordan, out of the place where the priests' feet stood, twelve stones and carry them over with you and lay them down in the camping-place, where you pass the night, that this may be a reminder to them. Then when your children ask from time to time: 'What do these stones mean to you?' you shall say to them, 'They are reminders that the waters of the Jordan were cut off before the ark of Jehovah, when it passed over the Jordan.' These stones shall be a constant reminder to the Israelites."

So the Israelites did as Joshua commanded and took up out of the middle of the Jordan twelve stones corresponding to the number of the tribes of the Israelites. They carried them over with them to the place where they camped and laid them down there.

Then the waters of the Jordan returned to their place and the river overflowed all its banks as before.

THE CAPTURE OF JERICHO AND AI

Now Jericho had closed its gates because of the Israelites, and no one went in or out. But Jehovah said to Joshua, "See, I have given Jericho to you with its king and its able warriors. You shall march around the city, all the soldiers going about the city once. You shall do this for six days, and on the seventh day the people shall make the attack, each man going up straight before him."

Then Joshua said to the people, "March around the city and let the armed men pass on before the ark of Jehovah. You shall not shout the battle-cry nor let your voice be heard; not a word shall escape from your mouth until the day I say to you, 'Shout the battle-cry'; then you shall shout!"

So he had the ark of Jehovah carried around the city once; then they returned to the camp and spent the night there. The second day they also marched around the city once and returned to the camp. Thus they did six days. The seventh day they rose early at dawn and made the circuit of the city in the same way, only on that day they marched about the city seven times. The seventh time the priests blew the trumpets, and Joshua said to the people, "Shout the battle-cry; for Jehovah has given you the city. The city and all that is in it shall be sacrificed to Jehovah; only Rahab and those who are with her in her house shall live, because she hid the messengers whom we sent."

So the people shouted the battle-cry and the wall fell down and they went straight up into the city and captured it. But Joshua spared the lives of Rahab and her father's family and all that she had, because she hid the messengers whom Joshua sent to explore Jericho; and they have lived among the Israelites even to this day.

Then Joshua set out with all the warriors to go up to Ai. And he selected thirty thousand brave soldiers and sent them out at night with this command, "Hide somewhere beyond the town, not very far from it, but be ready to act. I and all the people who are with me will go toward the town, but when they come out against us, we will flee before them. They will come out after us, until we have drawn them away from the town; for they will say, 'They are fleeing before us.' Then you shall rise up from where you are hiding, and take the town. When you have captured it, set it on fire."

So Joshua sent them out, and they went to the place where they were to hide and placed themselves on the west side of Ai. Joshua spent that night among the people, and rose early the next morning and gathered them, and he went up, together with the rulers of Israel, before the people to Ai. And the warriors who were with him went up and came before the town. When the king of Ai saw it, the men of the town quickly rose up and went out to fight against the Israelites, but the king did not know that men were hiding behind the town to rise up and attack him.

Then Joshua and the Israelites pretended to be beaten and fled toward the wilderness; and all the people that were in the town were called together to pursue them. So they left the town unguarded and pursued the Israelites. Then the men who were hiding rose quickly out of their place and set the town on fire. When the men of Ai looked back, they saw the smoke of the town rising to heaven; and they had no chance to flee this way or that, for the Israelites who had been fleeing to the wilderness turned back upon those who were following them. When the smoke of the town rose up, the rest of the Israelites came out of the town against them; so they were surrounded by the Israelites, some on this side, and some on that, so that they let none of the people of Ai remain or escape.

WOMEN WHO SAVED A NATION

Later Sisera, who had nine hundred iron chariots, cruelly oppressed the Israelites for twenty years. Then the prophetess Deborah, the wife of Lappidoth, delivered Israel. She used to sit under the palm-tree of Deborah between Ramah and Bethel in the highlands of Ephraim; and the Israelites went to her to have her decide their disputes.

She sent and called Barak, the son of Abinoam, from Kadesh Naphtali and said to him, "Does not Jehovah the God of Israel command you: 'Go, march to Mount Tabor and take with you ten thousand of the Naphtalites and of the Zebulunites? Then I will draw out to you at the brook Kishon Sisera with his chariots and his troops, and I will deliver him into your hands.'" Barak said to her, "If you will go with me, I will go, but if you will not go with me, I will not go." She replied, "I will certainly go with you, only you will not have the glory in this expedition on which you are going, for Jehovah will deliver Sisera into the hands of a woman."

So Deborah arose and went with Barak to Kadesh. Barak called the Zebulunites and the Naphtalites together at Kadesh and ten thousand men followed him; and Deborah also went up with him.

Now Heber the Kenite had left the Kenites, the children of Jethro the father-in-law of Moses, and had pitched his tent as far away as the oak which is near Kadesh.

When it was reported to Sisera that Barak the son of Abinoam had gone up to Mount Tabor, Sisera gathered together all his chariots, nine hundred iron chariots, and all his people from the heathen city Harosheth to the brook Kishon. Then Deborah said to Barak, "To the attack! for to-day Jehovah has delivered Sisera into your hands. Has not Jehovah gone out before you?"

So Barak went down from Mount Tabor followed by ten thousand men; and at the attack of Barak's swordsmen Jehovah put to flight Sisera and his chariots and all his forces, and Sisera got down from his war-chariot and fled on foot. But Barak pursued the chariots and the forces to Harosheth; and all the army of Sisera was destroyed by the sword; not a single man was left.

On that day Deborah and Barak, the son of Abinoam, sang this song:

"O Jehovah, when thou wentest from Seir,
Marching from the region of Edom,
Earth trembled, the heavens swayed,
The clouds also dripped water;
The hills quaked before Jehovah,
Yon Sinai, before Israel's God.
"In the days of Anath's son, Shamgar,
In Jael's days the roads were unused,
And travellers walked through byways.
Leaders disappeared in Israel,
Until you, O Deborah, rose,
Till you rose as a mother in Israel.

"My heart is with the commanders of Israel,
Who volunteered among the people. Bless Jehovah!
You who ride on tawny asses,
Who sit upon rich saddle-cloths;
You who walk by the way, tell of it.
Far from sounds of dividing the spoil,
In the places where water is drawn,
Let them tell of Jehovah's righteous acts,
And the righteous deeds of his leaders!

"Then the people of Jehovah
Went down to the gates, crying:
'Awake, awake, O Deborah,
Awake, awake, sing a battle-song!
Rise up, rise up, O Barak,
Take your captives, O son of Abinoam!'
"So they went down against the powerful,
The Lord's people against the mighty.
From Machir, commanders went down,
From Zebulun, standard-bearers,
Issachar's princes with Deborah,
And with Barak, the men of Naphtali;
Into the valley they streamed after him.

"Zebulun risked its life,
Naphtali on the heights of the field.
Rulers came, they fought,
The rulers of Canaan fought
At Taanach by the waters of Megiddo.
"They took no booty of silver,
For from heaven the very stars fought,
From their courses they fought against Sisera.

The brook Kishon swept them away,
That ancient brook, the brook Kishon.
O my soul, march on with strength!
Then did their horse hoofs pound
With the gallop, gallop of steeds.

"Blessed above women shall Jael be,
That wife of Heber, the Kenite,
More blessed than all nomad women!
Water he asked, milk she gave,
Curdled milk she brought him
In a bowl well fitted for lords!
She put her hand to the tent-pin,
Her right hand to the workman's hammer.
She struck Sisera, crushing his head,
She shattered, she pierced his temples.
At her feet he sank down and lay still,
At her feet he sank, he fell;
There he fell, a victim slain!

"Through the window she peered and cried,
Through the lattice, the mother of Sisera:
'Why so long his chariot in coming?
Why tarry the hoof-beats of steeds?'
Then the wisest of her ladies replied,
She herself also answered her question,
'Are they not dividing the spoil?
A woman or two for each warrior,
For Sisera a spoil of dyed stuffs,
A spoil of dyed stuffs embroidered,
Some pieces of lace for his neck?'
"So perish thy foes, O Jehovah!

But may those who love him be as the sun,
Rising up in invincible splendor!"

GIDEON'S BRAVE BAND

In course of time the Midianites conquered the Israelites. To escape them the Israelites made for themselves dens in the mountains and caves and strongholds. When the Israelites had sown their crops, the Midianites would come up and leave nothing for the Israelites to live on, neither sheep, nor ox, nor ass; for they came up with their cattle and their tents. The Israelites were so robbed by the Midianites, that they cried to Jehovah for help.

Then the angel of Jehovah came and sat down under the oak which was in Ophrah that belonged to Joash the Abiezerite; and his son, Gideon, was beating out wheat in the wine-press to hide it from the Midianites. The angel of Jehovah appeared to him and said, "Jehovah is with you, able warrior!" Gideon said to him, "O my lord, if Jehovah is with us, why then has all this overtaken us? Where are all his wonderful acts of which our fathers told us, saying, 'Did not Jehovah bring us from Egypt?' But now Jehovah has cast us off and given us into the power of the Midianites."

Then Jehovah turned to him and said, "With this strength which you have go and save Israel from the rule of the Midianites: do I not send you?" But Gideon said to him, "O Jehovah, how can I save Israel? See, my family is the poorest in Manasseh, and I am the least in my father's house." Jehovah said to him, "I will surely be with you, and you shall overthrow the Midianites as if they were only one man."

Then the spirit of Jehovah took possession of Gideon, and he sounded the war trumpet, and the Abiezerites assembled under his leadership. He also sent messengers throughout all the land of the Manassites, and they assembled under his leadership; and he sent messengers to the Asherites, the Zebulunites, and the Naphtalites, and they went up to join him. But

Jehovah said to Gideon, "You have too many people with you; if I give the Midianites up to the Israelites they will boast, 'We have saved ourselves!' Therefore, proclaim to your people, 'Whoever is afraid may go home.'"

Then Gideon separated them, so that twenty-two thousand of the people went back home, but ten thousand stayed. But Jehovah said to him, "The people are still too many; take them down to the water, and I will try them out for you there. Every one of whom I say to you, 'This one shall go with you,' shall go with you; and every one of whom I say to you, 'This one shall not go with you,' shall not go."

So Gideon brought the people down to the water. And Jehovah said to him, "You shall put by themselves all who lap the water with their tongues, as a dog laps, and all who kneel down on their knees to drink by themselves." The number of those who lapped with their tongue, putting their hand to their mouth, were three hundred men; but all the rest of the people knelt down on their knees to drink. Then Jehovah said to Gideon, "By the three hundred men who lapped I will save you and deliver the Midianites into your hands. Let all the rest of the people go home." So they took the food that the people had in their hands, and their trumpets; and Gideon sent home all the other Israelites, keeping only the three hundred men.

Then Gideon came to the Jordan and crossed it, and the three hundred men were with him, faint yet pursuing. And he said to the men of Succoth, "Give, I beg of you, loaves of bread to the people who follow me, for they are faint and I am pursuing after Zebah and Zalmunna, the kings of Midian." But the rulers of Succoth said, "Are Zebah and Zalmunna already in your power that we should give bread to your band?" Gideon replied, "When Jehovah has delivered Zebah and Zalmunna into my power, for this insult I will thrash your bare flesh with desert thorns and briers." He went on from there to Penuel and made the same request of the men of Penuel, but they made the same answer as the men of Succoth. To the men of Penuel he also said, "When I come back victorious, I will break down this tower."

Zebah and Zalmunna were in Karkor, and their forces were with them, in all about fifteen thousand men. Gideon went up by the caravan road and surprised the horde as it was encamped with no fear of being attacked. He divided the three hundred men into three companies. Into the hands of all of them he put horns and empty earthen jars. In each jar was a torch. He also said to them, "Watch me and do as I do. When I reach the outside of the camp and those who are with me blow a blast on the horn, then you also shall blow your horns on every side of the camp and cry, 'For Jehovah and Gideon!'"

So Gideon and the hundred men with him reached the outside of the camp at the beginning of the middle watch, when guards had just been posted; and they blew the horns and broke in pieces the jars that were in their hands. The two other companies also broke their jars, took the torches in their left hands and their swords in their right, and cried, "The Sword of Jehovah and of Gideon." And as they stood where they were, about the camp, the entire horde awoke, sounded the alarm, and fled. Zebah and Zalmunna also fled; but Gideon followed and captured the two kings of Midian and threw all the horde into a panic.

When Gideon returned from the battle, he captured a young man who lived at Succoth. At Gideon's request he wrote down for him the names of the rulers of Succoth and its leading men. There were seventy-seven in all. When Gideon came to the men of Succoth, he said, "See, here are Zebah and Zalmunna about whom you mocked me, saying, 'Are Zebah and Zalmunna already in your power that we should give bread to your men who are weary?'" Then he took desert thorns and briers, and with these he thrashed the leading men of Succoth. He also broke down the tower of Penuel and put to death the men of the town.

Then Gideon said to Zebah and Zalmunna, "What kind of men were those whom you killed at Tabor?" They replied, "They were just like you; each of them looked like a prince." Gideon said, "They were my own brothers, the sons of my mother. As surely as Jehovah lives, if you had saved them alive, I would not kill you now."

Then he said to Jether, his oldest son, "Up and kill them." But the boy did not draw his sword, because he was afraid, for he was only a boy. Then Zebah and Zalmunna said, "Get up yourself and fall upon us; for a man has a man's strength!" So Gideon rose and killed Zebah and Zalmunna, and took the crescents that were on their camels' necks.

Then the men of Israel said to Gideon, "Rule over us, and not only you but your son and your son's son after you, for you have saved us from the power of the Midianites." Gideon said to them, "I will not rule over you, nor shall my son rule over you; Jehovah shall rule over you; but let me make one request of you: let every man give me the ear-rings from his spoil" (for they had golden ear-rings, because they were desert dwellers). They answered, "Certainly, we will give them." So they spread out a blanket and each man threw into it the ear-rings from his spoil. The weight of the golden ear-rings for which he had asked was nearly seventy pounds of gold. Then Gideon made of the gold a priestly robe to wear when asking questions of Jehovah, and placed it in his own city, Ophrah.

Gideon died at a good old age and was buried in the tomb of Joash, his father, in Ophrah of the Abiezerites.

JEPHTHAH'S FOOLISH PROMISE

Jephthah, the Gileadite, was an able warrior, but he was the son of a wicked woman, and had fled from his relatives and lived in the land of Tob. There certain rascals gathered about him, and they used to go out on raids with him.

After a time the Ammonites made war against the Israelites. Then the elders of Gilead went to bring Jephthah from the land of Tob, and they said to him, "Come and be our commander, that we may fight against the Ammonites." But Jephthah said to the elders of Gilead, "Are you not the men who hated me and drove me out of my father's house? Why then do you come to me now when you are in trouble?" But the elders of Gilead said to Jephthah, "This is why we have now turned to you, that you may go with us and fight against the Ammonites, and you shall be our chief, even over all the people who live in Gilead." Then Jephthah said to the rulers of Gilead, "If you take me back to fight against the Ammonites and Jehovah gives me the victory over them, I shall be your chief." The elders of Gilead replied, "Jehovah shall be a witness between us; we swear to do as you say."

Then Jephthah went with the elders of Gilead, and the people made him chief and commander over them. Jephthah also made this vow to Jehovah: "If thou wilt deliver the Ammonites into my power, then whoever comes out of the door of my house to meet me, when I return victorious from the Ammonites, shall be Jehovah's, and I will offer that one as an offering to be burned with fire."

So Jephthah went out to fight against the Ammonites; and Jehovah gave him the victory over them, and delivered them into his hands. But when he came home to Mizpah, his daughter was just coming out to meet him with tambourines and choral dances. She was his only child; besides this one he had neither son nor daughter. So when he saw her, he tore his clothes and said, "Oh, my daughter, you have stricken me! It is you who are the cause of my woe! for I have made a solemn vow to Jehovah and cannot break it." She said to him, "My father, you have made a solemn vow to Jehovah; do to me what you have promised, since Jehovah has punished your enemies the Ammonites. But let this favor be granted me: spare me two months that I may go out upon the mountains with those who would have been my bridesmaids and lament because I will never become a wife and mother." He said, "Go."

So he sent her away for two months with her friends, and she mourned on the mountains because she would never become a wife and mother. At the end of two months she returned to her father, who did what he had vowed to do, even though she had never been married. So it became a custom in Israel: each year the women of Israel go out for four days to bewail the death of the daughter of Jephthah, the Gileadite.

SAMSON WHO DID TO OTHERS AS THEY DID TO HIM

There was a certain man of Zorah, of the clan of the Danites, named Manoah; and he and his wife had no children. But the angel of Jehovah appeared to the woman and said to her, "See, you have no children; but now be careful not to drink any wine nor strong drink, and do not eat anything unclean, for you are about to have a son. No razor shall be used upon your son's head, for from birth the boy shall belong to God." So the woman had a son and named him Samson.

Once Samson went down to Timnah and saw there a Philistine woman. When he came back he said to his father and mother, "I have seen a Philistine woman in Timnah. Get her as a wife for me." But his father and mother said to him, "Is there no woman in your own tribe or among all our people, that you must marry a wife from among the heathen Philistines?" But Samson said to his father, "Get her for me, for she suits me."

So Samson went with his father and mother to Timnah; and just as they came to the vineyards of Timnah, a full-grown young lion came roaring toward him. The spirit of Jehovah came upon Samson and, although he had nothing in his hand, he tore the beast in two as one tears a kid. But he did not tell his father and mother what he had done.

Then he went down and talked with the woman, and she suited him. When he returned after a while to marry her, he turned aside to see what was left of the lion, and there was a swarm of bees and honey in the carcass. He scraped the honey out into his hands and went on, eating it as he went. When he came to his father and mother, he gave some to them, and they ate; but he did not tell them that he had taken the honey out of the carcass of the lion.

Then Samson went down to the woman; and he gave a feast there (for so bridegrooms used to do). When the Philistines saw him, they provided thirty comrades to be with him. And Samson said to them, "Let me now tell you a riddle. If you can tell me what it is within the seven days of the feast, I will give you thirty fine linen robes and thirty suits of clothes; but if you cannot tell me, then you shall give me thirty fine linen robes and thirty suits of clothes." They said to him, "Tell your riddle, that we may hear it." And he said to them:

> "Out of the eater came something to eat,
> And out of the strong came something sweet."

But for six days they could not solve the riddle.

On the seventh day they said to Samson's wife, "Tease your husband until he tells us the riddle, or else we will burn up you and your father's house. Did you invite us here to make us poor?" So Samson's wife wept before him and said, "You only hate me and do not love me at all! You have told a riddle to my fellow countrymen and not told me what it is." He said to her, "See, I have not told it to my father or my mother, and shall I tell you?" So she wept before him as long as their feast lasted, but on the seventh day he told her, because she kept asking him; and she told the riddle to her fellow countrymen.

So the men of the city said to him on the seventh day before the sun went down, "What is sweeter than honey? And what is stronger than a lion?" And he said to them:

> "If with my heifer you did not plough,
> You had not solved my riddle now."

Then he was suddenly given divine strength, and he went down to Ashkelon and killed thirty of their men and took the spoil from them and gave the suits of clothes to those who had guessed the riddle. But he was very angry and returned to his father's house. And his bride was given to his comrade who had been his best man.

After a while, at the time of wheat harvest, Samson went to visit his wife with a kid as a present; but when he said, "Let me go into the inner room to my wife," her father would not let him go in, but said, "I thought that you must surely hate her, so I gave her to your best man. Is not her younger sister fairer than she? Take her then, instead." But Samson said to him, "This time I shall be justified if I do the Philistines an injury." So he went and caught three hundred foxes, turned them tail to tail, and put a torch between every pair of tails. When he had set the torches on fire, he let them go into the standing grain of the Philistines and burned up not only the shocks and the standing grain, but the olive orchards as well.

Then the Philistines said, "Who has done this?" The reply was, "Samson, the son-in-law of the Timnite, because that man took Samson's wife and gave her to his best man." So the Philistines went up, and burnt her and her father. Then Samson said to them, "If this is the way you do, I will not stop until I have had my revenge on you!" So he fought fiercely and killed many of them; then he went and stayed in a cavern in the cliff of Etam.

When the Philistines went up and camped in Judah and made a raid on Lehi, the Judahites said, "Why have you come up against us?" They replied, "We have come up to bind Samson, to do to him what he has done to us." Then three thousand men of Judah went down to the cavern in the cliff of Etam and said to Samson, "Do you not know that the Philistines are our rulers? What are you doing to us?" He replied, "I have done to them as they did to me." They said to him, "We have come down to bind you, to turn you over to the Philistines." Samson said to them, "Swear to me that you will not attack me yourselves." They said to him, "No; we will simply bind you securely and deliver you to them; but we will not kill you." So they bound him with two new ropes, and brought him up from the cliff.

When he came to Lehi, the Philistines shouted when they met him. Then he was suddenly given divine strength, and the ropes that were on his arms became like flax that has been burned in the fire, and his bonds melted from his hands. And he found a fresh jaw-bone of an ass, and having seized it, he killed a thousand men with it. Then Samson said:

"With the jaw-bone of an ass have I piled them, mass on mass;
A thousand warriors have I slain with the jaw-bone of an ass."

A STRONG MAN WHO LOST HIS STRENGTH

Afterward, Samson fell in love with a woman in the valley of Sorek, named Delilah. Then the rulers of the Philistines came to her and said, "Find out by teasing him how it is that his strength is so great and how we may overpower and bind him that we may torture him. Then we will each one of us give you eleven hundred pieces of silver." So Delilah said to Samson, "Tell me how it is that your strength is so great and how you might be bound to torture you?" Samson said to her, "If they should bind me with seven green bowstrings which have not been dried, I would become weak like any other man."

Then the rulers of the Philistines brought her seven green bowstrings which had not been dried, and she bound him with them. She had the men lying in wait in the inner room, but when she said to him, "The Philistines are upon you, Samson!" he snapped the bowstrings as a piece of yarn is snapped when it comes near the fire; so they did not find out the secret of his strength.

Then Delilah said to Samson, "You have deceived me and lied to me; now tell me with what you can be bound fast." He said to her, "If they should bind me securely with new ropes with which no work has been done, I would become weak like any other man." So Delilah took new ropes and bound him with them and said to him, "The Philistines are upon you, Samson!" Men were also lying in wait in the inner room; but he snapped the ropes from his arms like thread.

Again Delilah said to Samson, "So far you have deceived me and lied to me; tell me now with what you can be bound fast." He said to her, "If you should weave the seven braids on my head along with the web and beat it into form with the weaving pin, I would become weak like any other man." So while he was asleep, she took the seven braids of his hair and wove it with the web and beat it into form with the pin, and said to him, "The Philistines are upon you, Samson!" But he awoke out of his sleep and pulled up the loom and the web.

Then she said to him, "How can you say, 'I love you,' when you do not trust me? You have deceived me three times already and have not told me the secret of your great strength." But in time, since she daily begged and urged him, he was wearied to death, and told her all that he knew, saying, "A razor has never touched my head; for I have belonged to God from my birth. If I should be shaved, my strength would be gone, and I would become weak like any other man."

When Delilah saw that he had told her all that he knew, she sent and called for the rulers of the Philistines and said, "Come at once, for he has told me all that he knows." Then the rulers of the Philistines came up to her and brought the money with them. After she had put Samson to sleep on her knees, she called for a man and had him shave off the seven braids on his head. Then she began to tease him, and his strength went from him; and she said, "The Philistines are upon you, Samson!" And he awoke out of his sleep and thought, "I will get up as I have done at other times and shake myself free"; for he did not know that Jehovah had left him. So the Philistines seized him and bored out his eyes. Then they brought him down to Gaza and bound him with chains of brass, and then he was set to grinding in the prison. But the hair of his head began to grow again as soon as he was shaved.

Then the rulers of the Philistines assembled to offer a great sacrifice to their god Dagon and to rejoice, for they said, "Our god has given Samson, our enemy, into our power." When the people saw him, they also praised their god, saying:

"Our god has laid low our foe,
He who brought our country woe,
He who slew us with many a blow."

When they were in high spirits, they said, "Call Samson that he may amuse us." So they called Samson from the prison and he amused them; and they placed him between the pillars.

Then Samson said to the young man who held him by the hand, "Let me touch the pillars on which the building rests, that I may lean against them." Now the building was full of men and women, and all the rulers of the Philistines were there, and on the roof about three thousand men and women were looking on while Samson amused them. Samson called on Jehovah and said, "O Jehovah, remember me and strengthen me, I pray thee, just this once, O God, that by one act I may avenge myself on the Philistines for the loss of my two eyes."

Then Samson took hold of the two middle pillars upon which the building rested, one with his right hand and the other with his left, and leaned against them. And Samson said, "Let me die with the Philistines." Then he bent over with all his strength, and the house fell upon the rulers and upon all the people who were in it. So those whom he killed at his death were more than those whom he killed during his lifetime.

Then his brothers and all his family came down and took him away and buried him between Zorah and Eshtaol in the burying-place of Manoah his father.

THE DEVOTION OF RUTH

During the days of the judges, there was once a famine in the land; and a certain man from Bethlehem in Judah took his wife and two sons to live in the territory of Moab. His name was Elimelech and his wife's Naomi, and his two sons were Mahlon and Chilion. After they had been living in Moab for some time, Elimelech died, and Naomi was left with her two sons. They married Moabite women, named Orpah and Ruth. After they had lived there about ten years, Mahlon and Chilion both died, and Naomi was left without husband or children.

So she set out with her daughters-in-law to return from the land of Moab, for she had heard that Jehovah had remembered his people and given them food. As they were setting out on the journey to Judah, Naomi said to her daughters-in-law, "Go, return each of you to the home of your mother. May Jehovah be kind to you, as you have been kind to the dead and to me. Jehovah grant that each of you may find peace and happiness in the house of a new husband."

Then she kissed them; but they began to weep aloud and said to her, "No, we will return with you to your people." But Naomi said, "Go back, my daughters; why should you go with me? Can I still have sons who might become your husbands? Go back, my daughters, go your own way, for I am too old to have a husband. Even if I should say, 'I have hope,' even if I should have a husband to-night and should have sons, would you wait for them until they were grown up? Would you remain single for them? No, my daughters! I am sorry for you, for Jehovah has afflicted me." Then they again wept aloud, and Orpah kissed her mother-in-law good-by, but Ruth stayed with her.

Naomi said, "See, your sister-in-law is going back to her own people and to her own gods; go along with her!" But Ruth answered, "Do not urge me to leave you or to go back, for wherever you go I will go, and wherever you stay I will stay; your people shall be my people, and your God my God; I will die where you die and be buried there. May Jehovah bring a curse upon me, if anything but death separate you and me." When Naomi saw that Ruth had made up her mind to go with her, she ceased urging her to return.

So they travelled on until they came to Bethlehem. When they arrived there, the whole town was interested, and the women said, "Is this Naomi?" But she said to them, "Do not call me Naomi which means Sweetness: call me Mara which means Bitterness, for the Almighty has given me a bitter lot. I had plenty when I left, but Jehovah has brought me back empty-handed. Why should you call me Naomi, now that Jehovah has turned against me, and the Almighty has afflicted me?" So Naomi and

Ruth returned from Moab; and they came to Bethlehem at the beginning of the barley harvest.

Now Naomi was related through her husband to Boaz, a very wealthy man of the family of Elimelech. Ruth, the Moabitess, said to Naomi, "Let me now go into the fields and pick up the scattered heads of grain after him whose favor I should win." Naomi said to her, "Go, my daughter."

So she went to pick up grain in the field after the reapers; and it was her good fortune to pick up grain in that part of the field which belonged to Boaz, who was of the family of Elimelech. When Boaz come from Bethlehem and said to the reapers, "Jehovah be with you," they answered him, "May Jehovah bless you." Then Boaz said to his servant who had charge of the reapers, "Whose maiden is this?" The servant replied, "It is the Moabite maiden who came back with Naomi from the land of Moab; and she said, 'Let me pick up the scattered grain and gather sheaves after the reapers.' So she came and has worked all the time until now, and she has not rested a moment in the field."

Then Boaz said to Ruth, "Listen, my daughter. Do not go to pick up grain in another field nor leave this place, but stay here with my maidens. I have told the young men not to trouble you. When you are thirsty, go to the jars and drink of that which the young men have drawn."

Then she bowed low and said to him, "Why are you so kind to me, to take interest in me who am from another land?" Boaz replied, "I have heard what you have done for your mother-in-law since the death of your husband, and how you left your father and mother and your native land to come to a people that you did not know before. May Jehovah repay you for what you have done, and may you be fully rewarded by the God of Israel, under whose wings you have come to take refuge." Then she said, "I trust I may please you, my lord, for you have comforted me and spoken kindly to your servant, although I am not really equal to one of your own servants."

Ruth
Painted by Henry Ryland

At noonday Boaz said to her, "Come here and eat some of the food and dip your piece of bread in the wine." So she sat beside the reapers; and he passed her the roasted grain, and she ate until she had had enough and had some left. When she rose to gather grain, Boaz gave this order to his young men: "Let her gather grain even among the sheaves and do not disturb her. Also pull out some for her from the bundles and leave it for her to gather and do not find fault with her."

So she gathered grain in the field until evening, then beat out that which she had gathered; and it was about a bushel of barley. Then she took it up and went into the city and showed her mother-in-law what she had gathered. She also brought out and gave her that which she had left from her meal after she had had enough.

Her mother-in-law said to her, "Where did you gather grain to-day and where did you work? A blessing on him who took interest in you!" Then she told her mother-in-law where she had worked, and said, "The name of the man with whom I worked to-day is Boaz." Naomi said to her daughter-in-law, "May the blessing of Jehovah rest upon him who has not ceased to show his love to the living and to the dead." Naomi also said to her, "The man is a near relative of ours." Ruth the Moabitess added, "He said to me, 'You must keep near my young men until they have completed all my harvest.'" Naomi said to Ruth, "It is best, my daughter, that you should go out with his maidens and that no one should find you in another field." So she gathered grain with the maidens of Boaz until the end of the barley and wheat harvest; but she lived with her mother-in-law.

Then Naomi said to her, "My daughter, shall I not try to find a home for you where you will be happy and contented? Is not Boaz, with whose maidens you have been, a relative of ours? This very night he is going to winnow barley on the threshing-floor. So bathe and anoint yourself and put on your best clothes and go down to the threshing-floor; but do not make yourself known to the man until he is through eating and drinking. Then when he lies down, you mark the place where he lies. Go in, uncover his feet, lie down, and then he will tell you what to do." Ruth said to her, "I will do as you say."

So she went down to the threshing-floor and did just as her mother-in-law told her. When Boaz was through eating and drinking and was in a happy mood, he went to lie down at the end of the heap of grain. Then Ruth came softly and uncovered his feet and lay down. At midnight the man was startled and turned over, and there was a woman lying at his feet. He said, "Who are you?" She answered, "I am Ruth your servant; spread therefore your skirt over your servant, for you are a near relative." He said, "May you be blest by Jehovah, my daughter; for you have shown me greater favor now than at first, for you have not followed young men, whether poor or rich. My daughter, have no fear; I will do for you all that you ask; for all my townsmen know that you are a good woman. Now it is true that I am a near relative; yet there is one nearer than I. Stay here to-night, and then in the morning, if he will marry you, well, let him do it. But if he, being your nearest relative, will not marry you, then as surely as Jehovah lives, I will do so. Lie down until morning."

So she lay at his feet until morning, but rose before any one could tell who she was, for Boaz said, "Let it not be known that a woman came to the threshing-floor." He also said, "Bring the cloak which you have on and hold it." So she held it while he poured into it six measures of barley and laid it on her shoulders. Then he went into the city.

When Ruth came to her mother-in-law, Naomi said, "Is it you, my daughter?" Then Ruth told Naomi all that the man had done for her. She said, "He gave me these six measures of barley; for he said, 'Do not go to your mother-in-law empty-handed.'" Naomi said, "Wait quietly, my daughter, until you know how this will turn out, for the man will not rest unless he settles it all to-day."

Then Boaz went up to the gate and sat down. Just then the near relative of whom Boaz had spoken came along. To him Boaz said, "Ho!" calling him by name, "come here and sit down." So he stopped and sat down. Boaz also took ten of the town elders and said, "Sit down here." So they sat down.

Then he said to the near relative, "Naomi, who has come back from the country of Moab, is offering for sale the piece of land which belonged to our relative Elimelech, and I thought that I would lay the matter before you, and ask you to buy it in the presence of these men who sit here and of the elders of my people. If you will buy it and so keep it in the family, do so; but if not, then tell me, that I may know; for no one but you has the right to buy it, and I am next to you." He said, "I will buy it."

Then Boaz said, "On the day you buy the field from Naomi, you must also marry Ruth the Moabitess, the widow of Mahlon, that a son may be born to bear his name and to receive this field." The near relative said, "I cannot buy it for myself, for fear I should lose what already belongs to me. You take my right of buying it as a relative, for I cannot do so."

Now in those days this was the custom in Israel: to make an agreement between two men the one drew off his shoe and gave it to the other. So when the near relative said to Boaz, "Buy it for yourself," Boaz drew off the man's shoe.

Then Boaz said to the elders and to all the people, "You are witnesses at this time that I have bought all that was Elimelech's and all that was Chilion's and Mahlon's from Naomi. Moreover, I have secured Ruth, the Moabitess, the widow of Mahlon, to be my wife so that she may have a son who will receive this land and carry on Mahlon's name. You are witnesses this day."

Then all the people who were at the gate and the elders said, "We are witnesses. May Jehovah make the woman who is coming into your house like Rachel and Leah, and make you also famous in Bethlehem."

So Boaz married Ruth, and she became his wife; and Jehovah gave to her a son. Then the women said to Naomi, "Blessed be Jehovah who has not left you at this time without a near relative, and may his name be famous in Israel. This child will bring back your strength and take care of you in your old age; for your daughter-in-law who loves you, who is worth more to you than seven sons, has a son!"

So Naomi took the child in her arms and she became its nurse. Her neighbors also said, "Naomi has a son!" and they named him Obed; he became the father of Jesse, who was the father of David.

SAMUEL THE BOY PROPHET

Elkanah, a Zuphite of the hill country of Ephraim, lived at Ramah with his two wives, Hannah and Peninnah. Peninnah had children, but Hannah had none.

This man used to go up from his village each year to worship and offer a sacrifice to Jehovah of hosts at Shiloh. Whenever the day came for Elkanah to offer a sacrifice he gave portions to his wife Peninnah and to all his sons and daughters; but although he loved Hannah, he gave her only one portion, for Jehovah had given her no children. Peninnah made her angry by mocking her, for Jehovah had given her no children. Elkanah did this year after year; but whenever Hannah went up to the temple of Jehovah, Peninnah made her so angry that she wept and would not eat. So Elkanah her husband said to her, "Hannah, why do you weep and why do you not eat? Why are you so troubled? Am I not more to you than ten sons?"

After they had eaten in Shiloh, Hannah arose and stood before the temple of Jehovah, while Eli the priest was sitting on his seat beside the door posts of the temple. With a sad heart she prayed earnestly to Jehovah and wept bitterly. She also made this sacred promise:

"O Jehovah of hosts!
If thou wilt look at my affliction,
And remember, not forgetting thy servant,
But wilt give thy servant a son,
Then I will give him to thee,
Throughout all the days of his life;
And no razor shall touch his head."

While she continued praying before Jehovah, Eli watched her mouth. She spoke to herself; her lips moved, but her voice was not heard, so that Eli thought that she was drunk and said to her, "How long will you act like a drunken woman? Put away your wine and go from the presence of Jehovah." But Hannah answered, "No, my lord, I am an unhappy woman; I have not drunk wine nor any strong drink, but I have been pouring out my heart before Jehovah. Do not think that your servant is a wicked woman, for I have gone on speaking until now because my grief and vexation are so great." Eli answered, "Go in peace, and may the God of Israel grant what you have asked of him." She said, "May your servant have your approval!" So the woman went away and ate, and her face was no longer sad.

Early in the morning she and her husband rose; and after they had worshipped Jehovah, they returned to their home at Ramah. In the course of the year Hannah had a son and named him Samuel, saying, "I asked him of Jehovah."

Elkanah and all his household again went to offer the yearly sacrifice to Jehovah, but Hannah did not go up, for she said to her husband, "When the child is weaned, then I will take him, and he shall go to Jehovah's temple and live there the rest of his life." Elkanah said to her, "Do what seems best to you; wait until you have weaned him; only may Jehovah help you to do what you have promised."

So the woman waited and nursed her son until she weaned him. Then she took him with her, and a three-year-old ox, a bushel of flour, and a skin of wine, and brought him to the temple of Jehovah at Shiloh. Then they killed the ox, and Hannah brought the child to Eli and said, "Oh, my lord, as surely as you live, I am the woman who stood near you here praying earnestly to Jehovah. This is the boy for whom I prayed. Jehovah has granted what I asked of him. Therefore I have given him to Jehovah; as long as he lives he belongs to Jehovah."

Elkanah returned to his home in Ramah, but the boy stayed to serve Jehovah under the direction of Eli the priest. So Samuel—a young boy dressed in a linen robe—did the duties of a priest in the temple. His mother also made him a little robe and each year brought it to him when she came up with her husband to offer the yearly sacrifice.

Eli blessed Elkanah and said, "Jehovah repay you with children from this woman for the gift which she has given to Jehovah." Then they returned to their home; and Hannah had three more sons and two daughters. Meantime the boy Samuel grew up in the temple of Jehovah.

The sons of Eli were very wicked. They knew not Jehovah, and they despised the offerings which were brought to him. Eli was very old, and whenever he heard that his sons were doing wrong he said to them, "Why do you do such things, for I hear of your wicked deeds from all the people. No, my sons: it is not a good report that I hear from the people of Jehovah." But they did not listen to the words of their father.

The boy Samuel grew and won the favor both of Jehovah and of men. He continued to serve Jehovah under the direction of Eli; but in those days not many messages came from Jehovah.

One day Eli was lying in his room. His eyes had begun to grow dim so that he could not see. While the lamp of God was still burning, and Samuel was lying in the temple of Jehovah where the ark of God was, Jehovah called, "Samuel! Samuel!" He answered, "Here am I." Then he ran to Eli and said, "Here am I, for you called me." But Eli said, "I did not call, lie down again." So he went and lay down. Then Jehovah called again, "Samuel! Samuel!" Samuel rose and went to Eli and said, "Here am I, for you called me." But Eli answered, "I did not call, my son; lie down again."

Now Samuel did not yet know Jehovah nor had a message from Jehovah been given to him. So when Jehovah called Samuel again the third time, he rose and went to Eli and said, "Here am I, for you called me!" Then Eli knew that Jehovah was calling the boy. So he said to Samuel, "Go, lie down, and if you are called, say, 'Speak, Jehovah, for thy servant is listening.'" So Samuel went and lay down in his place.

Then Jehovah came and called as at other times, "Samuel! Samuel!" And Samuel answered, "Speak, for thy servant is listening." Jehovah said to Samuel, "See, I am about to do a thing in Israel that will make the ears of every one who hears it tingle. On that day I will do to Eli all that I have said that I would do to his family from the first to the last. For I have told him that I will punish his family forever for the crime of which he knew his sons were guilty, for they did not do what God commanded and he did not stop them."

Samuel lay until morning, and then he opened the doors of the temple of Jehovah. He was afraid to tell the vision to Eli. But when Eli called him and said, "Samuel, my son," he said, "Here am I." Eli asked, "What is the thing that Jehovah said to you? Keep nothing from me; may God do to you whatever he will, if you keep from me a word of all that he said to you." So Samuel told him everything, and kept nothing from him. And Eli said, "It is Jehovah; let him do what seems good to him."

THE ARK AMONG THE PHILISTINES

In those days the Israelites went out to meet the Philistines, and in a hard-fought battle the Israelites were defeated by the Philistines.

When the people returned to the camp, the leaders of Israel said, "Why has Jehovah let us be beaten to-day by the Philistines? Let us bring the ark of our God from Shiloh. He may then go out with us and deliver us from our enemies."

So the people sent to Shiloh and took from there the ark of Jehovah of hosts. When it came to the camp, all the Israelites shouted so loud that the earth resounded.

The Philistines heard the sound of the shouting and said, "What does this sound of great shouting in the camp of the Hebrews mean?" When they knew that the ark of Jehovah had come to the camp, they were afraid, for they said, "Their god has come to their camp. Woe to us! for it has never been so before; but be strong and act like men." So the Philistines fought, and the Israelites were defeated and each fled to his tent.

The same day a Benjamite from the ranks ran to Shiloh with his clothes torn and with earth on his head. As he came, Eli was sitting on his seat by the gate watching the road, for his heart was trembling for the ark of God.

When the man came and told the people of the city, they all cried out. Eli heard the sound of crying and said, "What is this uproar?" So the man came quickly and told Eli, "I am the man who came from the battle, for I fled from the ranks." Eli said, "How did it go, my son?" The messenger answered, "Israel fled from the Philistines, and many people were killed, and your two sons are dead, and the ark of God has been captured." When he spoke of the ark of God, Eli fell off his seat backward beside the gate, and his neck was broken, for he was old and heavy, and he died.

The Philistines took the ark of God and brought it to the temple of Dagon in Ashdod and set it up by the side of Dagon. When the people of Ashdod rose early the next day and came to the temple of Dagon, there was Dagon on the ground flat on his face before the ark of Jehovah. Then they raised up Dagon and set him in his place again. But when they rose early on the following morning, there was Dagon on the ground flat on his face before the ark of Jehovah. The head of Dagon and both his hands were broken off on the door sill, and only his body was left.

Jehovah severely punished the people of Ashdod, for he punished them with boils. When the men of Ashdod saw this, they said, "The ark of the god of Israel shall not stay with us, for he is severely punishing us and Dagon our god." So they sent for all the rulers of the Philistines and asked, "What shall we do with the ark of the god of Israel?" They answered, "Let it be carried around to Gath."

So they carried the ark of the God of Israel around to Gath. Then Jehovah punished the men of that city, both young and old, with boils. Therefore they sent the ark of the God of Israel to Ekron; but when it came to Ekron, the Ekronites cried out, "They have brought around the ark of the god of Israel to kill us and our people!" They sent, therefore, and gathered all the rulers of the Philistines and said, "Send the ark of the god of Israel back to its own place, so that it will not kill us and our people!"

Then the Philistines called the priests and diviners and asked, "What shall we do with the ark of Jehovah? Tell us with what we shall send it to its place." They said, "If you send back the ark of the god of Israel, you must not send it away empty, but must return to him an offering to repay him for all that you have done to the ark. Then you shall be healed, and you shall know why he has continued to punish you." They said, "What offering shall we send back in order to repay him?"

They said, "Five golden boils and five golden mice, the same number as the rulers of the Philistines; for one plague was upon you as well as upon your rulers. Now therefore prepare a new cart and two milch cows that have never worn a yoke, and fasten the cows to the cart, but leave their calves behind them at home. Then take the ark of Jehovah and place it upon the cart and put in a box at its side the golden objects which you are sending to them as an offering to repay him. Then send it away. If it goes on the way to its own border, to Bethshemesh, then it is Jehovah who has done us this great harm; but if not, then we shall know that it is not he who has punished us; it was only an accident."

The men did so, and the cows took a straight course along the Bethshemesh road. They went along the highway, lowing as they went, and did not turn aside to the right nor to the left. The rulers of the Philistines also went after them as far as Bethshemesh.

The inhabitants of Bethshemesh were harvesting their wheat in the valley, and when they looked up and saw the ark, they rejoiced at the sight. When the ark came into the field of Joshua, the Bethshemeshite, it stood still there. And a great stone was there; so they split up the wood of the cart and offered the cows as a burnt-offering to Jehovah. When the five rulers of the Philistines saw it, they returned to Ekron the same day.

HOW SAMUEL FOUND A LEADER

There was a rich Benjamite named Kish, who lived at Gibeah. He had a son named Saul, a man full grown and handsome; no one among the Israelites was more handsome than he. From his shoulders and upward he was taller than any of the people.

Now the asses of Kish, Saul's father, were lost. So Kish said to Saul, "Take one of the servants with you and go, look for the asses." They went through the highlands of Ephraim and the land of Shalishah, but did not find them. Then they crossed into the land of Shaalim, but the asses were not there. They also went through the land of Benjamin, but did not find them.

They had come into the land of Zuph when Saul said to his servant who was with him, "Come, let us go back, that my father may not stop thinking of the asses and be anxious about us." The servant answered him, "There is a man of God in this town who is held in honor; all that he says is sure to come true. Now let us go there; perhaps he can tell us the way we should go."

Saul said to his servant, "But, suppose we go, what shall we take to the man, for the bread is gone from our sacks, and there is no present to take to the man of God? What have we?" The servant answered Saul again and said, "See, I have with me a quarter of a silver shekel. Give it to the man of God that he may tell us our way." Then Saul said to his servant, "Your advice is good; come, let us go." So they went to the town where the man of God was.

As they were going up to the town, they met young women going out to draw water and said to them, "Is the seer here?" They answered them, "He is there; he is before you. Make haste, for he has just come into the town, for the people have a sacrificial feast to-day at the sacred place on the hilltop. As soon as you come to the town, you will find him before he goes up to the high place to eat, for the people will not eat until he comes, for he blesses the sacrifice, and then the guests eat. Therefore go up now, for at this time you will find him."

So they went up to the town, and when they came inside the gate, Samuel was just coming out toward them to go up to the high place. Now Jehovah had told Samuel the day before Saul came, "About this time to-morrow I will send you a man out of the land of Benjamin, and you shall anoint him to be a prince over my people Israel. He shall deliver my people from the power of the Philistines; for I have seen the suffering of my people, because their cry has come to me."

When Samuel saw Saul, Jehovah told him, "This is the man of whom I spoke to you! He it is who shall rule over my people." So when Saul met Samuel in the gate, and said, "Tell me, if you will, where the seer's house is," Samuel answered Saul, "I am the seer; go up before me to the high place, for you shall eat with me to-day; and in the morning I will let you go and will tell you all that is in your mind. As for your asses that were lost three days ago, do not trouble yourself about them for they have been found. And to whom belongs all that is best in Israel? Does it not belong to you and to your father's house?" Saul answered and said, "Am I not a Benjamite, of the smallest of the tribes of Israel, and is not my family the least of all the families of the tribe of Benjamin? Why then do you speak to me in this way?"

But Samuel took Saul and his servant and brought them into the hall and made them sit at the head of the guests (who were about thirty in number). Samuel also said to the cook, "Bring the part which I gave you and told you to put aside." So the cook took up the leg and what was on it and placed them before Saul. Then Samuel said, "See what has been kept for you! Set it before you and eat, for it was kept for you until the appointed time, that you might eat with the people whom I have invited." So Saul ate with Samuel that day.

After they came down from the high place into the town, they spread a bed for Saul on the roof, and he lay down. Then at daybreak Samuel called to Saul on the roof, saying, "Rise, that I may send you away." So Saul rose, and he and Samuel went out into the street. As they were going out of the town, Samuel said to Saul, "Tell the servant to go on before us, but you stand here that I may tell you the message from God."

Then Samuel took the flask of oil and poured it on Saul's head, and kissed him and said, "Has not Jehovah anointed you to be a prince over his people Israel? You shall rule over Jehovah's people and deliver them from the power of their enemies on every side. This is the sign that

Jehovah has anointed you to be a prince over his own people: when you go from me to-day you shall find two men at Rachel's tomb; and they will say to you, 'The asses that you went to seek are found, and now your father is thinking no more about the asses but is worrying about you, saying, "What shall I do for my son?"' Then you shall go on from there and come to the oak of Tabor. There three men going up to God at Bethel will meet you, one carrying three kids, another carrying three loaves of bread, and another carrying a skin of wine. They will greet you and give you two loaves of bread which you shall take from their hand. After that you shall come to Gibeah. As you come to the city you will meet a band of prophets coming down from the high place with a lyre, a tambourine, a flute, and a harp before them, while they prophesy. Then the spirit of Jehovah will come suddenly upon you, and you shall prophesy with them, and shall be changed into another man. When these signs come to you, do whatever you can, for God is with you." So when Saul turned away from Samuel, God gave him a new heart, and all those signs came to pass that day.

Saul's uncle also said to him and to his servant, "Where did you go?" He said, "To seek the asses; and when we saw that they were not to be found, we went to Samuel." Saul's uncle said, "Tell me what Samuel said to you." Saul replied, "He told us that the asses were surely found." But Saul did not tell him that Samuel had said he should become the ruler.

After about a month, Nahash, the Ammonite, came up and besieged Jabesh in Gilead; and all the men of Jabesh said to Nahash, "Make terms with us and we will serve you." But Nahash, the Ammonite, said to them. "On this condition will I make terms with you: that I bore out the right eye of each of you, and so bring disgrace upon all Israel." The elders of Jabesh said to him, "Let us have seven days in which to send messengers through all the land of Israel. Then, if there are none to save us, we will come to you."

So the messengers came to Gibeah where Saul lived and told the facts in the hearing of the people, and they all set up a loud wail. Just then Saul was coming from the field behind the oxen, and he said, "What is the trouble with the people that they are wailing?" Then they told him what the men of Jabesh had said. When he heard it, the spirit of Jehovah came suddenly upon him and he became very indignant. He took a pair of oxen, cut them in pieces, and sent them through all the land of Israel by messengers, who said, "Whoever does not come out after Saul and after Samuel, the same shall be done to his oxen!"

Then a terror from Jehovah fell upon the people, and they all gathered together. And Saul said to the messengers who came, "Say to the men of Jabesh in Gilead, 'To-morrow by the time the sun grows hot help shall come to you.'"

So the messengers went and told the men of Jabesh, and they were glad. Therefore the men of Jabesh said to the Ammonites, "To-morrow we will come out to you, and you shall do to us whatever you please." So on the following day, Saul divided the people into three divisions; and they went into the midst of the camp early in the morning, and fought against the Ammonites until noon. The Ammonites who stayed behind were so scattered that not two of them were left together.

Then all the people went to Gilgal and there in the presence of Jehovah made Saul their ruler, and they offered sacrifices there to Jehovah; and Saul and all the men of Israel were very happy.

JONATHAN'S BRAVE DEED

Saul picked out three thousand men from the Israelites. Two thousand were with Saul in Michmash and on the highland of Bethel, and a thousand were with his son Jonathan in Gibeah. But Saul had sent the rest of the people each to his home.

Then Jonathan attacked the company of the Philistines in Gibeah; and the Philistines heard of it. But Saul sounded a call to arms throughout all the land, saying, "Let the Hebrews hear!" So all Israel heard the report that Saul had attacked the Philistines, and also that Israel was hated by them.

Then the Philistines were gathered together to fight with Israel: three thousand chariots, six thousand horsemen, and foot soldiers as many as the sand of the seashore. They came up and camped in Michmash. When the men of Israel saw that they were in a tight place (for the people were hard pressed), the people hid themselves in caves, in holes, in the rocks, in tombs, and in pits. Also many people crossed over the Jordan to the land of Gad and Gilead.

Then Saul counted the people who were with him and found that there were about six hundred men. And Saul and his son Jonathan, together with the people who were with them, remained in Gibeah, while the Philistines camped in Michmash. Then the Philistines came out of the camp in three divisions to steal whatever they could find: one division turned toward Ophrah, in the land of Shual, another toward Bethhoron, and another toward the hill that looks down over the valley of Zeboim. But the garrison of the Philistines went out to the pass of Michmash.

Now on that day Jonathan the son of Saul said to the young man who carried his armor, "Come, let us go over against the Philistines' garrison that is on the other side." But he did not tell his father.

Meantime Saul was sitting just outside of Gibeah under the pomegranate-tree which is near the threshing-floor, and there were with him about six hundred men. But the people did not know that Jonathan had gone.

Along the ravine by which Jonathan tried to go over against the Philistines there was a steep rock on one side, and a steep rock on the other; one was named The Shining, and the other The Thorny. One rock rose up north of Michmash, and the other south of Geba.

So Jonathan said to the young man who carried his armor, "Come, let us go over to the camp of these heathen Philistines. Perhaps Jehovah will act for us, for there is nothing that can keep Jehovah from delivering his people either by many or by few." His armor-bearer replied, "Do whatever you wish, I will do my best to help you." Then Jonathan said, "See, we will cross over to the men and show ourselves to them. If they say to us, 'Stand still until we can reach you,' then we will stand still in our place, and will not go up to them. But if they say, 'Come up to us,' then we will go up; for this shall be the proof that Jehovah has given them into our power."

When both of them showed themselves to the Philistines, the Philistines said, "There are Hebrews coming out of the holes where they have hidden." So they called to Jonathan and his armor-bearer, "Come up to us, and we will show you something!" Then Jonathan said to his armor-bearer, "Come up after me, for Jehovah has given them into the power of Israel."

So Jonathan climbed up on his hands and feet and his armor-bearer after him. And the Philistines fell before Jonathan, and his armor-bearer followed and put them to death. In the first attack Jonathan and his armor-bearer killed about twenty men with spears and rocks from the field. Then there was a great panic in the camp, in the open field, and among all the Philistines. Even those who were out robbing were panic-stricken, and the earth quaked, so that it produced a God-sent panic.

The watchmen of Saul in Gibeah looked and saw the great company of Philistines melting away and rushing here and there. Then Saul said to the people who were with him, "Look now and see who is gone from us." When they searched they found that Jonathan and his armor-bearer were not there. So Saul said to Ahijah, "Bring the ark of God here," for at that time it was with the Israelites. While Saul was still speaking to the priest, the noise and disorder among the Philistines kept on increasing. Therefore, Saul said to the priest, "Do not wait to consult Jehovah!"

Then Saul and all the people that were with him gathered together and went into battle. And every Philistine's sword was turned upon his fellow, so that there was a very great confusion among them. The Hebrews who once were on the side of the Philistines and who had joined their army also went over to the side of the Israelites who were with Saul and Jonathan. Likewise all the men of Israel who were hiding in the highlands of Ephraim, when they heard that the Philistines had fled, closely followed them in the battle. So Jehovah delivered Israel that day, and the battle passed over beyond Bethhoron. But Saul made a great mistake that day, for he strictly commanded the people, saying, "The man who shall eat any food until evening and until I take vengeance on my enemies shall be punished." So none of the people tasted food.

Now there was honey on the surface of the ground; and when the people came to the forest, they saw a stream of honey, but no one put his hand to his mouth, for the people feared the punishment. But Jonathan had not heard when his father commanded the people. Therefore he reached out the end of the staff that was in his hand and dipped it in the honeycomb and put his hand to his mouth, and he felt refreshed. Then one of the people spoke up and said, "Your father strictly commanded the people, saying, 'The man who eats food this day shall be punished.'" But Jonathan replied, "My father has brought great trouble on the land. See how I have been refreshed because I tasted a little of this honey. If only the people had eaten freely to-day of the spoil of their enemies, many more of the Philistines would have been slain."

Saul and David
Painted by W. L. Taylor

Then Saul said, "Let us go down after the Philistines by night and take spoil until daybreak, and let us not leave one of them." They said, "Do whatever you think best." But the priest said, "Let us ask of God." So Saul asked of God, "Shall I go down after the Philistines? Wilt thou deliver them over to Israel?" But he did not answer him that day. Therefore Saul said, "Come here, all you leaders of the people, and find out who has done wrong to-day. For as surely as Jehovah the deliverer of Israel lives, even though it be Jonathan my son, he shall die." But not one of the people answered him.

Then he said to all Israel, "You be on one side, and I and Jonathan my son will be on the other." The people said to Saul, "Do what you think best." Therefore Saul said, "Jehovah, God of Israel, why hast thou not answered thy servant this day? If the sin be mine or that of Jonathan my son, Jehovah, God of Israel, show it by the lot marked Urim; but if the sin lies with thy people Israel, show it by the lot marked Thummim." Then the lot fell on Jonathan and Saul and not on the people. So Saul said, "Cast the lot between me and Jonathan my son. He whom Jehovah selects must die." The people said to Saul, "It shall not be so!" But Saul made the people do as he said, and they cast the lot between him and Jonathan his son; and it fell on Jonathan.

Then Saul said to Jonathan, "Tell me what you have done." So Jonathan told him, "I did indeed taste a little honey with the end of the staff that was in my hand. Here I am! I am ready to die." Saul said, "God do so to me and more too; Jonathan, you shall surely die!" But all the people said to Saul, "Shall Jonathan die who has brought this great deliverance to Israel? Far from it! As surely as Jehovah lives, not one hair of his head shall fall to the ground, for he has done this day what God wished." So the people saved Jonathan from death.

DAVID'S VICTORY OVER THE GIANT

As long as Saul lived there was bitter war with the Philistines. Whenever Saul saw a strong or able man, he would take him into his service.

Now the spirit of Jehovah had left Saul and an evil spirit from Jehovah troubled him. So Saul's servants said to him, "See now, an evil spirit from Jehovah is troubling you. Let your servants who are here advise you, and let them seek a man skilled in playing the lyre. Then, whenever the evil spirit comes upon you, he shall play on the lyre, and you will be well." Saul said to his servants, "Find me a man who plays well, and bring him to me."

Then one of the young men said, "I have seen a son of Jesse the Bethlehemite who is a skilled musician, a strong and able man, a soldier, careful in speech, handsome, and Jehovah is with him." So Saul sent messengers to Jesse with the command, "Send me David your son, who is with the flock."

Then Jesse took ten loaves of bread, a skin of wine, and a kid, and sent them to Saul by his son David. So David came to Saul and entered his service; and Saul loved him and he became his armor-bearer. Saul sent this message to Jesse: "Let David remain in my service, for I am well pleased with him." And whenever the evil spirit from God came upon Saul, David would take the lyre and play, and Saul would breathe more easily and would be well, and the evil spirit would depart from him.

Now the Philistines gathered their forces for war, and camped between Socoh and Ezekah in Ephesdammim. Saul and the men of Israel came together and camped in the valley of Elah; and they were drawn up ready for battle against the Philistines.

The Philistines were standing on the hill on one side, and the Israelites were standing on the hill on the other side with the valley between them. Then there came out from the ranks of the Philistines a champion named Goliath, who was about ten feet tall. He had a helmet of bronze on his head and wore a bronze breastplate of scales which weighed one hundred and fifty pounds. He also had bronze greaves upon his legs and a bronze back-plate between his shoulders. The shaft of his spear was like a weaver's beam, and the head of his iron spear weighed about twenty pounds; and his shield-bearer went before him.

He stood and called to the ranks of Israel: "Why have you come out to form the line of battle? Am I not a Philistine and you servants of Saul? Choose a man for yourselves and let him come down to me. If he is able to fight with me and kill me, then we will become your servants; but if I conquer and kill him, then you shall become our servants and serve us." The Philistine added, "I defy the ranks of Israel to-day; give me a man that we may fight together."

When Saul and all the Israelites heard these words of the Philistine, they were terrified. But David said to Saul, "Let not my lord's courage fail him; I will go and fight this Philistine." Saul said to David, "You are not able to go and fight against this Philistine, for you are only a youth and he has been a warrior from his youth." But David said to Saul, "Your servant kept his father's sheep, and whenever a lion or a bear came and took a lamb out of the flock, I would go out after him and kill him and rescue it from his mouth. If he attacked me, I would seize him by his throat and kill him with a blow. Your servant has killed both lion and bear. Now this heathen Philistine shall be like one of them, for he has defied the armies of the living God. Jehovah who saved me from the paw of the lion and from the paw of the bear will save me from the hand of this Philistine." So Saul said to David, "Go, and may Jehovah be with you."

Saul clothed David with his own garments, and put a helmet of bronze on his head and gave him a coat of mail. And David fastened on his sword over his coat and was not able to walk, for he was not used to them. So he said to Saul, "I cannot go with these, for I am not used to them." So David took them off.

Then he took his club in his hand, and he chose five smooth stones from the bed of the brook and put them in his bag, and he took his sling in his hand and drew near to the Philistine. When the Philistine looked and saw David, he despised him, for he was but a fair and ruddy youth. So the Philistine said to David, "Am I a dog that you come against me with a club?" And he cursed David by his gods, and said, "Come to me that I may give your flesh to the birds of the heavens and to the beasts of the field."

Then David answered the Philistine, "You come to me with a sword and spear and javelin, but I come to you in the name of Jehovah of hosts and of the God of the armies of Israel whom you have insulted this day. Jehovah will deliver you into my hand that I may kill you and cut off your head."

When the Philistine started to attack him, David put his hand into his bag and took from it a stone, and slung it and struck the Philistine in the forehead. The stone sank into his forehead, and he fell on his face to the earth. Then David ran and stood over the Philistine, and drawing his sword from its sheath, he killed him and cut off his head with it.

When the Philistines saw that their champion was dead, they fled. The men of Israel and of Judah rose up and raised the battle-cry and followed the Philistines to the entrance to Gath and to the gates of Ekron, so that the wounded of the Philistines fell all the way from the battle-field even to Gath and Ekron.

SAUL'S MEAN JEALOUSY

When the Israelites and David returned from slaying the Philistines, the women came out from all the cities of Israel, singing and dancing, to meet Saul with tambourines, with cries of rejoicing, and with cymbals. The women sang gaily to each other and said,

> "Saul has slain his thousands,
> And David his tens of thousands."

Saul was very angry, for their words displeased him, and he said, "To David they give credit for ten thousands, but to me only thousands; what more can he have but the rulership?" So Saul kept his eye on David from that day onward. Saul feared David and did not let him stay near him. He made him commander over a thousand men; and David went out and came in at the head of the soldiers. In all that he did David acted wisely and had success, for Jehovah was with him. When Saul saw that he acted wisely, he was still more afraid of him. But all Israel and Judah loved David, for he went out and came in at their head.

Michal, Saul's daughter, also loved David, and when they told Saul, he was pleased, for he said, "I will give her to him, that she may lead him to destruction and that the Philistines may capture him." So Saul commanded his servants, "Say to David secretly: 'See, the ruler is pleased with you and all his servants love you; now therefore become his son-in-law.'" When Saul's servants told this to David, he said, "Do you think it easy for me to become the son-in-law of a ruler when I am poor and have no reputation!" When Saul's servants told him David's answer, he commanded, "Say to David: 'Saul wishes no price for his daughter except the proof that you have killed a hundred Philistines;'" for Saul thought that David would be killed by them.

So David went with his men and killed a hundred Philistines; and Saul gave him his daughter Michal as his wife. Then Saul knew that Jehovah was with David and that all Israel loved him, so he feared David still more.

Then Saul commanded his son Jonathan and all his servants to put David to death. But Jonathan was very fond of David. And Jonathan spoke well of David to Saul his father and said to him, "Do not sin against your servant David, for he has not wronged you and his behavior toward you has been excellent; for he risked his life and killed the Philistine, so that Jehovah saved all Israel. You saw it and rejoiced. Why then will you sin by shedding innocent blood in killing David without cause?"

So Saul listened to Jonathan and gave his solemn promise: "As surely as Jehovah lives, he shall not be put to death."

Then Jonathan called David and told him all these things. And Jonathan brought David to Saul and he was with him as before.

But there was war again, and David went out and fought against the Philistines and killed so many of them that they fled before him. Then an evil spirit from Jehovah came upon Saul while he was sitting in his house with his spear in his hand and while David was playing on the lyre. Saul tried to pin David to the wall with the spear, but David slipped away so that Saul drove the spear into the wall; and David fled and so escaped.

That night Saul sent messengers to David's house to watch him, so as to kill him in the morning. But Michal, David's wife, told him, "If you do not save your life to-night, you will be killed to-morrow." So Michal let David down through the window; and he fled away and escaped. Then Michal took the household god and laid it in the bed, and she put a pillow of goat's hair under its head and covered it with a garment. And when Saul sent messengers to seize David, she said, "He is sick."

Again Saul sent the messengers to the house of David with the command, "Bring him up to me on the bed, that I may put him to death." When the messengers came in, there was the household god in the bed with the pillow of goat's hair under its head. Saul said to Michal, "Why have you deceived me thus and let my enemy go?" Michal answered Saul, "He said to me: 'Let me go; why should I kill you?'"

JONATHAN'S LOVE FOR DAVID

Then David went and found Jonathan and said, "What have I done? What is my guilt, and what is my sin in the mind of your father, that he is seeking my life?" Jonathan replied, "No, no! You shall not die. You know that my father does nothing great or small that he does not tell me, and why should my father hide this from me? He surely will not." David answered, "Your father well knows that you are fond of me, and he is saying to himself, 'Do not let Jonathan know this that he may not be grieved.' But as surely as Jehovah lives and as you live, there is only a step between me and death."

Then Jonathan said to David, "What do you wish me to do for you?" David answered, "To-morrow is the festival of the New Moon and I ought to sit at the table with Saul, but let me go and I will hide myself in the field until evening. If your father misses me, then say, 'David asked permission of me to run to Bethlehem, his native town, for the yearly sacrifice is there for all his family.' If he says, 'Good,' then it is well with your servant; but if he gets angry, then you will know that he is planning to harm me. Now show kindness to your servant, for in the presence of Jehovah you have made a solemn agreement with your servant. But if I am at all guilty, kill me yourself, for why should you bring me to your father?" Jonathan said, "That shall never be! If I learn that my father is planning to do you harm, I will tell you."

Then David said to Jonathan, "Who will tell me if your father answers you harshly?" Jonathan answered, "Jehovah the God of Israel be witness that about this time to-morrow I will find out how my father feels. If he feels kindly toward you, then I will send and tell you. Should my father wish to do you harm, God do to Jonathan whatever he will and more too if I do not tell you and send you away that you may go in peace. May Jehovah be with you, as he has been with my father. And if I am yet alive, O may you show me kindness like that of Jehovah himself! But if I should die, you must never cease to be kind to my family. And if, when Jehovah destroys all the enemies of David from the face of the earth, the family of Jonathan should be destroyed by the family of David, may Jehovah punish the crime by the hand of David's enemies." So Jonathan renewed his solemn promise to David, because he loved him; for he loved him as much as he loved his own life.

Then Jonathan said to him, "To-morrow is the festival of the New Moon and you will be missed, for your seat will be empty. On the third day, when you will be greatly missed, go to the place where you hid yourself when my father attacked you, and sit down beside the heap of stones. I will shoot three arrows on one side of it, as though I shot at a mark. Then I will send the boy, saying, 'Go, find the arrows.' If I call to the boy, 'See, the arrows are on this side of you; pick them up!'—then come; for all goes well with you, and as surely as Jehovah lives, there is nothing to fear. But if I call to the boy, 'See, the arrows are beyond you,' then go, for Jehovah sends you away. And as for the promises which you and I have made, Jehovah is witness between you and me forever."

So David hid himself in the field; and when the festival of the New Moon came, Saul sat down at the table to eat. He sat on his seat, as usual, by the wall, and Jonathan sat opposite, and Abner sat beside Saul; but David's seat was empty. Saul, however, did not say anything that day, for he thought, "It is an accident."

But on the next day when David's place was again empty, Saul said to Jonathan, "Why has not the son of Jesse come to the table, either yesterday or to-day?" Jonathan answered, "David asked permission to go to Bethlehem, for he said, 'Let me go, for we have a family sacrifice in the town, and my brother has commanded me to be there. Now if you approve, let me go away that I may see my family.' Therefore, he has not come to your table."

Then Saul's anger was aroused against Jonathan, and he said to him, "Son of a rebellious slave girl! Do I not know that you are making the son of Jesse your friend to your own shame and to your mother's shame? For as long as the son of Jesse lives, neither you nor your rule will be safe. Therefore, send now and bring him to me, for he is doomed to die."

Then Jonathan answered Saul his father and said, "Why should he be put to death? What has he done?" But Saul flung his spear at him to strike him. So Jonathan knew that his father had made up his mind to put David to death. And Jonathan rose from the table in hot anger and ate no food on the second day of the month, for he felt hurt because his father had insulted David.

The next morning Jonathan went out into the field to the place agreed upon with David, and a small boy was with him. He said to his boy, "Run, find now the arrows which I shoot." As the boy ran, he shot an arrow beyond him. When the boy came to the place where the arrow which Jonathan had shot lay, Jonathan called to him, "Is not the arrow beyond you? Hurry, be quick, do not stop!" So Jonathan's lad gathered up the arrows, and brought them to his master. But the boy knew nothing about the signal. Only Jonathan and David understood.

THE COST OF A LIE

Then David went to Nob, to Ahimelech the priest who came trembling to meet David and said to him, "Why are you alone, and no one with you?" David answered Ahimelech the priest, "Saul has given me orders about some business and has said to me, 'Let no one know anything about the business on which I am sending you and about which I have given you orders.' I have also directed the young men to meet me at a certain place. Therefore, if you have at hand five loaves of bread, give them to me or whatever can be found." The priest answered David, "There is no plain bread at hand, but only holy bread." So the priest gave him holy bread, for there was no other bread there except that which had been removed from the temple to be replaced at once by hot bread.

Now Doeg, the Edomite, the chief of Saul's herdsmen, was there that day. And David said to Ahimelech, "Have you not here at hand a spear or sword? For I did not bring my sword or my weapons with me, since the king's business required haste." The priest said, "The sword of Goliath the Philistine whom you slew in the valley of Elah is there, wrapped in a cloth. If you wish to take that, do so, for there is no other except that here." David answered, "There is none like that; give it to me."

Then David went from there and escaped to the stronghold of Adullam. When his brothers and all his father's clan heard of it, they went down there to him. Every one who was in trouble and every one who was in debt, and every one who was discontented gathered about him, and he became their leader. About four hundred men were with him.

When Saul heard that David and the men with him had been found, he was sitting in Gibeah, under the tamarisk-tree at the high place, with his spear in his hand. And all his servants were standing about him. Saul said to his servants who stood about him, "Hear, O Benjamites! Will the son of Jesse give all of you fields and vineyards? Will he make all of you commanders of thousands and commanders of hundreds? Is it not true that all of you have plotted against me so that no one tells me that my son has made an agreement with the son of Jesse, and that none of you has pity upon me or tells me that my son has made my servant David my enemy as he now is?" Then Doeg the Edomite, who was standing by the servants of Saul, spoke up and said, "I saw the son of Jesse go to Nob, to

Ahimelech, the son of Ahitub. And the priest inquired of God for him and gave him food and the sword of Goliath the Philistine."

Then Saul sent for Ahimelech the priest, and all his family and the priests who were in Nob; and all of them came to him. Then Saul said, "Listen, son of Ahitub!" He answered, "Here I am, my lord!" Saul said to him, "Is it not true that you and the son of Jesse have plotted against me and that you have given him bread and a sword and have inquired of God for him, that he might rebel against me?" Ahimelech answered Saul, "Who among all your servants is trusted like David, your son-in-law, chief over your subjects, and honored in your household? Is this the first time I have inquired of God for him? Far be it from me to be disloyal! Do not think that I or any of my clan have any evil intention, for your servant does not know the slightest thing about all this." But Saul said, "Ahimelech, you shall surely die, you and all your family."

Then Saul said to the guards who were standing about him, "Turn and kill the priests of Jehovah, for they have plotted with David; and although they knew that he was fleeing, they did not tell me." But Saul's servants would not raise their hands to kill the priests of Jehovah. Then Saul said to Doeg, "Turn and kill the priests." So Doeg, the Edomite, turned and killed them. On that day he killed eighty-five men who wore the priestly robes.

But Abiathar, one of the sons of Ahimelech, escaped and fled to David. When Abiathar told David that Saul had killed the priests of Jehovah, David said to him, "I knew that day, because Doeg the Edomite was there, that he would surely tell Saul. I myself am responsible for the death of all your family. Stay with me, have no fear, for whoever seeks your life must first take mine, for you are placed in my charge."

A SOLDIER WHO SPARED HIS ENEMY

Now when David was told, "The Philistines are fighting against Keilah and are robbing the threshing-floors," he inquired of Jehovah, "Shall

I go and attack these Philistines?" Jehovah said to David, "Go, attack the Philistines and save Keilah." But David's men said to him, "See, we are afraid here in Judah; how much more will we be if we go to Keilah against the armies of the Philistines?" When David again inquired of Jehovah, Jehovah answered him, "Arise, go down to Keilah, for I will give the Philistines into your hand." So David and his men went to Keilah and fought with the Philistines and drove away their cattle and killed a great many of them. In this way David delivered the people of Keilah.

Now when Abiathar, the son of Ahimelech, fled to David in Keilah, he came down with the priestly robe used in consulting Jehovah in his hand. And when Saul was told that David had come to Keilah, Saul said, "God has given him into my power, for by entering a town that has doors and bars he has let himself be trapped."

So Saul called all the people to arms to go down to Keilah to besiege David and his men. But when David knew that Saul was plotting evil against him, he said to Abiathar the priest, "Bring here the priestly robe." Then David said, "O Jehovah, the God of Israel, thy servant has surely heard that Saul is planning to come to Keilah, to destroy the town because of me. Will Saul come down, as thy servant has heard? O Jehovah, God of Israel, tell thy servant." Jehovah said, "He will come down." Then David said, "Will the men of Keilah turn me and my men over to Saul?" Jehovah said, "They will." Then David and his men, who were about six hundred, left Keilah, and wandered from one place to another. When it was reported to Saul that David had escaped from Keilah, he no longer followed him. So David lived in the Wilderness of Ziph and stayed in the mountain strongholds.

Then the Ziphites came to Saul at Gibeah, saying, "Is not David hiding in the hill country of Hachilah?" So Saul went down to the Wilderness of Ziph with three thousand men of Israel to hunt for David. And Saul camped in the hill country of Hachilah; but David stayed in the wilderness. When David saw that Saul was following him into the wilderness, he sent out scouts and learned that Saul had come to the place just in front of him. David then arose and went to the place where Saul had camped. And he saw the place where Saul lay, with Abner the son of Ner, the commander of his army; and Saul was within the barricade, and the people were camped about him.

Then David turned to Ahimelech the Hittite and to Abishai the son of Zeruiah, Joab's brother, and said, "Who will go down with me to Saul's camp?" Abishai said, "I will go with you." So David and Abishai came to the people by night, and Saul was lying asleep inside the barricade, with his spear stuck into the earth at his head and with Abner and the soldiers lying about him.

Then Abishai said to David, "God has given your enemy to you today. Now let me pin him to the earth with his spear at one stroke, for I will not need to strike him twice!" David replied, "As surely as Jehovah lives, either Jehovah will smite him, or his day will come to die, or he will go down into battle and meet his end. Jehovah forbid that I should harm him whom Jehovah has called to rule! But now take the spear that is at his head and the jug of water, and let us go." So David took the spear and the jug of water from Saul's head, and they departed. But no man saw it or knew it, for they were all asleep, and no one awoke, for a deep sleep from Jehovah had fallen upon them.

Then David went across and stood on the top of a hill at a distance with a great space between them. And David called to the soldiers and to Abner, the son of Ner, and said, "Do you make no answer, Abner?" Abner answered, "Who are you that calls?" David said to Abner, "Are you not a man, and who is like you in Israel? Why then have you not kept guard over your lord the ruler of Israel? For one of the people came to destroy your lord. You have not done what is right. As surely as Jehovah lives you ought to be put to death, for you have not kept watch over your master whom Jehovah has called to rule. Now see where his spear is and his jug of water that was at his head."

Saul knew David's voice and said, "Is this your voice, my son David?" David replied, "It is my voice, my lord." And he added, "Why is it that my lord is following his servant? For what have I done? Or of what am I guilty? Now therefore let my lord listen to me. If Jehovah has stirred you up against me, let him accept an offering. But if men have stirred you up against me, let them be cursed before Jehovah, for they have driven me out to-day, saying, 'Go serve other gods,' so that I have no share in the land which Jehovah has given to his people. May I not meet my end far away from the presence of Jehovah, for the ruler of Israel has come out to seek my life, as one hunts a partridge on the mountains."

Then Saul said, "I have done wrong. Come back, my son David, for I will do you no more harm, for you have spared my life to-day. I have acted foolishly and have made a great mistake." David answered, "Here is Saul's spear! Let one of the young men come over and take it. May Jehovah reward each one who does right and is faithful; for Jehovah gave you to me to-day, but I would not harm one whom Jehovah had called to rule. Just as your life was of great value in my sight so may my life be of great value in Jehovah's sight, and may he deliver me from all trouble."

Then Saul said to David, "May you be blessed, my son David! You shall do great deeds and shall surely succeed!" So David went his way, but Saul returned home.

ABIGAIL'S SENSIBLE ADVICE

Then David went away into the Wilderness of Maon. Now there was a man in Maon, whose property was in Carmel. The man was very rich; he had three thousand sheep and a thousand goats, and he was shearing his sheep at Carmel. His name was Nabal, and his wife's name was Abigail. The woman was sensible and beautiful, but the man was rough and ill-mannered; and he was a Calebite.

When David heard in the wilderness that Nabal was shearing his sheep, he sent ten young men with the command, "Go up to Carmel and enter Nabal's house and greet him in my name. You shall say to him and to his family, 'Peace and prosperity be to you and your family and to all that you have. Now I have heard that you have sheep-shearers. Your shepherds were with us, and we did not insult them, and nothing of theirs was missing all the while they were in Carmel. Ask your young men and they will tell you. Therefore receive my young men favorably, for we have come on a feast-day. Give also whatever you have at hand to your servants and to your son David.'"

When David's young men came, they spoke to Nabal for David as they were told, and then waited. But Nabal answered David's servants, "Who is David? And who is the son of Jesse? Many are the slaves these days who break away from their masters! Should I then take my bread and my water and my meat that I have prepared for my shearers and give it to men of whom I know nothing?" So when David's young men returned and told him, he said to them, "Let every man put on his sword." So they all put on their swords. David also put on his sword; and about four hundred men followed David, and two hundred stayed with the baggage.

But one of the young men told Abigail, Nabal's wife, "David has just sent messengers from the wilderness to greet our master, but he insulted them. The men have been very good to us and we have not been harmed nor have we missed anything, as long as we were with them in the open country. They were as a wall about us both night and day all the time we were near them guarding the sheep. Now therefore decide what you will do, for evil is planned against our master and against all his household, for he is such an ill-tempered man that no one can say a word to him."

Then Abigail quickly took two hundred loaves of bread, two skins of wine, five roasted sheep, five baskets of parched grain, a hundred bunches of raisins, and two hundred cakes of figs, and loaded them on asses. She said to her young men, "Go on ahead of me; see, I am coming after you." But she said nothing about it to her husband Nabal. As she was riding on the ass and coming down under cover of a hill, David and his men were coming down toward her, so that she met them. David had just said, "It was in vain that I guarded all that belongs to this fellow in the wilderness, so that nothing of his was missing, for he has returned me evil for good. May God bring a similar judgment upon David and more too, if by daybreak I leave a single man of all those who belong to him."

When Abigail saw David, she dismounted quickly from her ass and bowed down before him with her face to the ground. As she fell at his feet she said, "Upon me, my lord, upon me be the blame. Only let your servant speak to you, and listen to her words. Let not my lord pay any attention to that mean man Nabal, for as his name is, so is he. 'Fool' is his name and folly rules him. But your servant did not see the young men of my lord, whom you sent. Now, my lord, as surely as Jehovah lives and as you live, since Jehovah has kept you from murder and from avenging yourself by your own hand, may your enemies and those who seek to harm my lord be like Nabal. Let this present which your servant has brought to my lord be given to the young men who follow him. I beg of you, forgive the wrong done by your servant, for Jehovah will certainly make my lord's family strong, for my lord is fighting for Jehovah, and you shall not be guilty of any evil deed as long as you live. Should a man rise up to pursue you and seek your life, Jehovah your God will care for you, but he will cast away the lives of your enemies as from a sling. When Jehovah has done for you all the good that he has promised and has made you ruler over Israel, you will not have to be sorry that you shed blood without cause or that you were revenged by your own hand. When Jehovah gives prosperity to my lord, then too remember your servant."

David said to Abigail, "Blessed be Jehovah the God of Israel, who sent you this day to meet me, and blessed be your good sense. A blessing on you, who have kept me this day from murder and from avenging myself by my own hand. For as surely as Jehovah the God of Israel lives, who has kept me from doing you harm, unless you had quickly come to meet me, truly by daybreak not one man would have been left to Nabal."

So David received from her all which she had brought him. And he said to her, "Go back in peace to your house. See, I have listened to your advice and granted your request."

When Abigail returned to Nabal, he was holding a feast in his house like a king. He was feeling merry, for he was very drunk; so she told him nothing whatever until daybreak. But in the morning, when the effects of the wine were gone, his wife told him what she had done. Then his heart stopped beating and he became like a stone. About ten days later he had a stroke from which he died.

When David heard that Nabal was dead, he said, "Thanks be to Jehovah who has punished Nabal's insult to me and has kept me from doing wrong, for Jehovah has visited Nabal's crime upon his own head."

Then David sent to ask Abigail to become his wife. When his servants came to her at Carmel and said, "David has sent us to you to take you to him to be his wife," she rose and bowed her face to the earth and said, "See, your slave is willing to be even a servant to wash the feet of my lord's servants." Then Abigail quickly rose and mounted an ass; and five of her maids followed as servants. So she went with the messengers of David, and became his wife.

MAKING THE BEST OF TROUBLE

Then David said to himself, "I shall be killed some day by the hand of Saul. There is nothing better for me than to escape into the land of the Philistines. Then Saul will give up hope and search no more for me in all the land of Israel; and so I will escape from him." David, therefore, with the six hundred men who were with him went over to Achish, king of Gath. And David and his men lived with Achish at Gath, each with his family. When Saul was told that David had fled to Gath, he gave up looking for him.

David said to Achish, "If now you will grant me the favor, give me a place in one of the towns in the open country, that I may live there; for why should your servant live in the royal city with you?" So Achish gave him Ziklag, and David lived in the open country of the Philistines a year and four months.

And David and his men went up and made a raid upon the Geshurites, the Girzites, and the Amalekites; for these tribes live in the land which extends from Telem to the land of Egypt. As often as David made a raid on the land, he did not leave alive man or woman, but taking the sheep, the oxen, the asses, the camels, and the clothing, he returned and went to Achish. Then when Achish said, "Where have you made a raid to-day?" David answered, "Against the South Country of Judah, or against the South Country of the Jerahmeelites, or against the South Country of the Kenites." And Achish trusted David, thinking, "He has made his people Israel hate him; therefore he will be my servant forever."

Now in those days the Philistines gathered their forces to make war against Israel. And Achish said to David, "You and your men shall surely go with me in the army." David replied, "You shall then know what your servant can do." Achish said to David, "In that case I will make you the captain of my body-guard from this time on."

Then the Philistines gathered all their forces at Aphek, and the Israelites camped at the fountain in Jezreel. When the rulers of the Philistines were marching past, by hundreds and by thousands, and David and his men were marching in the rear with Achish, the commanders of the Philistines said, "What are those Hebrews doing here?" Achish said to them, "Is this not David, the servant of Saul the ruler of Israel, who has been with me these two years, and I have found no fault in him from the time that he came to me to the present?"

But the commanders of the Philistines were displeased and said to him, "Send the man back to the place where you had stationed him. Do not let him go down with us into battle, lest we have a foe in the camp; for how could this fellow better win back the favor of his master than with the heads of these men? Is not this the David of whom they sang to one another in the dances:

"'"Saul has slain his thousands,
And David his ten thousands?"'"

Then Achish called David and said to him, "As surely as Jehovah lives, you are upright, and your conduct toward me both in and out of the camp has been satisfactory, for I have found nothing wrong in you from the time that you came to me to the present; but you are not trusted by the other rulers. Go back home, therefore, in peace, that you may do nothing to displease the rulers of the Philistines." David said to Achish, "But what have I done? What have you found in your servant from the day that I entered your service, that I may not go out and fight the enemies of my lord the king?" Achish answered, "I know that you are as faithful to me as an angel of God, but the commanders of the Philistines have said, 'He shall not go with us into battle.' Therefore, you and those who came with you are to rise early in the morning, and go to the place where I have stationed you. Do not plan any evil, for I trust you, but rise early in the morning and, as soon as it is light, depart."

So David and his men arose early in the morning to return to the Philistine land, but the Philistines went up to Jezreel.

On the third day, when David and his men returned to Ziklag, the Amalekites had made a raid on the South Country and on Ziklag, and had attacked Ziklag and burned it with fire, and had also carried away captive all who were in it, including the women and children. They had not killed any but had carried them away with them. Then David and the people who were with him wept aloud until they were no longer able to weep.

David was in great trouble, for the people spoke of stoning him, because they all felt bitter, having lost their sons and daughters: but David took courage, for he trusted in Jehovah his God. So David with his six hundred followers went on to the Brook Besor, where those who were too tired to cross the brook stayed behind.

They found there an Egyptian in the open field and brought him to David and gave him food to eat and water to drink. Then David said to him, "To whom do you belong, and where do you come from?" He replied, "I am an Egyptian lad, an Amalekite's servant, and my master left me behind because three days ago I fell sick. We marched into the South Country of the Cherethites and into that which belongs to Judah and into the South Country of Caleb, and Ziklag we destroyed by fire." David said to him, "Will you guide me to this robber band?" He replied, "Swear to me by your God, that you will neither kill me nor turn me over to my master, and I will guide you to this band."

When he had brought him down, the Amalekites were scattered over all the land, eating and drinking and dancing, because of all the great spoil that they had taken from the land of the Philistines and from the land of Judah. David fought against them from twilight to the evening of the next day, and only four hundred young men who were mounted on camels escaped.

So David took from the Amalekites all that they had carried away and rescued his two wives; nothing at all was missing. Then he took all the flocks and the herds and drove those animals before the people, and they said, "This is David's spoil."

When David came to the two hundred men who had been so faint that they could not follow him, all the wicked, mean fellows who went with him said, "Because these men did not go with us, let us not give them any of the spoil that we have taken, except that each man may take his wife and children and depart." David answered, "My brothers, you shall not do so with that which Jehovah has given us, after he has saved our lives and given this robber band that attacked us into our power. Those who stay with the baggage shall have an equal share with those who fight." So from that day to the present he made this a law and a rule in Israel.

When David came to Ziklag, he sent some of the spoil to the leaders of Judah and to his relatives, saying, "See! a present for you from the spoil of the enemies of Jehovah."

THE DEATH OF TWO BRAVE WARRIORS

Samuel had died and all Israel had mourned for him and had buried him in his own town Ramah. Saul, too, had put the mediums and those who had messages from the spirits of the dead out of the land.

Then the Philistines came and camped in Shunem, and Saul gathered all the Israelites and camped in Gilboa. But when he saw the army of the Philistines, he was terrified and filled with fear. So he asked of Jehovah whether he should go against them, but Jehovah did not answer him either by dream or by lot or by the prophets. Then Saul said to his servants, "Find for me a woman who is a medium, that I may go and ask through her." His servants said to him, "There is such a woman at Endor."

So Saul did not let any one know who he was, but put on other clothes and went, taking two men with him. And they came to the woman at night. He said, "Ask for me through some departed spirit and bring up for me the one for whom I shall ask." The woman said to him, "You know what Saul has done, how he has driven from the land the mediums and those who have messages from the spirits of the dead. Why then are you trying to catch me, to put me to death?" But Saul swore to her by Jehovah, saying, "As surely as Jehovah lives, no punishment will come to you from this act." Then the woman said, "Whom shall I bring up to you?" Saul said, "Bring up Samuel."

When the woman saw Samuel, she screamed and said to Saul, "Why have you deceived me, for you are Saul?" Saul replied, "Do not be afraid! What do you see?" The woman said to Saul, "I see a god coming out of the earth." Saul asked, "What does he look like?" She said, "An old man is coming up, and he is wrapped in a cloak." Then Saul knew that it was Samuel; and he bowed with his face to the earth and worshipped.

Samuel said to Saul, "Why have you disturbed me by bringing me up?" Saul answered, "I am in great trouble, for the Philistines are making war against me, and God has turned from me and answers me no more, neither by prophets nor by dreams. So I have called you to tell me what I shall do." Samuel said, "Why do you ask of me when Jehovah has turned from you and become your enemy? He has taken the authority from your hand and given it to another, even to David. To-morrow you, with your sons beside you, shall fall, and Jehovah will deliver the army of Israel into the power of the Philistines."

Then Saul fell at full length upon the earth, for the words of Samuel filled him with fear, so he had no strength left, for he had not eaten any food all that day and night. When the woman came to Saul and saw that he was in great trouble, she said to him, "See, I have taken my life in my hand and have done what you asked me. Now therefore, listen also to my advice and let me set before you a little food, and eat that you may have strength to go on your way." Saul refused and said, "I will not eat"; but his servants, as well as the woman, urged him, until he listened to their advice. Then he rose from the earth and sat upon the couch. And the woman had a fat calf in the house which she quickly killed. And she took flour and kneaded it and baked from it bread without yeast. She set it before Saul and his servants, and they ate. Then they rose up and went away that night.

The Philistines fought against Israel, but the Israelites fled from them and fell dead on Mount Gilboa. Then the Philistines closely followed Saul and his sons; and they killed Jonathan and Abinadab and Malchishua, the sons of Saul. So the battle went against Saul, and when the archers found out where he was, he was severely wounded. Then Saul said to his armor-bearer, "Draw your sword and kill me with it, so that these heathen Philistines may not come and make sport of me." But his armor-bearer would not, for he was very much afraid. Saul, therefore, took his own sword and fell upon it. When his armor-bearer saw that Saul was dead, he also fell upon his sword and died with him. So Saul and his three sons and his armor-bearer died on the same day.

When the Israelites who were in the towns of the lowland and across the Jordan saw that the Israelites had fled and that Saul and his sons were dead, they left their towns and fled, and the Philistines came and took them.

On the next day, the Philistines came to rob the dead, and found that Saul and his three sons had fallen on Mount Gilboa. They cut off his head and stripped off his armor and sent messengers through all the land of the Philistines to bring the good news to their idols and to the people. And they put his armor in the temple of Ashtarte and fastened his body on the wall of Bethshan.

When the inhabitants of Jabesh in Gilead heard what the Philistines had done to Saul, their brave men rose up and marched all night, and they took the bodies of Saul and his sons from the wall of Bethshan and brought them to Jabesh and mourned over them there. Then they took their bones and buried them under the oak-tree in Jabesh and ate no food for seven days.

On the third day after David returned to Ziklag, after defeating the Amalekites, a man came from the camp of Saul with his clothes torn and with earth upon his head. When he came to David, he fell on the ground before him. David said to him, "Where do you come from?" He answered, "I have escaped from the camp of Israel." David said to him, "How did the battle go? Tell me." He answered, "The people fled from the battle-field, and many of them fell, and Saul and Jonathan his son are dead!"

Then David and all the men who were with him tore their clothes and mourned and wept and went without food until evening, because Saul and Jonathan his son and the people of Jehovah had fallen by the sword.

David then sang this dirge over Saul and Jonathan:

"Weep, O Judah!
Grieve, O Israel!
On your heights are the slain!
How the mighty have fallen!

"Saul and Jonathan, beloved and lovely!
In life and in death they were never parted;
They were swifter than eagles,
They were stronger than lions.

"O Jonathan, your death has mortally wounded me,
O Jonathan, my brother, for you I am sorrowing.
You were ever a friend to me most dear,
Your love meant far more than the love of women!

"How the mighty have fallen,
And the weapons of war vanished!"

A SHEPHERD BOY WHO WAS CALLED TO LEAD A NATION

After this David asked of Jehovah, "Shall I go up into one of the towns of Judah?" Jehovah answered, "Go up." When David asked, "To which shall I go?" he said, "To Hebron." So David went up with his two wives, Ahinoam and Abigail. And David brought the men who were with him, each with his family, and they lived in the towns about Hebron. Then the men of Judah came there and made David ruler over the people of Judah.

When they told David about the men of Jabesh in Gilead who had buried Saul, David sent messengers to them and said, "May you be blessed by Jehovah because you have shown this kindness to your master Saul and have buried him. Even so may Jehovah show kindness and faithfulness to you. I also will repay you for this kind deed which you have done. Therefore be brave and courageous; for Saul your master is dead, and the people of Judah have made me ruler over them."

Now Abner, the commander of Saul's army, had taken Ishbaal the son of Saul and brought him over to Mahanaim and made him ruler over Gilead and all Israel. But the people of Judah remained loyal to David.

There was constant war between the followers of Saul and those of David. But David kept growing stronger while the followers of Saul grew weaker.

Then Rechab and Baanah, the sons of Rimmon, went about midday to the palace of Ishbaal, as he was taking his rest at noon. The doorkeeper of the palace was cleaning wheat, but he grew drowsy and slept. So Rechab and Baanah his brother slipped in and, attacking Ishbaal, they killed him and cut off his head.

Then all the tribes of Israel came to David at Hebron and said, "See, we are your relatives. When Saul was ruler over us, it was you who led the Israelites, and Jehovah has said to you, 'You shall be shepherd of my people Israel, and you shall become the leader of Israel.'" So all the leading men of Israel came to David, and he made an agreement with them in Hebron in the presence of Jehovah, and they made David ruler over Israel. David was thirty years old when he began to rule and he ruled forty years.

When the Philistines heard that they had made David ruler over Israel, all the Philistines went up to search for David; but when he heard of this he went down to the fortress.

Three of David's thirty warriors went down to him to the top of the rock, to the fortress of Adullam, while a force of the Philistines was camped in the Valley of Rephaim. David was at that time in the fortress, and a company of the Philistines was in Bethlehem. And David said, longingly, "O that some one would bring me a drink of water from the well of Bethlehem which is near the gate!" Then the three famous warriors broke through the line of the Philistines and drew water out of the well of Bethlehem which was near the gate and brought it to David. He would not drink of it, however, but poured it out as an offering to Jehovah and said, "Jehovah forbid that I should drink it. This is the blood of the men who went at the risk of their lives." Therefore he would not drink it.

When the Philistines came and spread out over the Valley of Rephaim, David asked of Jehovah: "Shall I go out against the Philistines? Wilt thou give them into my hand?" Jehovah said to David, "Go; for I will certainly give the Philistines into your hand." So David went to Baal-perazim, and defeated them there; and he said, "Jehovah has broken down my enemies before me, like waters which break through their banks."

Then the Philistines came up again and spread out over the Valley of Rephaim. When David asked of Jehovah, he said, "You shall not make a direct attack. Go around behind them and attack them opposite the balsam-trees. When you hear the sound of marching in the tops of the balsams, act quickly, for then Jehovah will have gone out before you to overthrow the army of the Philistines." David did as Jehovah commanded him and drove the Philistines from Gibeon as far as Gezer.

JERUSALEM MADE THE CAPITAL CITY

David and his men went to Jerusalem against the Jebusites, the people of the land who had said to David, "You shall not come in here, for the blind and the lame will turn you back," for they thought, "David cannot come in here."

But David took the fortress of Zion, and lived there. He also built a wall around it, and called it the City of David.

David continued to grow more powerful, for Jehovah of hosts was with him. And Hiram, king of Tyre, sent messengers to him, and cedar-trees and carpenters and masons, and they built a palace for him. So David knew that Jehovah had made him ruler over Israel and his kingdom powerful for the sake of his people Israel.

David again gathered all the chief men of Israel, thirty thousand in all, and went with all the people to Baal-Judah, to bring up from there the ark of God. They placed the ark of God upon a new cart and brought it out of the house of Abinadab on the hill. Uzzah and Ahio, the sons of Abinadab, guided the cart. Uzzah went beside the ark of God, while Ahio went before it. David and all the people of Israel danced before Jehovah with all their might to the music of harps and lyres and drums and castanets and cymbals.

When they came to the threshing-floor of Nachon, Uzzah stretched out his hand to hold up the ark of God, for the oxen stumbled. Then the anger of Jehovah was aroused against Uzzah and he struck him down there, because he had stretched out his hand to the ark; so he died there in the presence of God. David was afraid of Jehovah that day, and said, "How can the ark of Jehovah come to me?" So David was not willing to remove the ark of Jehovah to the City of David, but carried it aside to the house of Obed-edom, the Gittite, and it remained there three months. But Jehovah blessed Obed-edom and all his family.

When the report came to David, "Jehovah has blessed Obed-edom and all his family because of the ark of God," David joyfully brought up the ark from the house of Obed-edom to the City of David. When the bearers of the ark of Jehovah had gone six paces, David offered an ox and a fat animal as a sacrifice; and he danced before Jehovah with all his might, and he had about his waist a priestly garment made of linen. So David and all the house of Israel brought up the ark of Jehovah with shouting and the blare of trumpets.

When they had brought in the ark of Jehovah and had set it in its place in the tent that David had built for it, he offered burnt-offerings and sacrifices to Jehovah. When David had finished offering these sacrifices, he blessed the people in the name of Jehovah of hosts and gave to each of the many Israelites who were there, to both men and women, a roll of bread, a portion of meat, and a cake of raisins. Then all the people went back to their homes.

This message also from Jehovah came to Nathan, the prophet: "You shall say to my servant David: 'Jehovah of hosts declares, I took you from the pasture from following the sheep to be chief over my people Israel.

I have been with you wherever you went, to destroy all your enemies before you, and I will make you a name, like that of the great in the earth. When your life is ended and you are buried with your fathers, I will raise up your son after you, and I will make his rule strong. I will be a father to him, and he shall be my son. When he goes astray I will gently correct him. I will not withdraw my favor from him as I withdrew it from Saul. Your house and your dominion shall always stand firm before me; your authority shall stand forever.'"

DAVID'S KINDNESS TO JONATHAN'S SON

Then David asked, "Is any one left of the family of Saul to whom I may show kindness for Jonathan's sake?" And there was a servant of Saul named Ziba. When they called him before David, he said to him, "Are you Ziba?" He replied, "Your servant." David said, "Is there any one else belonging to the family of Saul to whom I may show kindness like that which God shows to us?" Ziba answered, "A son of Jonathan is still living, but he is lame in his feet." David inquired, "Where is he?" Ziba replied, "He is in the house of Machir in Lodebar."

Then David sent and brought him from the house of Machir; and when Meribaal the son of Jonathan came to David, he bowed down to the ground before him. David said, "Meribaal!" He answered, "Here is your servant!" David said to him, "Fear not, for I will surely show you kindness for the sake of your father Jonathan, and I will give back to you all the land of your grandfather Saul; and you shall always eat at my table." Meribaal bowed down and said, "What is your servant that you should look favorably upon one as unworthy as I?"

Then David called to Ziba, Saul's servant, and said to him, "I have given to your master's son all that belongs to Saul and to his family. You with your sons and servants shall cultivate the land for him and harvest the fruits, that your master's son may have food to eat; but Meribaal, your master's son, shall always eat at my table." Now Ziba had fifteen sons and twenty servants; and he said to David, "Your servant will do all that my lord commands."

So Meribaal ate at David's table like one of his own sons. Meribaal also had a young son, whose name was Mica. And all who lived in the house of Ziba were Meribaal's servants. So Meribaal lived in Jerusalem, and though he was lame in both feet, he always ate at David's table.

A RICH MAN WHO WAS A THIEF

One evening, while Joab was besieging Rabbath Ammon, David rose from his bed and walked upon the roof of the royal palace. From the roof he saw a woman bathing; and she was very beautiful. And David sent to ask about the woman; and some one said, "Is not this Bathsheba, the wife of Uriah the Hittite?" Then David sent messengers to bring her; and she came to him, but later returned to her home.

Then David wrote a letter to Joab and sent it by Uriah. In the letter, he said, "Place Uriah in the front line where there is the fiercest fighting, then draw back from behind him, that he may be struck down and die." So Joab, in posting guards over the city, sent Uriah to the place where he knew there were brave men. When the men of the city went out to fight against Joab, some of the soldiers of David fell, and Uriah the Hittite was killed.

Then Joab sent to tell David all about the war, and he gave this command to the messenger: "If, after you have finished telling the ruler all about the war, he is angry and says to you, 'Why did you go so near to the city to fight? Did you not know that they would shoot from the wall? Who struck down Abimelech the son of Jerubbaal? Did not a woman cast an upper millstone upon him from the wall, so that he died at Thebez? Why did you go near the wall?' then say, 'Your servant Uriah the Hittite is dead also.'"

So the messenger of Joab went to Jerusalem and told David all that Joab commanded him. Then David said to the messenger, "Say to Joab,

'Let not this thing trouble you, for the sword takes one and then another. Go on fighting against the city and capture it,' and encourage him."

When Bathsheba heard that Uriah her husband was dead, she mourned for him as was the custom. When the mourning was over, David sent for her, and she became his wife and she had a son.

What David had done displeased Jehovah and he sent the prophet Nathan to David. Nathan went to him and said, "There were two men in one city, the one rich and the other poor. The rich man had many flocks and herds; but the poor man had nothing except one little ewe lamb which he had bought. He fed it, and it grew up with him and with his children. It used to eat of his own small supply of food and drink out of his own cup, and it lay in his bosom and was like a daughter to him.

"Now a traveller came to the rich man; and he spared his own flock and did not take an animal from it nor from his own herd to make ready for the traveller who had come to him, but took the poor man's lamb and prepared it for the guest who had come."

Then David was very angry, and he said to Nathan, "As surely as Jehovah lives, the man who has done this deserves to die; he shall repay seven times the value of the lamb, because he showed no pity."

Nathan said to David, "You are the man! Jehovah the God of Israel declares: 'I made you ruler over Israel and I delivered you out of the hand of Saul. I gave you your master's house and your master's wives to be your own, and I gave you the nations of Israel and Judah. If that were too little, I would add as much again. Why have you despised Jehovah by doing that which is wrong in his sight? You have struck down Uriah the Hittite with the sword, and have taken his wife to be your wife, and have killed him with the sword of the Ammonites. Now, therefore, the sword shall never cease to smite your family, because you have despised me and have taken the wife of Uriah the Hittite to be your wife.'"

David said to Nathan, "I have sinned against Jehovah!" Then Nathan said to David, "Jehovah has also put away your sin so that you shall not die. Yet, because by this deed you have shown contempt for Jehovah, the child that is born shall surely die." Then Nathan went to his house.

And Jehovah smote Bathsheba's child so that it fell sick. David prayed to God for the child, and ate no food but went in and lay all night in sackcloth upon the earth. The older men in his house stood over him to raise him up from the earth; but he would not rise nor eat with them. When on the seventh day the child died, the servants of David were afraid to tell him that the child was dead, for they said, "While the child was yet alive, we spoke to him and he paid no attention to our voice. How can we tell him that the child is dead, for he will do some harm!"

But when David saw that his servants were whispering together, he knew that the child was dead, and said to his servants, "Is the child dead?" They replied, "He is dead." Then David rose from the earth, washed and put oil on himself, changed his clothes, and went into the temple of Jehovah and worshipped. After that he went to his own house; and he asked for bread, and when they set it before him, he ate.

His servants said to him, "What is this you have done? You ate no food and cried for the child while it was alive, but when the child died, you rose and ate bread." He replied, "While the child was yet alive, I ate no food and cried aloud, for I said, 'Who knows whether Jehovah will have mercy, so that the child will live?' But now that he is dead, why should I eat no food? Can I bring him back? I am going to him, but he will not come back to me."

ABSALOM THE UNGRATEFUL SON

Some time later Absalom, David's son, prepared a chariot and horses and fifty men to run before him. He used to rise early and stand beside the highway which led to the city gate. He would call to him every man who had a suit that was to come before the ruler for judgment and say, "Of what city are you?" When the man replied, "Your servant is from one of the tribes of Israel," Absalom would say to him, "Your claims are good and right; but the ruler has not appointed any one to hear you. Oh, that some one would make me judge in the land, so that every man who has any complaint or cause would come to me, and I would see that he received justice!" And whenever a man came near to bow before him, he would put out his hand and take hold of him and kiss him. In this way Absalom treated all the Israelites who came to David for justice. Thus, Absalom stole from David the hearts of the Israelites.

At the end of four years, Absalom said to his father, "I should like to go and keep my promise, which I have made to Jehovah in Hebron." David said to him, "Go in peace." So he went to Hebron; but Absalom sent messengers to all the tribes of Israel to say, "As soon as you hear the sound of the trumpet, cry, 'Absalom has become ruler in Hebron.'" With Absalom there went two hundred men from Jerusalem, who were invited and went innocently, knowing nothing at all of what he was going to do. Absalom also sent for Ahithophel, David's adviser, from the city of Giloh, while he was offering the sacrifices. And the plot was strong, for more and more people kept going over to Absalom.

When a messenger came to David, saying, "The hearts of the men of Israel have gone over to Absalom," David said to all his servants who were with him at Jerusalem, "Up, let us flee; for, if we do not, none of us will escape from Absalom. Go at once, or he may quickly overtake us and bring evil upon us and kill the people of the city." Then David's servants said to him, "It shall be done as our lord wishes; we are your servants."

So David and all the people who followed him went out and stood at the last house, while all the officers and the royal body-guard and all the men of Ittai the Gittite, the six hundred who had followed him from Gath, passed on before him.

Then David said to Ittai, "Why do you also go with us? Go back and stay with the new ruler, for you are a foreigner and away from your own land. Yesterday you came, and to-day shall I make you go up and down the land with us, while I go where I may? Go back and take your men with you, and may Jehovah show you kindness and faithfulness." But Ittai answered, "As surely as Jehovah lives and as my lord the ruler of Israel lives, wherever my lord is, whether dead or living, there your servant will be!" David said to Ittai, "March on." So Ittai marched on with all his men and with all the children who were with him.

All the people were weeping aloud while David stood in the Kidron valley, and they went by before him on the way to the wilderness. And Zadok and Abiathar came carrying the ark of Jehovah and set it down until all the people had passed. Then David said to Zadok, "Carry the ark of God back into the city. If I win Jehovah's favor, he will bring me back and show me both it and the place where he dwells. But if he declares, 'I have no trust in you, then here am I, let him do to me as he thinks best.'" So Zadok and Abiathar carried the ark of God back to Jerusalem and stayed there.

But David went up, weeping as he climbed the Mount of Olives with his head covered and his feet bare. All the people who were with him covered their heads and went up, weeping as they went.

And when David came to the summit, where one worships God, Hushai the Archite with his garment torn and earth upon his head, came to meet him. David said to him, "If you go on with me you will be a burden to me. But if you go back to the city, and say to Absalom, 'Your brothers have gone away and your father has gone after them; I will be your servant, O king; as I have been your father's servant in the past, so now I will be your servant,' you can defeat for me the advice of Ahithophel. And have you not there with you Zadok and Abiathar the priests? See, they have there with them their two sons, Ahimaaz, Zadok's son, and Jonathan, Abiathar's son. By them you shall send word to me of everything that you hear." So Hushai, David's friend, went into the city, when Absalom came to Jerusalem.

Then David and all the people who were with him, reached the Jordan tired out, but he refreshed himself there.

And Absalom, with all the men of Israel, came to Jerusalem, and Ahithophel was with him. When Hushai, David's friend, came to Absalom,

Hushai said to him, "May the king live, may the king live!" But Absalom said to Hushai, "Is this your love for your friend? Why did you not go with your friend?" Hushai answered, "No! to him whom Jehovah and his people and all the men of Israel have chosen, to him will I belong and with him will I stay. Also whom should I serve? Should it not be his son? As I have served your father, so will I serve you."

The advice which Ahithophel gave in those days was thought by David and Absalom to be the same as if it had come from God himself. And Ahithophel said to Absalom, "Let me now pick out twelve thousand men, and set out and follow David to-night. Thus I will come upon him when he is tired and weak and will frighten him, and all the people who are with him will flee. Then I will kill only the king, and I will bring back all the people to you as the bride turns to her husband. Seek only the life of one man, and all the people will be at peace." This advice pleased Absalom and all the leaders of Israel.

Then Absalom said, "Call now Hushai and let us hear also what he has to say." When Hushai came to Absalom, Absalom said to him, "Thus Ahithophel has spoken; shall we act as he advises? If not, you advise us." Then Hushai said to Absalom, "The advice that Ahithophel has given this time is not good. You know that your father and his men are mighty warriors and are now angry, like a bear robbed of her cubs. Your father is also a soldier and will not stay at night with the people. Even now he has hidden himself in one of the caves or in some other place. If some of the people fall at first, whoever hears it will say, 'There is a slaughter among the people who follow Absalom.' Then even he who is brave, whose heart is like the heart of a lion, will completely lose courage; for all Israel knows that your father is a great warrior, and they who are with him are brave men. But I advise, let all the Israelites be gathered to you, from Dan to Beersheba, as many as the sand that is by the sea, with you yourself marching in the midst of them. In this way we will come upon him in some place where he will be found, and we will fall upon him as the dew falls on the ground;

and of him and of all the men who are with him not even one shall be left. If he goes into a city, then all Israel will bring ropes to that city, and we will pull it down into the valley, until not even a small stone is found there."

Absalom and all the men of Israel said, "The advice of Hushai is better than the advice of Ahithophel." For Jehovah had planned to defeat the good advice of Ahithophel, so that Jehovah might bring evil upon Absalom.

Then Hushai said to Zadok and to Abiathar the priests, "This is what Ahithophel advised Absalom and the leaders of Israel; and this is what I advised. So now send quickly and say to David, 'Do not spend this night at the fords of the wilderness, but by all means cross over, for fear that David and all the people with him be killed.'"

Now Jonathan and Ahimaaz were staying at Enrogel; and a maid-servant was to go and bring them news, and they were to go and tell David, for they must not be seen coming into the city. But a boy saw them and told Absalom. Then they both went away quickly and entered into the house of a man in Bahurim, who had a well in his courtyard into which they descended. The women took and spread the covering over the mouth of the well, and scattered dried fruit upon it, so that nothing was known. And when Absalom's servants came to the woman at the house and said, "Where are Ahimaaz and Jonathan?" the woman answered, "They have gone over the brook." When they had searched and could find nothing, they returned to Jerusalem.

But as soon as the men had gone away, Ahimaaz and Jonathan came up out of the well, and went and told David and said, "Get up, cross quickly over the water, for so has Ahithophel advised in regard to you." Then David and all the people who were with him rose and crossed the Jordan. By daybreak there was not one left behind.

A BROKEN-HEARTED FATHER

After Absalom and all the men of Israel crossed the Jordan, David counted the troops who were with him, and put over them commanders of thousands and of hundreds. And he divided the troops into three divisions; one was under the command of Joab, another under Abishai, and another under the command of Ittai. Then David said to the people, "I too will surely go out with you." But the people said, "You shall not go out; for if we are defeated, or if half of us die, it will make no difference, for you are equal to ten thousand of us. It is therefore more important for you to be ready to help us from the city." David said to them, "I will do what you think best!" So he stood beside the gate, while all the troops marched out by hundreds and by thousands.

David commanded Joab and Abishai and Ittai, "Deal gently for my sake with the young man, with Absalom!" All the people heard when he gave the commanders this order about Absalom.

So the troops went out into the field against Israel. The battle was fought in the forest of Ephraim. And the soldiers of Israel were defeated there by those who were loyal to David, and the loss of life on that day was great—twenty thousand men. The battle spread over the whole country; and the dense thickets killed more people than were killed by the sword.

Absalom happened to meet the soldiers of David while riding upon his mule, and the mule went under the thick branches of a great oak, and Absalom's head caught fast in the oak, and he was hung between heaven and earth, while the mule that was under him went on. A certain man saw it and told Joab, "I saw Absalom hanging in an oak." Joab said to the man who told him, "You saw him! Why did you not strike him to the ground? I would have given you ten pieces of silver and a belt." But the man said to Joab, "If I were to feel the weight of a thousand pieces of silver in my hand, I would not raise my hand against the ruler's son, for in our hearing he commanded you and Abishai and Ittai, 'Take care of the young man

Absalom.' If I had treacherously taken his life, nothing would have been hidden from the ruler of Israel, and you yourself would not have tried to save me." Joab answered, "I will not waste time with you."

So he took three spears in his hand and drove them into Absalom's heart, while he was still alive in the midst of the oak. Then Joab said to a negro slave, "Go, tell the ruler of Israel what you have seen." And the negro bowed before Joab and ran off.

Now David was sitting between the two gates, and when the negro came, he said, "Let my lord receive the good news; Jehovah has punished for you this day all those who rose up against you."' David said to the negro, "Is it well with the young Absalom?" The negro answered, "May the enemies of my lord and all who rebel against you to harm you be as that young man!"

Then David was very sad and went up to the chamber over the gate and wept. As he wept he said, "My son Absalom, my son, O my son Absalom! Oh that I had died for you, Absalom, my son, my son!" And it was reported to Joab, "The ruler of Israel is weeping and mourning for Absalom." So for all the people the victory that day was turned to mourning, because they heard that David was mourning for his son. Therefore, the people stole away into the city, as people who are ashamed steal away when they have run away in battle. But David covered his face and cried aloud, "My son Absalom, Absalom, my son, my son!"

HOW SOLOMON BECAME THE RULER OF ISRAEL

Now when David was old, Adonijah thought, "I will be ruler of Israel." So he prepared for himself chariots and horsemen and fifty men to run before him. His father, David, had never in his life troubled him by saying, "Why have you done thus and so?" Adonijah was very good-looking and was the next younger son after Absalom. He also had made an agreement with Joab and with Abiathar the priest to help him. But

Zadok the priest and Benaiah and Nathan the prophet, as well as Shimei and Rei and David's famous warriors, were not on his side.

Adonijah held a feast and killed for it sheep, oxen, and fat beasts by the Serpent's Stone, which is beside the Fuller's Spring; and he invited to the feast all his brothers and all the royal officials of Judah; but he did not invite the prophet Nathan nor Benaiah nor the famous warriors nor his brother Solomon.

Then Nathan said to Bathsheba the mother of Solomon, "Have you not heard that Adonijah has been made ruler without David our lord knowing it? Now, therefore, let me advise you that you may save your own life and the life of your son Solomon. Go at once to David and say to him, 'Did you not, my lord, solemnly promise your servant that Solomon your son should rule after you? Why then has Adonijah been made ruler?' While you are still talking with him, I will come in and repeat your words."

So Bathsheba went into David's room; he was very old, and Abishag the Shunamite was caring for him. When David said, "What do you wish?" she said to him, "My lord, you solemnly promised your servant by Jehovah: 'Solomon your son shall rule after me.' But now Adonijah has been made ruler without your knowledge, my lord! Now, my lord, all the Israelites are looking to you, to tell them who shall rule after you. If you do not tell them, then, when my lord dies, I and my son Solomon will be treated as criminals."

While she was still talking with David, Nathan the prophet came in. And they told David, "Nathan the prophet is here." So he came in and bowed before David with his face to the ground. Then Nathan said, "My lord, have you said, 'Adonijah shall rule after me?' For he has gone down this day and killed many oxen and fat beasts and sheep and has invited all your sons and the commanders of the army and Abiathar the priest; and there they are eating and drinking before him and saying, 'May the new ruler Adonijah live!' But he has not invited me, even me your servant, nor Zadok, the priest, nor Benaiah nor your servant Solomon. If you have done this, my lord, you have failed to show your servants who is to rule after my lord."

David answered, "Call Bathsheba to me." So she came in and stood before him. Then David made this solemn promise; "As surely as Jehovah lives, who has delivered me from all trouble, as I have solemnly promised to you by Jehovah, the God of Israel, saying, 'Solomon your son shall rule after me'; so I will certainly do to-day." Then Bathsheba bowed her face to the earth and said, "May my lord live forever."

Then David said, "Call to me Zadok the priest, Nathan the prophet, and Benaiah the son of Jehoiada." When they came before him, he said to them, "Take with you the servants of your lord. Let Solomon my son ride upon my own mule, bring him down to Gihon, and there let Zadok the priest and Nathan the prophet make him ruler over Israel and blow the trumpet and say, 'May Solomon the ruler live!' Then you shall go up after him, and he shall go in and sit upon my throne, for he shall rule after me; and I have appointed him to be chief over Israel and Judah." Benaiah answered David, "So may it be! May Jehovah confirm the words of my lord. As Jehovah has been with my lord, even so may he be with Solomon, and may he make his throne greater than the throne of my lord David!"

Then Zadok, Nathan, and Benaiah together with the Philistine body-guards, went down and put Solomon on David's mule and brought him to Gihon. Zadok the priest took the horn of oil out of the tent and poured oil on Solomon's head, and they blew the trumpet, and all the people said, "May Solomon live!" Then all the people followed him and the people played on flutes and rejoiced so loudly that the earth seemed to be shaken by the sound that they made.

Adonijah and all the guests who were with him heard it just as they had finished eating. And they were terrified and each rose up and went away. But Adonijah in his fear of Solomon went and caught hold of the horns of the altar. When it was reported to Solomon, "See, Adonijah fears Solomon the ruler, for he has caught hold of the horns of the altar and says, 'Let Solomon solemnly promise me first that he will not kill his servant with the sword,'" Solomon said, "If he shall show himself a worthy man, not one of his hairs shall be touched, but if he is found guilty of disloyalty, he shall die." So Solomon had him brought from the altar. And he came and bowed before Solomon the ruler. And Solomon said to him, "Go to your home."

Then David died and was buried in the City of David, after having ruled over Israel forty years.

A YOUNG MAN'S WISE CHOICE

Solomon went to Gibeon to offer a sacrifice there, for that was the great high place. He offered upon that altar a thousand animals as a burnt-offering.

In Gibeon Jehovah appeared to Solomon in a dream by night and said, "Ask what I shall give you." Solomon said, "Thou hast showed to thy servant David my father great kindness. Now, O Jehovah my God, thou hast made thy servant ruler in the place of David my father, although I am but a child who does not know how to go out or come in. Give thy servant, therefore, an understanding mind to rule thy people, that I may see clearly what is good and what is evil; for who is able to rule this thy great people?"

Jehovah was pleased that Solomon had asked this; and God said to him, "Because you have asked this and have not asked for yourself long life nor riches nor the life of your enemies, but have asked for yourself understanding to see clearly what is just, I have now granted what you ask; I have given you a wise and understanding mind. I have also given you that which you have not asked, both riches and honor." When Solomon awoke, he found that it was a dream; and he returned to Jerusalem.

Once two women came to Solomon and stood before him. The one woman said, "Oh, my lord, this woman and I live in the same house. While with her in the house I had a child. Three days later this woman also had a child, and we were alone by ourselves in the house. While we two were alone this woman's child died in the night, because she lay upon it.

"'Then she rose at midnight and took my son from beside me, while your servant slept, and laid it on her breast and laid her dead child on mine. When I rose at dawn to nurse my child, there it was dead; but when I looked at it closely in the morning, I found that it was not my son." Then the other woman said, "No; the living is my son, and the dead child is your son." So they quarrelled before Solomon.

Then Solomon said, "One says, 'This one who is alive is my son, and your son is dead.' But the other says, 'No; your son is dead, and my son is the one that is alive.' Bring me a sword." So they brought him a sword. Then he said, "Divide the living child in two and give half to the one and half to the other." At that the woman to whom the living child belonged spoke to Solomon—for she loved her son with all her heart—and said, "Oh, my lord, give her the living child and on no account put it to death." But the other said, "It shall be neither mine nor yours! Divide it!" Then Solomon said, "Give the first woman the living child, and on no account put it to death; she is its mother."

When all Israel heard of the decision which Solomon had given, they had great respect for him, for they saw that he had divine wisdom to decide questions justly.

BUILDING A GREAT TEMPLE

In the fourth year of Solomon's rule over Israel he built the temple of Jehovah. The temple was ninety feet long, thirty feet wide, and forty-five feet high. The porch before the large room of the temple was thirty feet wide and fifteen feet deep. Solomon made windows for the temple with casings, broad on the inside and narrow on the outside.

The temple was built with stone which had been made ready at the quarry; neither hammer nor chisel nor any iron tool was heard while the temple was building. Against the wall of the temple on the outside Solomon built wings, both around the larger room and the inner room, and made side-chambers around the temple.

The entrance to the lower side-chambers was on the south side of the temple. Winding stairs led to the second floor, and from the second to the third. Solomon built the wings against the sides of the temple, each seven and a half feet high; and they were joined to the temple with timbers of cedar.

He covered the walls of the temple on the inside with boards of cedar from the floor of the temple to the rafters: and he covered the floor of the temple with boards of cypress.

He also made a room thirty feet square in the back part of the temple with boards of cedar reaching from the floor to the rafters. He built it as an inner room, even as the most holy place. The temple, that is the large room in front of the inner room, was sixty feet long. And there was cedar inside the temple with carving in the form of gourds and open flowers. All was cedar, no stone was seen. Solomon prepared the inner room as a place for the ark.

In the inner room Solomon made two winged bulls of olive wood. The height of each was fifteen feet. Each of their wings measured seven and a half feet across, fifteen feet from the end of one wing to the end of the other. He set these up in the inner room of the temple; and their wings were stretched out so that the wing of the one touched the one wall, while the wing of the other touched the other wall, and their wings touched each other in the middle of the temple; and he covered them with gold.

Then Solomon gathered in Jerusalem the leaders of Israel to bring up the ark of Jehovah out of Zion, the City of David, at the time of the autumn festival in September. When all the leaders of Israel had come, the priests took up the ark and the tent of meeting and all the sacred vessels that were in the tent. So the priests brought in the ark of Jehovah to its place in the inner room of the temple under the wings of the winged bulls. There was nothing in the ark except the two tables of stone which Moses put there at Horeb. And when the priests came out from the inner room, the cloud filled the temple of Jehovah, so that the priests could not stand and perform their service on account of the cloud, for the glory of Jehovah filled his temple.

Then Solomon said:

> "Jehovah has set the sun in the heavens,
> But has said that he will dwell in thick darkness.
> So I have built thee a temple as a lofty dwelling,
> A place for thee to abide in forever."

As Solomon stood before the altar of Jehovah in the presence of all the assembly of Israel, he spread out his hands toward heaven and said, "O Jehovah, the God of Israel, there is no God like thee in heaven above or on earth beneath, who keepest thy solemn agreement and showest kindness to thy servants who serve thee whole-heartedly, who hast kept with thy servant David my father the promise that thou didst make to him.

"But will God actually dwell on earth? Indeed heaven and the highest heaven cannot hold thee; how much less this temple that I have built!"

A RULER WHO WRONGED HIS PEOPLE

Solomon was building his palace thirteen years before he finished it. He also built the throne-hall where he judged the people. This room was the Hall of Judgment; and it was covered with cedar from floor to ceiling.

His palace where he lived, in another court farther in from the Hall of Judgment, was of the same workmanship. He made a palace, too, similar to this hall, for Pharaoh's daughter whom he had married. All these buildings were of costly stones, hewn according to measurements, sawed with saws, both on the inside and outside.

Solomon also gathered together chariots and horsemen; he had one thousand four hundred chariots and twelve thousand horsemen that he placed in the chariot cities and with him at Jerusalem. And Solomon had twelve officers over all Israel who provided food for him and for his household: each man had to provide food for a month in the year.

When the queen of Sheba heard of the fame of Solomon, she came to test him with puzzling questions. So she came to Jerusalem with a very large number of servants, with camels that carried spices and a great amount of gold and precious stones. As soon as she came to Solomon, she told him all that was in her mind. And Solomon answered all her questions: nothing was too difficult for him to answer.

When the queen of Sheba had seen all the wisdom of Solomon, the palace that he had built, the food on his table, the housing of his officers, the way his waiters served him, their clothing, his cup-bearers, and the burnt-offering which he offered at the temple of Jehovah, she was greatly surprised. She said to Solomon, "What I heard in my own land of your acts and of your wisdom was true. But I would not believe the words until I came and saw with my own eyes; but as it is, the half was not told me; your wisdom and prosperity are even greater than what was reported to me."

Now Solomon loved women; and he married many foreign wives—Moabites, Canaanites, Edomites, Sidonians, Hittites, and Ammonites. He had seven hundred wives of princely birth, and three hundred concubines. When Solomon was old, his wives influenced him to worship other gods, and he was not loyal to Jehovah his God. Solomon built a place of worship for Chemosh, the god of Moab, on the hill that is opposite Jerusalem, and for Milcom, the god of the Ammonites. He did the same for all his foreign wives, burning incense and offering sacrifices to their gods.

Then God raised up as a foe against him Rezon, the son of Eliada, who had fled from his master, Hadadezer, king of Zobah. He gathered men about him and became commander of a robber band, and he went to Damascus and lived and reigned there. He was a foe to Israel as long as Solomon lived.

Jeroboam, the son of Nebat, was a man of great ability. When Solomon saw that the young man was industrious, he placed him over all the men of the tribe of Joseph who were working for the ruler.

Once upon a time, when Jeroboam went away from Jerusalem, the prophet Ahijah of Shiloh met him on the way and took him aside. Now Ahijah had put on a new garment, and while they two were alone in the field, Ahijah took hold of the new garment he had on and tore it in twelve pieces. Then he said to Jeroboam, "Take for yourself ten pieces; for Jehovah, the God of Israel, declares, 'I will tear the kingdom out of the hand of Solomon and will give ten tribes to you, but he shall have only one tribe.'" So Jeroboam also rebelled against Solomon.

Solomon, therefore, wanted to kill Jeroboam. But Jeroboam arose and fled to Egypt, and he was in Egypt until the death of Solomon.

REHOBOAM'S GREAT MISTAKE

When Solomon died, Rehoboam his son ruled after him. As soon as Jeroboam, who was still in Egypt, heard that Solomon had died, he returned at once to his home town, Zeredah in Mount Ephraim.

Rehoboam went to Shechem, for all the Israelites had come to Shechem to make him ruler. But they said to Rehoboam, "Your father laid a heavy yoke upon us. Now make the hard service of your father and the heavy yoke that he laid upon us lighter, and we will serve you." He said to them, "Go away for three days; then come again to me." So the people went away.

Then Rehoboam asked advice from the old men who had been in the service of Solomon his father during his lifetime and inquired, "What answer do you advise me to give this people?" They said to him, "If now you will serve this people and give them a favorable answer, then they will be your servants forever."

But he rejected the advice which the old men had given him and asked the young men who had grown up with him and had been in his service. And he said to them, "What answer do you advise that we give to this people who have said to me, 'Make the yoke that your father laid upon us lighter'?" The young men who had grown up with him said to him, "Make this answer to them: 'My little finger is thicker than my father's loins! While my father loaded you with a heavy yoke, I will make your yoke heavier; my father punished you with whips, but I will punish you with scourges.'"

So when all the people came to Rehoboam the third day, as he had directed, he answered the people harshly and did not follow the advice which the old men had given him, but spoke to them as the young men had advised, saying, "My father made your yoke heavy, but I will make your yoke still heavier; my father punished you with whips, but I will punish you with scourges." So Rehoboam paid no attention to the demand of the people.

When all Israel saw that he paid no attention to their demand they gave him this answer: "What interest have we in David? We have nothing in common with the son of Jesse! To your tents, O Israel! Now look out for your house, O David!"

So the Israelites went to their homes.

Then Rehoboam sent to them Adoniram, who was over the men who did forced labor. But when all the Israelites stoned him to death, Rehoboam quickly mounted his chariot and fled to Jerusalem. So Israel has refused to obey the house of David to the present day.

As soon as all Israel heard that Jeroboam had returned, they sent and called him to the assembly of the people and made him ruler over all Israel. None remained loyal to the house of David except the tribe of Judah.

ELIJAH AND THE WIDOW'S SON

When Asa had been ruler of Judah for thirty-one years Omri became ruler over Israel, and he ruled twelve years. He bought the hill Samaria from Shemer for two talents of silver; and he built a city on the hill and named it Samaria, after Shemer, the owner of the hill.

When Omri died, Ahab his son ruled in his place. But Ahab displeased Jehovah more than all the kings who had ruled before him. He married Jezebel, the daughter of Ethbaal, king of the Sidonians, and then began to worship the Phœnician god Baal. He also built an altar for Baal in the temple of Baal, which he built in Samaria.

Then Elijah from Tishbe in Gilead said to Ahab, "As surely as Jehovah the God of Israel lives, whom I serve, there shall be no dew nor rain for years except as I announce it."

Then this message from Jehovah came to Elijah: "Go from here and hide yourself near the Brook Cherith that is east of the Jordan. You shall drink from the brook, and I have commanded the ravens to feed you there."

So he obeyed the command of Jehovah and lived near the Brook Cherith. The ravens brought him bread every morning and meat every evening, and he drank from the brook. But after a while the brook dried up, for there had been no rain in the land.

Then this message from Jehovah came to him, "Arise, go to Zarephath which belongs to Sidon, and live there. I have commanded a widow there to provide for you." So he went to Zarephath.

When he came to the gate of the city, a widow was there gathering sticks. Calling to her, he said, "Bring me, I beg of you, a little water in a vessel, that I may drink." As she was going to get it, he called after her, "Bring also a bit of bread with you." She replied, "As surely as Jehovah your God lives, I have nothing baked, and only one handful of meal in the jar and a little oil in the jug. Now I am gathering a few sticks, that I may go in and prepare it for myself and my son, that we may eat it and die." Elijah said to her, "Fear not; go and do as you have said, but first bake for me a little dough and bring it to me. Afterward make some for yourself and your son. For Jehovah the God of Israel declares: 'The jar of meal shall not be empty, nor the jug of oil fail, until Jehovah sends rain upon the earth.'"

So she did as Elijah directed; and she and her child, as well as Elijah, had food to eat. From that day the jar of meal was never empty and the jug of oil did not fail, as Jehovah had said through Elijah.

Now after this the woman's son fell sick; and his sickness was so severe that he stopped breathing. So she said to Elijah, "What have I to do with you, O man of God? You have come to me to remind me of my sin by taking the life of my son!" He said to her, "Give me your son." So he took him out of her arms and carried him up into the upper room where he was staying and laid him on his own bed. Then he prayed earnestly to Jehovah and said, "O Jehovah, my God, hast thou also brought misfortune upon this widow, with whom I am staying, by taking the life of her son?" And he stretched himself upon the child three times and prayed to Jehovah and said, "O Jehovah, my God, I pray thee, give back this child's life to him again."

So Jehovah listened to Elijah's prayer; and the life of the child came back to him, and he sat up. Then Elijah took the child and brought him down from the upper room into the house and gave him to his mother; and said, "See, your son lives!" The woman said to him, "Now I know that you are a man of God and that the message of Jehovah that you speak is true."

THE PROPHET OF FIRE

In the third year of the famine this command came from Jehovah to Elijah: "Go, show yourself to Ahab; and I will send rain upon the earth." So Elijah went to show himself to Ahab.

The famine was so severe in Samaria that Ahab had called Obadiah, the overseer of the palace. Obadiah was very loyal to Jehovah; for when Jezebel tried to kill the prophets of Jehovah, he took a hundred and hid them in a cave and kept them supplied with bread and water. Ahab said to Obadiah, "Come, let us go through the land to all the springs and to all the brooks, in the hope that we may find grass, so that we can save the horses and mules and not lose all of them." So they divided the land between them, Ahab going in one direction and Obadiah in another.

While Obadiah was on the way, Elijah suddenly met him. As soon as Obadiah knew him, he fell on his face and said, "Is it you, my lord Elijah?" He answered, "It is; go, tell your master: 'Elijah is here.'" But Obadiah said, "What sin have I done, that you would give your servant over to Ahab to kill me? As surely as Jehovah your God lives, there is no nation nor kingdom where my lord has not sent to find you; and when they said, 'He is not here,' he made each of the kingdoms and nations take an oath, that no one had found you. Now you say, 'Go, tell your lord, Elijah is here!' As soon as I have left you the spirit of Jehovah will carry you to a place unknown to me, so that when I come and tell Ahab and he cannot find you, he will put me to death, although I, your servant, have been loyal to Jehovah from my youth! Have you not been told what I did when Jezebel killed the prophets of Jehovah, how I hid a hundred by fifties in a cave and fed them continually with bread and water?" Elijah answered, "As surely as Jehovah of hosts lives, before whom I stand, I will show myself to Ahab to-day."

So Obadiah went to Ahab and told him; and Ahab went to meet Elijah. As soon as Ahab saw Elijah, he said to him, "Is it you, you who have brought trouble to Israel?" He answered, "I have not brought trouble on Israel, but you and your father's house have; because you have failed to follow the commands of Jehovah and have run after the Phœnician gods. Now therefore call together to me at Mount Carmel all the Israelites and the four hundred and fifty prophets of the god Baal who eat at Jezebel's table."

So Ahab sent for all the Israelites and gathered the prophets together at Mount Carmel. Then Elijah came to the people and said, "How long are you going to falter between worshipping Jehovah or Baal? If Jehovah is the true God, follow him, but if Baal, then follow him." But the people were silent. Then Elijah said to the people, "I, even I only, am left as a prophet of Jehovah, but there are four hundred and fifty prophets of Baal. Let us take two oxen; let them choose one ox for themselves and cut it in pieces and lay it on the wood, without lighting any fire, and I will dress the other ox and lay it on wood, without lighting any fire. Then you call on your god and I will call on Jehovah. The god who answers by fire is the true God." All the people answered and said, "It is a fair offer."

Then Elijah said to the prophets of Baal, "Choose one of the oxen for yourselves and dress it first, for you are many, and call on your god, without lighting any fire." So they took the ox which he gave them and dressed it, and called on their god from morning until noon, saying, "O Baal, hear us." But there was no voice nor answer, although they leaped about the altar which they had built.

When it was noon, Elijah mocked them, saying, "Call loudly, for he is a god; either he is thinking, or he has gone out, or he is on a journey, or perhaps he is sleeping and must be awakened!" Then they called loudly and cut themselves, as was their custom, with swords and lances until the blood gushed out upon them. When noon was past, they cried out in frenzy until the time of the offering of the evening sacrifice; but there was neither voice nor answer nor was any attention paid to their cry.

Then Elijah said to all the people, "Come near to me." And all the people drew near to him, and he rebuilt the altar of Jehovah which had been thrown down. Then around the altar he made a ditch that would hold about two bushels of seed. When he had placed the pieces of wood in order, he cut up the ox and laid it on the wood. Then he said, "Fill four jars with water and pour it on the burnt-offering and on the pieces of wood." And he said, "Do it the second time"; and they did it the second time. He said, "Do it the third time"; and they did it the third time, so that the water ran round the altar. And he also filled the ditch with water.

When it was time to offer the evening sacrifice, Elijah the prophet came near and said, "O Jehovah, God of Abraham, of Isaac, and of Israel, let it be known this day that thou art God in Israel, that I am thy servant, and that I have done all these things at thy command. Hear me, O Jehovah, hear me, that this people may know that thou, Jehovah, art God, and that thou mayst win their hearts."

Then the fire of Jehovah fell and burned up the burnt-offering and the wood, the stones and the dust, and licked up the water that was in the trench. When all the people saw it, they fell on their faces and cried, "Jehovah, he is God; Jehovah, he is God." But Elijah commanded them, "Take the prophets of Baal; do not let one of them escape!" So they took them down to the Brook Kishon and there put them to death.

Then Elijah said to Ahab, "Go, eat and drink; for there are signs of a heavy rain." So Ahab went to eat and drink. But Elijah went up to the top of Carmel and crouched down upon the earth, with his face between his knees. And he said to his servant, "Go up now, look toward the sea." So he went up and looked and said, "There is nothing." But seven times he said, "Go again." So the servant went back seven times, but the seventh time he said, "There is a cloud as small as a man's hand rising out of the sea." Then Elijah said, "Go, say to Ahab, 'Make ready your chariot; go down, that the rain may not stop you.'" In a little while the heavens grew black with clouds and wind, and there was a heavy rain. And as Ahab rode toward Jezreel, Elijah was given divine strength, so that he tightened his belt and ran before Ahab to the entrance to Jezreel.

GOD'S LOW WHISPER

Now when Ahab told Jezebel that Elijah had put the prophets to death with the sword, she sent a messenger to Elijah, saying, "As surely as you are Elijah and I am Jezebel, may the gods do to me what they will and more too, if I do not make your life as the life of one of those prophets by to-morrow about this time."

Then he was afraid and fled for his life. And he came to Beersheba, which belongs to Judah, and left his servant there. But he went on a day's journey into the wilderness and sat down under a desert tree, and he asked that he might die, saying, "It is enough; now, O Jehovah, take my life, for I am no better than my fathers."

Then he lay down and slept under the desert tree, but an angel touched him and said to him, "Rise, eat!" When he looked, he saw there at his head a loaf, baked on hot stones, and a jar of water. So he ate and drank and lay down again. But the angel of Jehovah came again the second time and touched him and said, "Rise, eat, or else the journey will be too long for you." So he rose and ate and drank and went in the strength of that food forty days and forty nights to Horeb the mountain of God.

Then Jehovah passed by, and a very violent wind tore the mountain apart and broke the rocks in pieces before Jehovah; but Jehovah was not in the wind. And after the wind an earthquake; but Jehovah was not in the earthquake. And after the earthquake a fire; but Jehovah was not in the fire. After the fire there was the sound of a low whisper. As soon as Elijah heard it, he wrapped his face in his mantle and went out and stood at the entrance of the cave. Then he heard a voice saying, "What are you doing here, Elijah?" He replied, "I have been very jealous for Jehovah the God of hosts, for the Israelites have forsaken thee, thrown down thine altars, and slain thy prophets with the sword, and I only am left; and they seek to take my life."

Then Jehovah said to him, "On your way back go to the wilderness of Damascus, and when you arrive there, anoint Hazael to rule over Aram, Jehu, the son of Nimshi, to rule over Israel, and Elisha, the son of Shaphat, to be prophet in your place. Then every one who escapes the sword of Hazael, Jehu shall put to death; and every one who escapes the sword of Jehu, Elisha shall put to death. Yet I will spare seven thousand in Israel—all who have not worshipped Baal and kissed his image."

After he had left, Elijah found Elisha the son of Shaphat, as he was ploughing with twelve pairs of oxen. When Elijah went up to him and threw his mantle upon him, he left the oxen and ran after Elijah and said, "Let me kiss my father and my mother, and then I will follow you." Elijah said to him, "Go back, for what have I done to you?" So Elisha turned back and took one pair of oxen and offered them as a sacrifice and, using the wooden ploughs and yokes as fuel, boiled their flesh, and gave it to the people to eat. Then he arose and followed Elijah and served him.

AHAB THE THIEF

Now Naboth, the Jezreelite, had a vineyard in Jezreel next to the palace of Ahab, who ruled at Samaria. So Ahab said to Naboth, "Give me your vineyard, that I may have it as a vegetable-garden, for it is near my palace; and I will give you a better vineyard for it; or, if it is more pleasing to you, I will pay you its value in money." But Naboth answered Ahab, "May Jehovah save me from the crime of giving you what has come down to me from my fathers!"

So Ahab went into his house sullen and in bad humor because of what Naboth had said to him. And he lay down on his bed and covered his face and would eat no food.

But Jezebel his wife came to him and said, "Why are you in such bad humor that you will not eat?" He replied, "Because I made this offer to Naboth, 'Give me your vineyard for its value in money, or else, if it is more pleasing to you, I will give you another vineyard for it.' But he answered, 'I will not give you my vineyard.'" Then Jezebel his wife said to him, "Are you not the one who now rules in Israel? Rise, eat, and set your mind at rest. I will give you the vineyard of Naboth."

So she wrote letters in Ahab's name and sealed them with his seal and sent the letters to the leaders and officials who lived in Naboth's city. In the letters she wrote, "Proclaim a fast and put Naboth in front of the people. Then set up two base men before him and let them bring this charge against him: 'You cursed God and the ruler of Israel.' Then carry him out and stone him to death."

The leaders and officials of Naboth's city did as Jezebel commanded in her letters to them. They proclaimed a fast and put Naboth in front of the people. Then the two base men came in and sat before him, and the scoundrels in the presence of the people said, "Naboth cursed God and the ruler of Israel." Then they carried him out of the city and stoned him to death. And they told Jezebel, "Naboth has been stoned to death."

As soon as Jezebel heard that Naboth had been stoned to death, she said to Ahab, "Rise, take the vineyard of Naboth which he refused to sell you, for Naboth is not alive but dead." As soon as Ahab heard that Naboth was dead, he went down to the vineyard of Naboth to take it. But this command came from Jehovah to Elijah, the Tishbite, "Rise, go down to meet Ahab, the ruler of Israel, who lives in Samaria; he is just now in the vineyard of Naboth, where he has gone to take it. Say to him, 'This is the message of Jehovah, "Have you killed and also taken his vineyard? In the very place where the dogs licked the blood of Naboth there they shall also lick your blood." '"Ahab said to Elijah, "Have you found me, O my enemy?" He answered, "I have. And Jehovah has declared: 'The dogs shall eat Jezebel in the district of Jezreel.'" When Ahab heard those words, he tore his clothes and put sackcloth on his flesh and ate no food.

MICAIAH'S COURAGE IN TELLING THE TRUTH

For three years there was no war between Aram and Israel. But in the third year, when Jehoshaphat the ruler of Judah came to visit the ruler of Israel, Ahab said to his followers, "Do you not know that Ramoth in Gilead belongs to us; yet we sit still instead of taking it from the king of Aram?" Then he asked Jehoshaphat, "Will you go with me to attack Ramoth in Gilead?" Jehoshaphat replied, "I am with you, my people are as your people, my horses as your horses."

And Jehoshaphat said to the ruler of Israel, "Ask now what Jehovah has to say." So Ahab gathered the prophets together (in all about four hundred men), and asked them, "Shall I go to fight against Ramoth in Gilead or shall I not?" They said, "Go up; for Jehovah will give it into your hands." But Jehoshaphat said, "Is there any other prophet of Jehovah, that we may ask him?" The ruler of Israel answered, "There is another by whom we may ask of Jehovah, Micaiah, the son of Imlah, but I hate him; for he prophesies for me nothing good, but only evil." Jehoshaphat said, "Do not say so."

Then the ruler of Israel called a servant and said, "Bring quickly Micaiah, the son of Imlah." The messenger who went to call Micaiah said to him, "See, the prophets have all of them promised the ruler of Israel success. Agree with them, and prophesy success." But Micaiah said, "As surely as Jehovah lives, I will speak what he says to me."

When he came to Ahab, he said to him, "Micaiah, shall we go to Ramoth in Gilead to fight, or shall we not?" He answered him, "Go up and conquer! Jehovah will give it into your hands!" But Ahab said to him, "How many times shall I warn you to speak nothing to me in the name of Jehovah but the truth?" He said, "I saw all the Israelites scattered upon the mountains as sheep that have no shepherd. And Jehovah said, 'These have no master; let each of them go home in peace!'"

The ruler of Israel said to Jehoshaphat, "Did I not tell you that he would prophesy for me nothing good, but only evil?" Micaiah said, "Hear then the message from Jehovah: I saw Jehovah sitting on his throne and all the host of heaven standing about him. And Jehovah said, 'Who will deceive Ahab, so that he will go up and fall at Ramoth in Gilead?' One suggested one thing and another, another, until a spirit came out and stood before Jehovah and said, 'I will deceive him.' Jehovah said to him, 'By what means?' He said, 'I will go out and become a lying spirit in the mouth of all his prophets.' Then Jehovah said, 'You shall succeed in deceiving him. Go out and do so.' So Jehovah has now put a lying spirit in the mouth of all these prophets of yours, for he has decided to bring evil upon you."

Then Zedekiah came near and struck Micaiah a blow on the cheek and said, "How was it that the spirit of Jehovah went from me to speak to you?" Micaiah replied, "Indeed, you shall see on the day when you shall go from one hiding-place to another." Then the ruler of Israel said, "Take Micaiah back to Amon, the governor of the city, and to Joash, the ruler's son, and say, 'This is the ruler's command: Put this fellow in prison and feed him with a scanty fare of bread and water until I return successful.'" Micaiah said, "If you indeed return successful, Jehovah has not spoken by me."

Then Ahab, the ruler of Israel, and Jehoshaphat, the ruler of Judah, went up to Ramoth in Gilead. And the ruler of Israel said to Jehoshaphat, "I will dress myself so that no one will know me, and go into the battle, but you can put on your robes."

But a certain man shot an arrow, and by chance it struck the ruler of Israel between the breastplate and the lower part of his armor. So Ahab said to the driver of his chariot, "Turn about and carry me out of the battle, for I am wounded." But the battle grew more intense, so that Ahab stayed until evening propped up in his chariot in the sight of the Arameans, and the blood ran out of the wound into the bottom of the chariot. And that evening he died.

About sunset the cry went out through the army, "Each to his town and each to his land, for the ruler is dead!" So they went to Samaria and buried Ahab there. And when they washed the chariot by the pool of Samaria, the dogs licked up his blood just as Jehovah had said.

THE MANTLE OF ELIJAH

When Jehovah took up Elijah to heaven in a whirlwind, he was going with Elisha from Gilgal. And Elijah said to Elisha, "Stay here, for Jehovah has sent me as far as Bethel." But Elisha said, "As surely as Jehovah lives and as you live, I will not leave you." So they went down to Bethel.

Then the followers of the prophets at Bethel came out to Elisha and said, "Do you know that to-day Jehovah will take away your master from you?" He said, "Yes, I know it; say no more." And Elijah said to him, "Elisha, stay here, for Jehovah has sent me to Jericho." But he said, "As surely as Jehovah lives and as you live, I will not leave you." So they came to Jericho.

The Parting of Elijah and Elisha
Painted by W. T. Taylor

Then the followers of the prophets at Jericho came near to Elisha and said, "Do you know that to-day Jehovah will take your master from you?" He answered, "Yes, I know it; say no more." And Elijah said to him, "Stay here, for Jehovah has sent me to the Jordan." But he said, "As surely as Jehovah lives and as you live, I will not leave you." So they both went on.

Fifty followers of the prophets stood opposite them at a distance, while they two stood by the Jordan. Then Elijah rolled up his mantle and with it struck the waters; and they were divided, so that they two went over on dry ground. When they had gone over, Elijah said to Elisha, "Ask what I shall do for you before I am taken from you." Elisha said, "Let a double portion of your spirit be upon me." He replied, "You have asked what is difficult; but if you see me when I am taken from you, it shall come to you; but if you do not, it shall not come."

As they were going on their way talking, a fiery chariot with horses of fire suddenly came and separated the two; and Elijah went up in a whirlwind to heaven. When Elisha saw it, he cried, "My father, my father! the chariots and the horsemen of Israel!" And he saw Elijah no more, but he took hold of his own robes and tore them in two. Then he took up the mantle that had fallen from Elijah.

ELISHA HEALING THE SICK BOY

One day Elisha went over to Shunem where a rich woman lived, and she asked him to be her guest. Afterward, whenever he passed by, he stopped there to eat. So she said to her husband, "Now I see that this is a holy man of God who is constantly passing by our door. Let us make a little chamber on the roof, and put there for him a bed, a table, a seat, and a candlestick, so that whenever he comes to us, he can stay there."

One day when he came, he went into the upper room and lay down there. Then he said to Gehazi his servant, "Call this Shunamite." So he called her, and she stood before him. Elisha said to Gehazi, "Say now to her, 'See, you have been so anxious to care for us; what can be done for you? May I ask the ruler or the commander of the army to do a favor for you?'" She answered, "I am living among my own people." Elisha said, "What then can be done for her?" Gehazi answered, "Verily, she has no son, and her husband is old." Then Elisha said, "Call her." So he called her, and she stood at the door. Then Elisha said, "At this time a year from now you shall hold a son in your arms!" But she said, "No, my lord, O man of God, do not deceive your servant!" But the next year the woman had a son at the very time Elisha had promised her.

When the child had grown up he went out one day to his father to the reapers. And he called to his father, "My head, my head!" So his father said to his servant, "Carry him to his mother." When he had been taken to his mother, the boy sat on her lap until noon and then died. His mother went up and laid him on the bed of the man of God, and shut the door as she went out.

Then she called her husband and said, "Send me one of the servants and one of the asses, that I may go quickly to the man of God and return." He said, "Why do you go to him to-day, for it is neither the feast of the new moon nor the sabbath?" She said, "I have good reason."

Then she saddled an ass and said to her servant, "Drive on fast, do not stop until I tell you." So she went to the man of God on Mount Carmel. But when Elisha saw her at a distance, he said to Gehazi, his servant, "See, there is the Shunamite! Run down to meet her and say to her, 'Is all well with you? Is your husband well? Is the child well?'" And she answered, "All is well." But when she came to the man of God on the mountain, she caught hold of his feet. When Gehazi tried to push her away, Elisha said, "Let her alone, for she is deeply troubled and Jehovah has not told me the reason." Then she said, "Did I ask a son of my lord? Did I not say, 'Do not deceive me?'"

Elisha said to Gehazi, "Tighten your belt, take my staff in your hand and go! If you meet any one, do not speak to him, and if any one speaks to you do not answer him, and lay my staff on the face of the child." But the mother of the child said, "As surely as Jehovah lives and as you live, I will not leave you." So he rose and went with her. And Gehazi had gone on before them and had laid the staff upon the face of the child, but there was neither sound nor sign of life in the boy. So he went back to meet him and told him, "The child has not awakened."

When Elisha came into the house, there was the child lying dead on his bed. So he went in and shut the door after them and prayed to Jehovah. He also went up and lay upon the child and put his mouth upon his mouth, his eyes upon his eyes, and his hands upon his hands. As he lay upon him, the flesh of the child became warm. Then he turned and walked backward and forward in the house, and again went up and lay upon him, and the child sneezed seven times, and then opened his eyes. Calling Gehazi, he said, "Call this Shunamite woman." So he called her. And when she came in to him, he said, "Take up your son." Then she went nearer, fell at his feet, and bowed to the ground; after that she took up her son and went out.

A SLAVE GIRL WHO HELPED HER MASTER

Naaman, the commander of the army of the king of Aram, was a man who was beloved by his master and was held in high honor, for through him Jehovah had given victory to Aram. He was an able man, but he was a leper.

Now the Arameans had gone out to rob and had brought away captive from the land of Israel a little maid who became the servant of Naaman's wife. She said to her mistress, "O that my master were with the prophet who is in Samaria! Then he would cure him of his leprosy." So Naaman went in and told the king what the maid from the land of Israel had said. The king of Aram said, "Go now, and I will send a letter to the ruler of Israel."

So Naaman set out and took with him a thousand pounds of silver and six thousand gold pieces and ten suits of fine clothes. He also brought to the ruler of Israel the letter, which read: "This letter is to tell you that I have sent Naaman, my servant, to you, that you may cure him of his leprosy." When the ruler of Israel read the letter, he tore his clothes and said, "Am I a god, who can kill and make alive, that this king sends a man to me to cure him of his leprosy? But you can clearly see that he is seeking a quarrel with me!"

When Elisha the man of God heard that the ruler of Israel was tearing his clothes, he sent this message to him: "Why are you tearing your clothes? Let him come now to me and he shall know that there is a prophet in Israel!" So Naaman came with his horses and chariots and stood at the door of Elisha's house. And Elisha sent a messenger to him to say, "Go and wash seven times in the Jordan and your flesh will again be well and clean."

But Naaman went away in a rage, saying, "I expected that he would surely come out to me and stand and call on the name of Jehovah his God and wave his hand over the place, and so cure the leper. Are not Amana and Pharpar, the rivers of Damascus, better than all the waters of Israel? Could I not wash in them and be clean?" So he turned and went away in a rage. But his servants came near and said to him, "If the prophet had told you to do some great thing, would you not have done it? Why not, then, when he says to you, 'Wash and be clean!'" So he went down and dipped himself seven times in the Jordan as the man of God commanded; and his flesh became again like the flesh of a little child, and he was cured of his leprosy.

Then Naaman, with all his followers, returned to the man of God. When he arrived, he stood before him and said, "Now I know that there is no god in all the earth, but in Israel; therefore accept a present from your servant." But Elisha said, "As surely as Jehovah lives, before whom I stand, I will take nothing." And although he urged him to take it, he would not. Then Naaman said, "If not, at least give your servant a load of earth, what two mules can draw, for your servant will from this time on offer burnt-offering and sacrifice to no other god but Jehovah." And Elisha said to him, "Go, and may good fortune attend you."

But when he had gone from him a short distance, Gehazi, the servant of Elisha the man of God, thought to himself, "My master has let this Naaman the Aramean go without accepting what he brought! As surely as Jehovah lives, I will run after him and take something from him." So Gehazi ran after Naaman; and when Naaman saw some one running after him, he stepped down from the chariot to meet him and said, "Is all well?" Gehazi replied, "All is well. My master has sent me to say, 'Just now two young men of the followers of the prophets have come to me from the highland of Ephraim. Give them a hundred pounds of silver and two suits of fine clothes.'" Naaman said, "Agree to take twice as much silver." So he urged him and bound up two hundred pounds of silver in two bags, with two suits of fine clothes, and laid them on two of his servants, and they carried them before Gehazi. But when he came to the hill, he took them from their hand and hid them in the house and let the men go.

Then he went in to Elisha; but when he stood before his master, Elisha said to him, "Where do you come from, Gehazi?" He answered, "Your servant has not been anywhere." But Elisha said to him, "Was I not in spirit with you when the man turned from his chariot to meet you? Now you have received money and you may get clothes, olive yards, vineyards, sheep, oxen, and slaves; but the leprosy of Naaman shall stick to you and to your children forever." Then Gehazi went from Elisha's presence a leper as white as snow.

ELISHA'S WAY OF TREATING ENEMIES

Once while the king of Aram was at war with Israel, he said to his officers, "In such and such a place we shall hide and surprise them." But Elisha, the man of God, sent word to the ruler of Israel, "Take care that you do not pass that place, for the Arameans are hiding there." So the ruler of Israel sent soldiers to the place of which the man of God had told him. Thus he warned him many times, so that he could there be on his guard.

The king of Aram was very much troubled by this, and he called his officers and said to them, "Can you not tell me who has betrayed us to the ruler of Israel?" One of his officers replied, "No one, my lord, O king, for Elisha, the prophet in Israel, tells the ruler of Israel the words that you speak in your bedchamber." The king said, "Go and see where he is, that I may send and seize him." And they told the king, "Elisha is now in Dothan."

So the king sent horses and chariots there and a great army. And they arrived at night and surrounded the city. When the man of God rose early the next morning and went out, an army with horses and chariots was about the city; so that his servant said to him, "Alas, my master! What shall we do?" He answered, "Fear not, for they who are with us are more than they who are with them." And Elisha prayed and said, "Jehovah open his eyes, that he may see." Then Jehovah opened the eyes of the young man, and he saw that the highlands around about Elisha were full of horses and chariots of fire.

When the Arameans came toward him, Elisha prayed to Jehovah, and said, "Make this people blind." So Jehovah made them blind, as Elisha asked. Then Elisha said to them, "This is not the way nor the city. Follow me, and I will bring you to the man whom you seek!" So he led them to Samaria.

But as soon as they came to Samaria, Elisha said, "O Jehovah, open the eyes of these men, that they may see." And Jehovah opened their eyes, so that they could see, and there they were in Samaria. When the ruler of Israel saw them, he said to Elisha, "My father, shall I cut them down?" Elisha answered, "You shall not cut them down; would you cut down those whom you have not taken captive with your sword nor with your bow? Set bread and water before them, that they may eat and drink and go to their master." So he prepared a great feast for them; and when they had had food and drink, he sent them back to their master. So the robber bands of Arameans no longer invaded the land of Israel.

Later, Benhadad, king of Aram, gathered all his army and besieged Samaria. The famine was so severe in Samaria while they were besieging it, that an ass's head was sold for eighty pieces of silver.

Once as the ruler of Israel was passing by on the wall, a woman cried out to him, "Help, my lord." He answered, "If Jehovah does not help you, from where can I bring help to you? From the threshing-floor or from the wine-press?" However, the ruler of Israel said to her, "What is the trouble with you?" She answered, "This woman said to me, 'Give your son, that we may eat him to-day, and we will eat my son to-morrow!' So we cooked my son and ate him, and I said to her on the next day, 'Give your son that we may eat him'; but she has hidden her son."

When the ruler of Israel heard the words of the woman, he tore his clothes; and as he was passing by on the wall, the people looked and saw that he wore sackcloth next to his skin.

Now Elisha was sitting in his house with the elders beside him; and while he was still talking with them, the ruler of Israel came down to him and said, "See, this is the evil that comes from Jehovah! Why should I put my hope in Jehovah any longer?" But Elisha said, "Hear the word of Jehovah, for he says, 'To-morrow about this time a peck of fine meal shall be sold for a piece of silver and two pecks of barley for a piece of silver in the gate of Samaria.'" Then the charioteer on whose arm the ruler of Israel leaned answered the man of God, "If Jehovah himself should make windows in heaven, could this be possible?" He said, "You shall see it with your own eyes."

Now there were four lepers just outside the gate; and they said one to another, "Why do we sit here until we die? If we say, 'We will enter the city,' then, since there is famine in the city, we shall die there; but if we sit here, we shall die too. Now, come, let us go over to the army of the Arameans. If they spare our lives, we shall live; and if they kill us, we shall but die."

So they set out in the evening to go over to the camp of the Arameans. But when they came to the edge of the camp of the Arameans, no one was there, for the Lord had made the army of the Arameans hear a noise of chariots and of horses and of a great army, and they said to one another, "Surely the ruler of Israel has hired the kings of the Hittites and the kings of the Egyptians to attack us." So they rose and fled in the twilight; and they left their tents, their horses and their asses, even the camp as it was, and fled for their lives. When these lepers came to the edge of the camp, they went into one tent and ate and drank and carried away silver and gold and clothing and hid them. Then they came back and entered another tent and carried away what was in it and went and hid that.

Then they said to one another, "We are not doing right; this day is a day of good news. If we keep still and wait until morning punishment will overtake us. Now, come, let us go and tell those in the palace." So they called the watchmen at the city gate and said to them, "We went to the camp of the Arameans, but there was no one there and no sound of men's voices. The horses and asses were tied and the tents were just as they had been."

The watchmen at the city gate shouted this news to those in the palace. And the ruler of Israel rose in the night and said to his servants, "I will now tell you what the Arameans have done: they know that we are hungry; so they have gone out of the camp to hide themselves in the field, thinking, 'When they come out of the city, we will take them alive and get into the city.'"

But one of his servants spoke up and said, "Let some men take a pair of the horses which are left here. If they die, they will be like most of the Israelites who are dying! Let us send and find out." So they took two men on horseback, and the ruler of Israel sent them after the army of the Arameans with the command, "Go and see." They followed them to the Jordan; and all the way was filled with clothes and weapons which the

Arameans had thrown away in their haste. So the messengers returned and told the ruler of Israel.

Then the people went and carried things away from the camp of the Arameans. So a peck of fine meal was sold for a piece of silver, and two pecks of barley for a piece of silver, just as Jehovah had said.

THE END OF AHAB'S SELFISH FAMILY

Elisha the prophet called one of the followers of the prophets and said to him, "Tighten your belt, take this flask of oil in your hand and go to Ramoth in Gilead. When you arrive there, look for Jehu, the son of Jehoshaphat, and when you go in take him into an inner room, away from those who are with him. Then from the flask pour oil on his head, and say, 'Jehovah declares, I have anointed you to rule over Israel.' Then open the door and flee without delay."

So the young man went to Ramoth in Gilead. When he arrived, the officers of the army were sitting together. And he said, "Commander, I have a message for you." Jehu said, "To which of us?" He replied, "To you, O commander." Then Jehu rose and went into the house; and the young man poured the oil on his head and said to him, "Jehovah the God of Israel says, 'I have anointed you to rule over Jehovah's people, over Israel!'" Then he opened the door and hurried away.

When Jehu came out to the servants of his master, they asked him, "Is all well? Why did this insane fellow come to you?" He answered, "You know the man and his message." But they said, "You are deceiving us. You must tell us." Jehu replied, "He said this to me: 'Jehovah says, I have anointed you to rule over Israel.'" Then each quickly took his garment, laid it at his feet on the bare stairs, and blew the horn and cried, "Jehu is the ruler of Israel." So Jehu plotted against Joram.

Now Joram, with all the Israelites, had been defending Ramoth in Gilead against Hazael king of Aram, but Joram had gone back to Jezreel to recover from the wounds which he had received from the

Arameans when he fought with Hazael king of Aram. So Jehu said, "If it is your will, let no one escape from the city to bring news to Jezreel." Then Jehu mounted his chariot and went toward Jezreel.

While the watchman was standing on the tower of Jezreel, he saw the cloud of dust about Jehu, as he came, and said, "I see a cloud of dust." Joram said, "Send a horseman to meet him and ask whether he comes with peaceful purpose." So the horseman went out to meet him and said, "The ruler of Israel asks, 'Do you come with peaceful purpose?'" Jehu replied, "What have you to do with peace? Turn and follow me." So the watchman said, "The messenger went to them, but does not return." Then Joram sent out a second horseman who went to them and said, "The ruler of Israel asks, 'Do you come with peaceful purpose?'" Jehu answered, "What have you to do with peace? Turn and follow me." So the watchman said, "He also went to them but does not return; however, the driving is like the driving of Jehu, for he drives very fast."

Then Joram said, "Get my chariot ready," and when it was ready he went to meet Jehu and found him in the field of Naboth the Jezreelite. When Joram saw Jehu, he said, "Do you come with peaceful purpose, Jehu?" Then Joram turned to flee, but Jehu drew his bow and struck Joram between the shoulders, so that the arrow went through his heart, and he fell down in his chariot.

Then Jehu said to Bidkar, his charioteer, "Take him up and throw him into the field of Naboth the Jezreelite, for I well remember that, as you and I rode together after Ahab, his father, Jehovah pronounced this sentence upon him: 'Surely I saw yesterday the blood of Naboth and his sons, and I will punish you on this same piece of land.' So throw him into this piece of land, as Jehovah said."

Then Jehu arrived at Jezreel. As soon as Jezebel heard of it, she painted her eyes, arranged her hair, and looked out of the window. As Jehu came in at the gate, she said, "Is all well with you, you traitor, you murderer of your master?" But he looked up to the window and cried, "Who is on my side? who?" Two or three slaves looked down at him, and he said, "Throw her down." And they threw her down and the horses trampled on her. When Jehu had gone in and had had something to eat and drink, he gave this command, "Look after this woman and bury her, for she is a king's daughter." But when they went to bury her, they found no more of her than the skull, the feet, and the hands. When they went back and told Jehu, he said, "This is what Jehovah declared by his servant Elijah when he said, 'On the piece of land at Jezreel the dogs shall eat Jezebel's flesh, and her body shall be as refuse on the surface of the field, so that no one can say, This is Jezebel.'"

THE BOY JOASH ON THE THRONE OF JUDAH

When Joram had ruled twelve years over Israel, Ahaziah the son of Jehoram began to rule over Judah. And he went down to Jezreel to visit Joram, who was ill. When Jehu struck down Joram, Ahaziah saw it and fled toward Beth-gannim. But Jehu followed after him with the words, "Shoot him down, too, in the chariot." So they shot him down on the way up to Gur, near Ibleam, but he escaped to Megiddo and died there.

When Athaliah, the mother of Ahaziah, learned that her son was dead, she rose and put to death all of Ahaziah's children except Joash, whom his aunt, Jehosheba, secretly took and placed with his nurse in the bedchamber. In this way she hid him from Athaliah, so that he was not put to death. He was with her, hid in the temple of Jehovah, six years, while Athaliah ruled over the land.

But in the seventh year Jehoiada the priest called together the officers of the royal guard and brought them into the temple of Jehovah. After he had made them make a solemn promise, he showed them Ahaziah's son, and gave them these orders, "This is what you shall do: a third part of you who go in on the Sabbath to guard the palace shall keep watch over it. Two divisions of you, including all who go out on the Sabbath to guard the temple of Jehovah, shall surround Joash, each with his weapons in his hand. And let every one who comes within the ranks be put to death. Thus you shall guard Joash, when he goes out and when he comes in."

The officers did as Jehoiada the priest commanded. And he brought out Ahaziah's son and put the crown and the royal ornaments upon him; and they made him ruler over Judah and poured oil upon his head and clapped their hands, crying, "Long live the ruler!"

But when Athaliah heard the people shouting, she came to them in the temple of Jehovah. When she saw Joash standing by the pillar, as was the custom, and the officers and the trumpeters by him, and all the people of the land rejoicing and blowing trumpets, she tore her clothes and cried, "Treason! Treason!" But Jehoiada the priest gave this order to the officers: "Bring her out between the ranks, and kill with the sword whoever follows her," for the priest said, "Let her not be put to death in the temple of Jehovah." So they seized her, and she was killed as she went through the horses' entry to the palace.

Jehoiada made a solemn agreement between Jehovah and the new ruler and the people, that they should be Jehovah's people; also between the ruler and the people, and Joash ruled forty years in Jerusalem.

The Prophet Isaiah
Painted by W. L. Taylor

Uzziah, Joash's grandson, was sixteen years old when he began to rule over Judah and he ruled fifty-two years in Jerusalem.

He fought against the Philistines, and broke down the wall of Gath and of Jabneh and of Ashdod and built cities near Ashdod and among the Philistines. And God helped him against the Philistines. The Ammonites also paid tribute to Uzziah, for he became very strong.

And Uzziah built towers in Jerusalem at the Corner Gate and at the Valley Gate and at the corner of the wall, and fortified them. He also built towers in the wilderness and dug many cisterns, for he had many herds in the lowland and farmers in the plain and vine-dressers in the mountains and in the fruitful fields, for he loved to cultivate the ground. But he was a leper to the day of his death. He lived in his own house, while Jotham, his son, was at the head of the royal household, ruling the people of the land. And Uzziah died; and they buried him with his fathers in the city of David, and Jotham, his son, became ruler in his place.

Isaiah said it was in the year that Uzziah, the ruler of Judah, died that I saw the Lord sitting on a high and lofty throne; and the train of his robe filled the temple. Guardian angels stood above him. Each had six wings, one pair to cover the face, another pair to cover the feet, and another pair with which to fly. And they cried to one another:

> "Holy, holy, holy, is Jehovah of hosts,
> The whole earth is full of his glory."

The foundations of the thresholds trembled at the voice of those who called, and the temple was filled with smoke. Then I said: "Woe is me! I am ruined; for I am a man with unclean lips, and I live among a people with unclean lips; for my eyes have seen the King, Jehovah of hosts!" But one of the guardian angels flew to me with a hot coal in his hand that he had taken from off the altar, and with it he touched my mouth and said: "See, this has touched your lips; your guilt is taken away and your sin forgiven."

Then I heard the voice of the Lord, saying:

> "Whom shall I send,
> And who will go for us?"

and I said, "Here am I, send me."

JEREMIAH'S CALL TO DO A HARD TASK

This was the message which came to me from Jehovah: "Before you were born I knew you and prepared you for your work. I have appointed you to be a prophet to the nations." But I (Jeremiah) said: "O Lord Jehovah! I do not know how to speak in public, for I am only a youth." Then Jehovah said to me: "Do not say, 'I am only a youth,' for you shall go to all to whom I send you, and you shall speak whatever I command you. Do not be afraid of them, for I am with you to protect you."

Then Jehovah stretched out his hand and touched my mouth and said to me: "See. I have put my words in your mouth, and I have appointed you this day over the nations and kingdoms, to tear up and break down, to destroy and to overthrow, to build and to plant."

Again this message came from Jehovah, "What do you see?" I answered, "A great kettle brewing hot, and it faces from the north." Then Jehovah said to me: "From the north trouble is brewing for all the people of the land. For I am about to call all the kingdoms of the north, and they shall come and each set up his throne at the entrance to the gates of Jerusalem and around its walls and against all the cities of Judah. And I will pass judgment upon Jerusalem and these cities for all their wickedness, for they have been disloyal to me and offered sacrifices to other gods and have worshipped that which their own hands have made.

"Therefore make ready, rise, speak to them all that I command you. Do not be afraid of them, for see, I myself will make you this day like a fortified city, and like a bronze wall against the rulers of Judah, its leaders, its priests, and the common people. Though they fight against you, they will not overcome you, for I am with you to protect you."

THE YOUNG JOSIAH AND THE BOOK OF THE LAW

Josiah was eight years old when he began to rule, and he ruled thirty-one years in Jerusalem. In the eighteenth year of his rule he sent Shaphan, the scribe, to the temple of Jehovah with the command, "Go up to Hilkiah, the chief priest, and see that, when he has taken the money that is brought into the temple of Jehovah and that which the doorkeepers have gathered from the people, they give it to the workmen who have charge of the temple of Jehovah. Then let them give it to the carpenters, the builders, and the masons who are in the temple of Jehovah, to repair the breaks in it and to buy timber and cut stone to restore it." But no account was asked of them for the money that was given to them, for they dealt honestly.

Then Hilkiah, the chief priest, said to Shaphan, the scribe, "I have found the book of the law in the temple of Jehovah." And Hilkiah gave the book to Shaphan, and he read it. Then Shaphan went to Josiah and told him, "Your servants have taken the money that was found in the temple and have turned it over to the workmen who have charge of the temple of Jehovah." Shaphan, the scribe, also said to Josiah, "Hilkiah, the priest, has given me a book." And Shaphan read it to him.

When Josiah had heard the words of the book of the law, he tore his clothes. Then he gave this command to Hilkiah, the priest, to Ahikam, the son of Shaphan, to Achbor, the son of Micaiah, to Shaphan, the scribe, and to Asaiah, his servant, "Go, ask of Jehovah for me and for the people and for all Judah about the words of this book that has been found; for Jehovah must be very angry with us, because our fathers have not listened to the words of this book nor done all that we are there commanded to do."

So Hilkiah, the priest, and Ahikam and Achbor went to Huldah, the prophetess, who lived in Jerusalem and talked with her. She said to them, "This is the message of Jehovah, the God of Israel: 'Tell the man who sent you to me, Jehovah says, I am now about to bring evil upon this place and upon its people even all that is written in the book which the ruler of Judah has read. But you shall say to him who sent you to ask of Jehovah, Jehovah the God of Israel declares, Because you listened and humbled yourself before Jehovah and have wept before me, I also have heard you,'" So they brought back word to Josiah.

Then at his command they got together all the leaders of Judah and of Jerusalem. And Josiah went up to the temple of Jehovah, and with him all the men of Judah and all the people of Jerusalem, as well as the priests and the prophets and all the people, including the children. And he read to them all the words of the book of the covenant which was found in the temple of Jehovah. And Josiah stood by the pillar and made a solemn promise before Jehovah to obey all the commands and carry out the rules written in this book. And all the people also agreed to do so.

Then Josiah commanded Hilkiah, the chief priest, and the second priest and the doorkeepers to bring out from the temple of Jehovah all the things that were made for Baal and for the Canaanite goddess of fortune, and for the Babylonian star gods. And he burned them outside Jerusalem in the lime-kilns by the Kidron, and carried their ashes to Bethel. He also put away the idolatrous priests, whom the rulers of Judah had appointed to offer sacrifice at the temples on the heights in the towns of Judah and in the places about Jerusalem; those also who offered sacrifices to Baal, to the sun, the moon, and the planets and all the starry host.

He also destroyed Topheth, which is in the valley of Ben-Hinnom, so that no man could ever make his son or his daughter pass through the fire to Molech. He removed the horses at the entrance of the temple of Jehovah, which the rulers of Judah had given to the sun, and burned the chariots of the sun. Josiah broke down and crushed in pieces the altars that were on the roof, which the rulers of Judah had made.

Josiah also tore down the altar and the old temple at Bethel, broke its stones in pieces, and beat it to dust.

Then he gave this command to all the people: "Keep the passover to Jehovah your God, as is commanded in this book of the covenant." Such a passover as this had not been kept from the days of the judges who ruled Israel and during the period of the rulers of Israel and of Judah;

but this passover was kept in Jehovah's honor in Jerusalem for the first time in the eighteenth year of Josiah's rule.

Josiah put away all the mediums, the wizards, the idols and all the evil things that were discovered in the land of Judah and in Jerusalem, that he might carry out the words of the law which were written in the book that Hilkiah, the priest, found in the temple of Jehovah. Josiah was the first ruler who turned to Jehovah with all his heart, with all his soul, and with all his strength in exact accord with the law of Moses, nor were any of the rulers that followed like him.

THE WRITING OF AN ANCIENT BOOK

When Jehoiakim, the son of Josiah, had been ruler for four years, this message came to Jeremiah from Jehovah, "Take a parchment roll and write on it all the words that I have spoken to you about Jerusalem and Judah and all the nations from the time of Josiah to the present. Perhaps the people of Judah will pay attention to all the evil which I intend to bring upon them, so that they will turn each from his evil way, that I may forgive their guilt and sin."

Then Jeremiah called Baruch, the son of Neriah; and Baruch wrote on a parchment roll as Jeremiah told him all the words which Jehovah had spoken to him. And Jeremiah commanded Baruch, saying, "I am not permitted to go to the temple of Jehovah. Therefore you go and read in the temple on the fast day the words of Jehovah from the roll which you have written at my command. You shall read them to all the people of Judah who have come from their towns. Perhaps they will pray to Jehovah and each turn from his evil way; for great is the anger and wrath of Jehovah against this people." So Baruch did as Jeremiah, the prophet, commanded him, reading in the temple from the writing the words of Jehovah.

The next year, when all the people who had come to Jerusalem from the cities of Judah were observing a fast in the temple courts, Baruch read to them all from the writing the words of Jeremiah.

When Micaiah, the grandson of Shaphan, had heard all the words of Jehovah, he went down to the palace, where all the court officials were sitting, and told them all that he had heard when Baruch read the book to the people.

Then all the nobles sent Jehudi, the son of Nethaniah, to Baruch to say: "Take the roll from which you have read to all the people and come here." So Baruch took the roll in his hand and went to them. And they said to him, "Sit down now and read it to us." So Baruch read it to them. But when they had heard all, they turned in fear to one another and said to Baruch, "We must surely tell Jehoiakim all this." So they asked Baruch, "Tell us now: how did you write all this?" Baruch answered, "Jeremiah told it all to me and I wrote it down in ink." Then the nobles said to Baruch, "Go, hide both yourself and Jeremiah, and let no one know where you are."

But after they had put the roll in the room of Elishama, the chancellor, they went to Jehoiakim's room, and told all these things to him. Then he sent Jehudi to bring the roll, and he brought it out of the room of Elishama, the chancellor. And Jehudi read it to him and to all the leaders who were with him.

Now Jehoiakim was sitting in the winter house with a brazier burning before him. When Jehudi had read three or four double columns, Jehoiakim cut it with a paper-knife and threw it into the fire that was on the brazier, and the entire roll was burned up. But neither he nor any of his servants who were present, were disturbed or tore their garments. Elnathan and Delaiah and Gemariah begged Jehoiakim not to burn the roll, but he would not listen to them. He also ordered Jerahmeel, his son, and Seraiah, the son of Azriel, and Shelemiah, the son of Abdeel, to seize Baruch, the scribe, and Jeremiah, the prophet, but Jehovah kept them hidden.

Then Jeremiah took another roll and gave it to Baruch, the scribe, who wrote on it as Jeremiah spoke to him, all the words of the book which Jehoiakim, the ruler of Judah, had burned in the fire; and many other similar words were added.

A PROPHET WHO SAVED A GREAT CITY

Once the king of Assyria sent a high official with a great army to Jerusalem. When they arrived at Jerusalem, they called for Hezekiah the ruler of Judah, Eliakim, the son of Hilkiah, Shebnah, the scribe, and Joah, the son of Asaph, and they came out to them. And the high official said to them, "Why are you so confident? To whom do you look for help that you have rebelled against me? You count on Egypt to help you. Pharaoh, king of Egypt, is as weak as a broken reed. But if you say, 'We trust in Jehovah our God,' is not he the one whose high places and altars Hezekiah has destroyed? Now therefore make a bargain with my master, the king of Assyria, and I will give you two thousand horses, if you are able on your part to set riders upon them. How then can you conquer one of the least of my master's servants? Have I now come up against this place to destroy it without Jehovah's approval? Jehovah it was who said to me, 'Go up against this land and destroy it.'"

Then Eliakim and Shebnah and Joah said to the high official, "Speak, I pray you, to your servants in the Aramaic language, for we understand it; but do not speak with us in the Jewish language in the hearing of the people who are on the wall." But the high official said to them, "Has my master sent me to your master and to you to speak these words? Is it not rather to the men who sit on the wall, who will suffer most from the siege?"

Then the high official stood and cried with a loud voice, in the Jewish language, saying, "Hear the message of the great king, the king of Assyria. 'Thus saith the king, Let not Hezekiah deceive you; for he will not be able to save you from my hand. Neither let Hezekiah make you trust in

Jehovah by saying, Jehovah will surely save us, and this city shall not be given into the power of the king of Assyria.'"

"Do not listen to Hezekiah, for thus says the king of Assyria, 'Make your peace with me and come over to me; then each one of you shall eat from his own vine and his own fig-tree and drink the waters of his own cistern, until I come and take you away to a land like your own land, a land full of grain and new wine, a land full of bread and vineyards, a land full of olive-trees and honey, that you may live and not die. But do not listen to Hezekiah, when he deceives you by saying, Jehovah will save us. Has any of the gods of the nations ever saved his land from the power of the king of Assyria? Have the gods of the land of Samaria saved Samaria from my power? Who are they among all the gods of the countries, that have saved their country from my power, that Jehovah should save Jerusalem from my power?'"

Then the people were silent and made no answer; for the ruler's command was, "Do not answer him." But Eliakim, the steward of the palace, and Shebnah, the scribe, and Joah, the son of Asaph, came to Hezekiah with torn clothes and told him the words of the high official. And as soon as Hezekiah heard it, he tore his clothes and covered himself with sackcloth and went into the temple of Jehovah. And he sent Eliakim, who was in charge of the palace, and Shebnah, the scribe and the oldest of the priests, covered with sackcloth, to Isaiah, the prophet. And they said to him, Hezekiah says, "This is a day of trouble, of discipline and of shame. It may be Jehovah your God will hear all the words of the high official, whom his master, the king of Assyria, has sent to defy the living God, and will punish him for them; therefore lift up your prayer for the people."

When the servants of Hezekiah came to Isaiah, Isaiah said to them, "Take back this answer to your master: Jehovah says, 'Do not be afraid of the words that you have heard, with which the servants of the king of Assyria have insulted me. I will put a spirit in him, so that he will hear bad news and return to his own land; and I will cause him to fall by the sword in his own land.'"

So the high official returned and found the king of Assyria making war against Libnah, for he had heard that he had gone from Lachish. But the king of Assyria had heard that Tirkakah, king of Ethiopia, had come out to fight against him. Now that very night the angel of Jehovah went out and struck down in the camp of the Assyrians a hundred and eighty-five thousand. And when men arose early the next morning, these were all dead.

Then Sennacherib, king of Assyria, went away and returned to Nineveh. While he was worshipping in the temple of Nisroch his god, his sons struck him down with the sword; and they escaped into the land of Ararat. And Esarhaddon, his son, became king in his place.

JEREMIAH'S COURAGE IN DANGER

The command came to Jeremiah from Jehovah, "Stand in the door of the temple and speak this message: 'Hear the word of Jehovah, all you people of Judah who enter these gates to worship him. Jehovah, the God of Israel, says: Change your ways and your deeds and I will let you live in this place. Trust not in misleading words, thinking, this is the temple of Jehovah. For if you really change your ways and your deeds, if you faithfully see that justice is done between a man and his neighbor, if you do no wrong to the foreigners who live among you, to the fatherless nor to the widow, and do not shed the blood of the innocent in this place nor follow other gods to your hurt, then I will let you stay in this place, in the land that I gave to your fathers, forever and ever.

"'But now you are trusting in misleading words that are useless. Will you steal, murder, tell lies and offer sacrifice to Baal, and follow other gods whom you have not known, and then come and stand before me in this house which bears my name and say, We are free to do all these shameful deeds? Is this my house, which bears my name, in your eyes a den of robbers? I myself have seen these shameful deeds,' says Jehovah.

"'Then go to my temple which was at Shiloh, where people used to worship me at first, and see what I did to it because of the wickedness of my people Israel. Now because you have done all these deeds, and have paid no attention, although I spoke to you earnestly and often; and have not answered, although I called you, I will destroy the temple which bears my name, in which you trust, and the place which I gave to you and to your fathers, as I did at Shiloh. I will also send you from my sight, as I have sent away your relatives, even all the Northern Israelites.'"

When Jeremiah had finished speaking all that Jehovah had commanded him to say, the priests and prophets seized him and said, "You must die. Why have you said in the name of Jehovah that this temple shall be like Shiloh and this city shall be deserted, with no one living in it?" And all the people were gathered about Jeremiah in the temple of Jehovah.

But when the public officials of Judah heard of these things, they came up from the palace to the temple of Jehovah and held court at the entrance, at the new gate of the temple. Then the priests and the prophets said to the officials and to the people, "This man should be put to death, for he has prophesied against this city as you have heard with your own ears." But Jeremiah answered the officials and all the people, "It was Jehovah who sent me to prophesy against this temple and city all that you have heard. Now therefore change your ways and your deeds and listen to Jehovah your God; and he will not do the evil things that he has threatened to do to you. But as for me, see, I am in your power; do to me as you think right and proper. Only remember that, if you put me to death, you will bring upon yourselves and upon this city and upon its inhabitants guilt for shedding innocent blood, for Jehovah has indeed sent me to you to tell you all these things."

Then the officials and all the people said to the priests and to the prophets, "This man does not deserve to die, for he has spoken to us in the name of Jehovah our God." Certain of the elders of the land rose and said to the assembly of the people, "Micah prophesied in the days when Hezekiah ruled over Judah, and said to the people of Judah, 'Jehovah of hosts says:

> "Zion shall be ploughed as a field,
> Jerusalem shall become a ruin,
> The temple-mount an overgrown hill."'

"Did Hezekiah and the people of Judah put him to death? Did they not rather fear Jehovah and ask him to forgive them, so that he did not do the evil things that he had threatened to do to them? But we are in danger of doing great harm to ourselves?"

THE SAD FATE OF A GUILTY NATION

Jerusalem was taken in the eleventh year of the rule of Zedekiah, on the ninth day of the fourth month. An opening was made through the walls, and all the princes of the king of Babylon came and sat in the middle gate. When Zedekiah, the ruler of Judah, and all the warriors saw them, they fled and left the city by night by the way of the royal garden, through the gate between the two walls, and went out toward the Arabah. But the army of the Chaldeans followed them and captured Zedekiah on the plains of Jericho. Then they brought him up to Nebuchadrezzar, king of Babylon, who was then at Riblah in the land of Hamath. And the king of Babylon killed the sons of Zedekiah before his eyes. And the king of Babylon put to death all the nobles of Judah. Moreover, he put out Zedekiah's eyes and bound him in chains to carry him to Babylon.

In the nineteenth year of the reign of Nebuchadrezzar, king of Babylon, Nebuzaradan, the commander of the body-guard, an officer of the king of Babylon, came to Jerusalem. He burned the temple of Jehovah and the royal palace and all the houses in Jerusalem. All the soldiers of the Chaldeans, who were with the commander of the body-guard, broke down the walls around Jerusalem. The rest of the people who were left in the city and the deserters who had gone over to the king of Babylon, Nebuzaradan carried away captive. But he left some of the poorest of the people to take care of the vineyards and farms.

The pillars of brass that were in the temple of Jehovah, and the stands and the bronze sea that were in the temple of Jehovah the Chaldeans broke in pieces and carried the brass from them to Babylon. Also the pots, the shovels, the snuffers, the bowls, and all the vessels of brass, with which sacrifices were offered in the temple, they took away. The fire-pans and the basins of silver and of gold, the commander of the body-guard also melted and took away.

The commander of the body-guard carried away Seraiah, the chief priest and Zephaniah, the second priest, and the three doorkeepers and brought them to the king of Babylon at Riblah. And the king of Babylon put them to death at Riblah in the land of Hamath. So the people of Judah were carried away captive from their own homeland.

Nebuchadrezzar made Gedaliah, the grandson of Shaphan, governor over the people he had left in the land of Judah.

Now Nebuchadrezzar, king of Babylon, had given this command about Jeremiah to Nebuzaradan, the commander of the body-guard, "Take good care of him, and do him no harm; but do to him as he shall tell you." So Nebuzaradan, the commander of the body-guard, said to him, "See, I release you this day from the chains which are upon your hand. If it seems best to you to come with me to Babylon, come, and I will look out for you. But if you do not wish to come with me to Babylon, do not come; go back to Gedaliah, whom the king of Babylon has made governor over the cities of Judah, and live with him among the people, or go wherever it seems right for you to go." So the commander of the body-guard gave Jeremiah food and a present, and sent him away. Then Jeremiah went to Gedaliah, who was at Mizpah, and lived with him among the people who were left in the land.

THE COURAGE OF FOUR CAPTIVES

Nebuchadrezzar, the king of Babylon, commanded Ashpenaz, the chief of his servants, to bring to him certain of the Israelites and some of their princes and nobles. They were to be young men who were strong and handsome, well taught and quick to learn and able to serve in the king's palace. And they were to be taught the learning and the language of the Chaldeans. The king gave to them each day some of his rich food and some of the wine which he drank. He also commanded that they should be taught for three years, and that at the end of that time they should enter the royal service.

Among these young men were: Daniel, Hananiah, Mishael, and Azariah; but the chief of the king's servants gave other names to them. To Daniel he gave the name Belteshazzar, and to Hananiah, Shadrach, and to Mishael, Meshach, and to Azariah, Abednego.

But Daniel made up his mind not to injure himself with the rich food of the king nor with the wine which he drank. So he asked the chief of the king's servants not to make him injure himself. And God helped Daniel to win the kindness and favor of the chief of the king's servants.

But the chief of the king's servants said to Daniel, "I fear that my lord, the king, who has given you your food and your drink will see that your faces are sadder than those of young men who are your own age, and so you will endanger my head with the king."

Daniel said to the guardian whom the chief of the king's servants had put over Daniel, Hananiah, Mishael, and Azariah, "Try your servants ten days; and let us have vegetables to eat and water to drink. Then compare the way we look with that of the young men who eat of the king's rich food. Then do to us as seems best." So he did as they asked and tried them ten days. At the end of ten days they looked better and they were fatter than all the young men who ate of the king's rich food. So the guardian took away their rich food and the wine and gave them vegetables.

To these four young men God gave knowledge, learning, and wisdom; and Daniel understood all kinds of visions and dreams.

At the end of the days which the king had fixed for bringing them in, the chief of his servants brought them in to Nebuchadrezzar, and the king talked with them. But not one of all the young men was found equal to Daniel, Hananiah, Mishael, and Azariah. So they began to serve the king. On every subject which called for wisdom and understanding and about which the king questioned them, he found them ten times better than all the wise men and magicians who were in his entire kingdom.

A KING'S STRANGE DREAM

Nebuchadrezzar in the second year of his reign had dreams, and his mind was so troubled that he could not sleep. Then the king sent for the magicians and the wise men, and those who studied the stars to tell him what his dreams meant. So they came in before the king, and he said to them, "I have had a dream and my mind is troubled, for I want to know what the dream means."

Then those who studied the stars said to the king: "O king, live forever! Tell the dream to your servants and we will tell you what it means." The king answered, "What I now say is certain: if you do not tell me the dream and what it means, you shall be torn limb from limb and your houses shall be made ash-heaps. But if you tell the dream and what it means, you shall receive from me gifts and rewards and great honors; therefore tell me the dream and what it means." They answered the second time, "Let the king tell the dream to his servants, and we will tell what it means." The king replied, "I see clearly that you wish to gain time, for you know that what I have said is certain, and that if you do not tell the dream to me, you will all suffer the same punishment. So you have planned to speak lying and false words before me, until the time when it is to happen has passed. Therefore tell me the dream, and I shall know that you can tell me what it means." The Chaldeans answered the king, "There is no man on earth who can do what the king asks, for no king, however great and powerful, has ever asked such a thing of any wise man or magician, or of one who studies the stars. What the king asks is too hard. There is no one else who can tell it to the king, except the gods, who do not live with men." This made the king very angry and he ordered all the wise men of Babylon put to death.

So the command was given that the wise men were to be put to death. And search was made for Daniel and his friends that they too might be put to death. Then Daniel spoke wisely, to Arioch, the captain of the king's guard, who had gone out to put the wise men of Babylon to death, and said, "Why is the king's command so harsh?" When Arioch told Daniel the facts, he went to the king and asked that he give him time to tell what the dream meant.

Then Daniel went to his house and told the facts to his friends, Hananiah, Mishael, and Azariah, that they might ask the God of heaven to be kind to them and to tell Daniel this secret, so that they might not die with the rest of the wise men of Babylon. Then the secret was told to Daniel in a vision at night, and he praised the God of heaven and said:

"Blessed be the name of God
From everlasting to everlasting!
For wisdom and power are his.
He gives wisdom to the wise,
And knowledge to those who have insight.
He shows the deep, secret things;
He knows what is in the darkness,
And the light of truth dwells in him.
I give thee thanks and praise,
For thou givest me wisdom and strength,
And hast made known the things we asked;
Thou hast made known to us the king's secret!"

Then Daniel went to Arioch, whom the king had commanded to kill the wise men of Babylon, and said to him, "Do not kill the wise men of Babylon. Take me to the king, and I will tell him what his dream means."

Then Arioch quickly brought Daniel to the king and said to him, "I have found a man among the captives from Judah who will tell you what this dream means." The king said to Daniel (whose name was Belteshazzar), "Can you make known to me the dream which I have had and what it means?" Daniel answered, "The secret which the king asks is something that neither wise men, magicians, nor those who study the stars can make known to him; but there is a God in heaven who tells secrets, and he has made known to King Nebuchadrezzar what shall come in the future. Your dream and the visions which you had as you lay asleep are these: You, O king, had a vision and saw a great image. That image was large and it was exceedingly bright as it stood before you, and its appearance was terrible. The head of the image was of fine gold, its breast and its arms of silver, its body and its thighs of brass, its legs of iron, its feet part of iron and part of clay. You looked at it until a stone was cut out, not by the hands of men, which struck the image on its feet of iron and clay and broke them in pieces. Then the iron, the clay, the brass, the silver, and the gold were all broken in pieces and became like the chaff which blows from the summer threshing-floors, and the wind carried them away so that nothing was left of them. But the stone that struck the image became a great mountain and filled the earth.

"This is the dream, and we will tell the king what it means: O king, you are the king of kings to whom God has given the rule, the power, the strength, and the glory. Over the whole world he has given into your power, men, the wild beasts and the birds, and has made you rule over them all. You are the head of gold.

"After you shall rise another kingdom not so strong as you are, and a third kingdom of brass, which shall rule over the whole earth. A fourth kingdom shall be strong as iron, for iron breaks in pieces and shatters all things, and like iron which crushes, it shall break in pieces and crush all things. As you saw the feet and toes, part clay and part iron, it shall be a divided kingdom; but there shall be in it some of the strength of the iron, for you saw the iron mixed with clay. As the toes of the feet were part iron and part clay, so the kingdom shall be partly strong and partly broken. You saw the iron mixed with clay, for the rulers will marry one another, but they will not stick together, even as iron does not stick to clay.

"During the reigns of these kings the God of heaven will set up a kingdom which shall never be destroyed, nor shall the power be left to another people; but it shall break in pieces and destroy all these kingdoms, and it shall stand forever. This is shown by the fact that you saw a stone cut out of the mountain, but not with the hands of men. And it broke in pieces the iron, the brass, the clay, the silver, and the gold.

"The great God has made known to the king what is to come, and the dream is real and this meaning true."

Then King Nebuchadrezzar fell upon his face and worshipped Daniel, and ordered that a sacrifice and sweet odors should be offered to him. The king also said to Daniel, "Your God is the God of gods and the Lord of kings, and one who tells his secrets to his servant, for you have been able to tell this great secret." Then the king gave Daniel a high position and many costly gifts, and made him ruler over all of Babylon and chief over all the wise men in Babylon. And at Daniel's request the king placed Shadrach, Meshach, and Abednego in charge of the province of Babylon; but Daniel stayed in the king's court.

THE TEST BY FIRE

Nebuchadrezzar, the king, made an image of gold ninety feet high and nine feet wide. He set it up in the plain of Dura, in the province of Babylon. Then he sent for the officers, the governors, the judges, the treasurers, and all the rulers of the provinces. So they all came together and stood before the image that Nebuchadrezzar had set up.

Then the herald cried aloud, "To you it is commanded, O peoples, nations: 'The moment you hear the sound of the trumpet, flute, lute, harp, bagpipe, and all kinds of musical instruments, you shall fall down and worship the golden image. Whoever does not fall down and worship shall be thrown into a burning, fiery furnace.'" So when all the people heard the sound of the trumpet, flute, lute, harp, bagpipe, and all kinds of musical instruments, all the peoples, nations, and races fell down and worshipped the golden image that King Nebuchadrezzar had set up.

But at that time certain Chaldeans came near to the king and made this charge against the Jews: "O king, live forever! O king, you have commanded that every man who hears the sound of the trumpet, flute, lute, harp, bagpipe, and all kinds of musical instruments shall fall down and worship the golden image, and that whoever does not fall down and worship shall be thrown into a burning, fiery furnace. There are certain Jews, Shadrach, Meshach, and Abednego, whom you have placed in charge of the province of Babylon. These men, O king, have not obeyed your command; they do not serve your gods nor worship the golden image which you have set up."

Then Nebuchadrezzar in his rage and fury gave command to bring in Shadrach, Meshach, and Abednego. When they were brought before the king, Nebuchadrezzar said to them, "Is it true, O Shadrach, Meshach, and Abednego, that you do not serve my god nor worship the golden image which I have set up? If you are now ready, as soon as you hear the sound of the trumpet, flute, lute, harp, bagpipe, and all kinds of musical instruments, to fall down and worship the image which I have made, well; but if you do not worship, you shall at once be thrown into a burning, fiery furnace. Where is there a god who can deliver you out of my hands?" Shadrach, Meshach, and Abednego replied, "O king, there is no need of our answering you about this. Our God whom we serve is able to save us from the burning, fiery furnace; he will save us out of your hand, O king. But if not, know, O king, that we will not serve your gods nor worship the golden image which you have set up."

Then Nebuchadrezzar was very angry and the appearance of his face changed, as he looked at Shadrach, Meshach, and Abednego. He ordered that the furnace should be heated seven times hotter than usual. He also commanded certain strong men who were in his army to bind Shadrach, Meshach, and Abednego, and throw them into the burning, fiery furnace. Then these men were bound in their cloaks, their tunics, their robes, and their other garments, and were thrown into the burning, fiery furnace. As the king's command was urgent and the furnace very hot, the flames destroyed the men who took up Shadrach, Meshach, and Abednego. But Shadrach, Meshach, and Abednego, fell down, bound, into the midst of the burning, fiery furnace.

Nebuchadrezzar, the king, was so astonished that he rose up hastily and said to his counsellors, "Did we not throw three men, bound, into the fire?" They answered, "True, O king." He said, "Now I see four men, unbound, walking in the midst of the fire, and they are unhurt, and the fourth looks like an angel."

Then Nebuchadrezzar went near the door of the burning, fiery furnace and said, "Shadrach, Meshach, and Abednego, servants of the Most High God, come out." Then Shadrach, Meshach, and Abednego came out of the fire. And the officers, governors, and counsellors who were there saw that the fire had no power over the bodies of these men, and that the hair of their heads was not singed and that their cloaks were not harmed, and that there was no smell of fire. And Nebuchadrezzar said, "Blessed be the God of Shadrach, Meshach, and Abednego, who has sent his angel to save his servants who trusted in him and refused to obey the king's command and have offered their bodies, that they might not serve nor worship any god except their own. Therefore I command that every people, nation, and race that shall say anything against the God of Shadrach, Meshach, and Abednego shall be cut in pieces and their house shall be made an ash-heap, for there is no other god who is so able to save as is this one." Then the king gave high positions, in the province of Babylon, to Shadrach, Meshach, and Abednego.

THE HANDWRITING ON THE WALL

Belshazzar, the king, made a great feast for a thousand of his nobles and drank wine before them all. Under the influence of wine, he gave command to bring the gold and silver utensils which his father, Nebuchadrezzar, had taken from the temple at Jerusalem, that the king, his nobles, his wives, and the others of his household might drink from them. So they brought the golden vessels which were taken from the temple of God which was at Jerusalem. And the king, his nobles, his wives, and the others of his household drank from them. They drank wine and praised the gods of gold, of silver, of brass, of iron, of wood, and of stone.

At that moment the fingers of a man's hand appeared and wrote opposite the candlestick upon the plaster of the wall of the king's palace; and the king saw the palm of the hand that wrote.

Then the king grew pale, and his thoughts troubled him, his legs trembled and his knees knocked together. The king called for the magicians and those who study the stars and said to the wise men of Babylon, "Whoever shall read this writing and tell what it means shall be clothed in purple and have a chain of gold about his neck and shall be the third ruler in the kingdom." Then all the king's wise men came in, but they could not read the writing nor tell the king what it meant. So King Belshazzar was greatly troubled, and his face grew pale, and his nobles were thrown into confusion.

Now the queen, because of what the king and his nobles had said, came into the banquet-house and said, "O king, live forever; let not your thoughts trouble you nor let yourself grow pale. There is a man in your kingdom in whom is the spirit of the holy gods, and in the days of your father he was found to have light and understanding and wisdom, like the wisdom of the gods. Now let Daniel be called, and he will tell what it means."

So Daniel was brought in before the king, and the king said to him, "Are you that Daniel, one of the men who were carried away captive, whom the king, my father, brought from Judah? I have heard that the spirit of the gods is in you, and that you have understanding and great wisdom. The wise men and the magicians have been brought in before me to read this writing and to tell what it means; but they are not able. I have heard that you can tell what dreams mean and answer hard questions. Now if you can read the writing and tell what it means, you shall be clothed with purple and have a chain of gold about your neck and shall be the third ruler in the kingdom."

Then Daniel answered the king, "Keep your gifts and give your rewards to another. Without them I will read the writing to the king, and tell what it means. O king, the Most High God gave Nebuchadrezzar, your father, the kingdom and power, glory and majesty. Because of the power that he gave him, all peoples, nations, and races trembled and feared him. He killed or kept alive as he wished; and he raised up or put down whom he pleased. But when he became proud and haughty, he was made to come down from his kingly throne and his glory was taken from him, and he was driven away from men, and his mind became like that of the beasts, and he lived with the wild asses; he was fed with grass like oxen, and his body was wet with the dew of heaven, until he learned that the Most High God rules over the kingdom of men and that he sets up over it whom he will.

"But you, his son, O Belshazzar, have not been humble, though you knew all this, but you have raised yourself against the Lord of heaven, and have had the utensils of his temple brought before you, and you, your nobles, your wives, and the others of your household have drunk wine from them. You have given praise to the gods of silver, of gold, of brass, of iron, of wood, and of stone, which cannot see nor hear nor know; and you have not praised the God in whose control are your very breath and all that you do."

"Then the hand was sent out before him and traced this writing:

MENE, TEKEL, PERES

"This is what it means: Mene: God has numbered your kingdom and brought it to an end. Tekel: you are weighed in the scales and found wanting. Peres: your kingdom is divided and given to the Medes and Persians."

Then at Belshazzar's command Daniel was clothed with purple and a chain of gold was put about his neck, and he was proclaimed the third ruler in the kingdom. But on that very night Belshazzar, the Chaldean king, was killed, and Darius, the Mede, received the kingdom.

DANIEL IN THE LIONS' DEN

Daniel's Answer to the King
Painted by Briton Riviere

It pleased Darius to set over the kingdom a hundred and twenty officers who ruled the whole kingdom, and over them three chief officials, of whom Daniel was one, that these officers might report to them and that the king should lose nothing. Daniel was better than the other chief officials and the officers, for he had a fine spirit; and the king intended to set him over the whole empire.

Then the chief officials and the officers tried to find a way to accuse Daniel of not having done his duty, but they could not find anything against him, for he was faithful and was not guilty of any mistake or wrong-doing.

Then these men said, "We shall not find any way to accuse this Daniel unless we find it in connection with the law of his God." So these chief officials and officers all went to the king, and said to him, "King Darius, live forever. All the chief officials of the kingdom, the counsellors and the officers, the judges and the governors, have consulted together to have the king make a law and give a strong command that whoever shall ask a petition of any god or man for thirty days, except of you, O king, shall be thrown into a den of lions. Now, O king, give the command and sign the law that, like the law of the Medes and Persians, it may not be changed." So King Darius signed the law and the command.

When Daniel knew that the law was signed, he went into his house. His windows were open in his room toward Jerusalem, and he knelt upon his knees three times a day and prayed, and gave thanks to his God as he had done before. Then these men rushed in and found Daniel praying and calling upon his God. So they went before the king and spoke to him about the royal command: "Have you not signed a command, that every man who shall ask a petition of any man or god within thirty days, except of you, O king, shall be thrown into the den of lions?" The king answered, "The rule is fixed according to the law of the Medes and Persians, which cannot be changed." Then they went on to say to the king, "That Daniel, who is one of the captives from Judah, pays no attention to you, O king, nor to the command that you have signed, but prays three times a day."

When the king heard these words, he was greatly displeased, and set his heart on saving Daniel, and he worked until the sun set to save him. Then these men all went to the king and said to him, "Know, O king, that it is a law of the Medes and Persians, that no command nor law which the king gives may be changed."

So the king gave his command, and they brought Daniel and threw him into the den of lions. But the king said to Daniel, "Your God, whom you always serve, will save you." Then a stone was brought and laid at the entrance to the den; and the king sealed it with his own seal-ring and with those of his nobles, that no change might be made so as to rescue Daniel. Then the king went to his palace and passed the night fasting.

At dawn, as soon as it was light, the king rose and hurried to the den of lions. When he came near to the den where Daniel was, he cried with a very sad voice, "O Daniel, servant of the living God, has your God, whom you always serve, been able to save you from the lions?" Daniel said to the king, "O king, live forever. My God has sent his angel and has closed the lions' mouths, and they have not hurt me, for I was innocent before him; and also before you, O king, I have done no wrong." Then the king was very glad and commanded that they should take Daniel up out of the den. So Daniel was taken up out of the den, and it was found that he was not injured, for he had trusted in his God.

Then the king commanded that those men who had accused Daniel should be brought and thrown into the den of lions.

And King Darius wrote to all the peoples, nations, and races in all his kingdom, "May your peace be great! I make a law that throughout all my kingdom, men tremble and fear before the God of Daniel; for he is the living God, and is the same forever, and his kingdom is one that shall not be destroyed; and his rule shall be without end. He saves and rescues, and does wonderful things in heaven and earth; it is he who has saved Daniel from the power of the lions." So Daniel was successful and happy during the reign of Darius.

QUEEN ESTHER'S LOVE FOR HER PEOPLE

After Xerxes had been king of Persia for three years, he gave a feast for all his officials, officers, and servants. The commanders of the armies of Persia and Media, the nobles and governors were before him; while for one hundred and eighty days he showed them the wonderful riches of his kingdom and the costliness of his magnificent regalia.

When these days were ended, the king made a seven days' feast in the enclosed garden of the royal palace, for all classes of people who were in the royal palace at Susa. Vashti, the queen, also gave a feast for the women in the royal palace which belonged to King Xerxes.

On the seventh day, when King Xerxes had been drinking wine, he commanded his seven court attendants to bring Vashti, the queen, before him with the royal crown on her head, to show the peoples and the officials her beauty, for she was very fair. But Queen Vashti refused to come as the king commanded. Therefore the king was very angry.

In his anger the king said to the wise men, "According to law what shall we do to Queen Vashti?" Memucan, one of the seven high officials, said before the king and his officers, "Vashti, the queen, has done wrong not only to the king but also to all the officials and to all the peoples in all of the king's provinces. For the refusal of the queen will be reported to all the women so that they will disobey their husbands, for they will say, 'King Xerxes commanded Vashti, the queen, to be brought in before him, but she did not come!' And this very day the ladies of Persia and Media who have heard of the refusal of the queen will tell it to all the king's officials, and there will be contempt and strife! If it seems best to the king, let him send out a royal command, and let it be written among the laws of Persia and Media, in order that it may not be changed, that Vashti may never again come before King Xerxes; and let the king give her place as queen to another who is better than she. And when the king's command shall be heard throughout his kingdom—great as it is—the wives of all classes will give honor to their husbands!"

The plan pleased the king and the officials, and the king did as Memucan advised. Then the king's pages who waited upon him said, "Let beautiful young girls be sought for the king, and let the king appoint officers to all the provinces of his kingdom to gather them all to the palace at Susa. Then give them what is needed to make them beautiful, and let the girl who pleases the king be queen instead of Vashti." The plan pleased the king and he did so.

There was in the royal palace at Susa, a certain Jew named Mordecai, who had been carried away from Jerusalem with the captives by Nebuchadrezzar, the king of Babylon. He had adopted Esther, his uncle's daughter, for she had neither father nor mother. The girl was attractive and beautiful, and after her father and mother died, Mordecai took her as his own daughter.

So when the king's command was made known, and when many girls were brought to the royal palace at Susa, Esther also was taken into the king's palace and placed in the charge of Hegai, who took care of the women. The girl pleased him and won his favor, so that he quickly gave her what she needed to make her more beautiful and her allowance of food and the seven maids chosen from the king's household. He also moved her and her maids to the best place in the women's quarters. Esther had not told who were her people or her family, for Mordecai had told her not to tell. Every day Mordecai used to walk in front of the court of the women's quarters to ask after Esther's health and what had been done with her.

When Esther's turn came to go in to the king, he loved her more than all the other women, and she became his favorite and won his love, so that he placed the royal crown on her head and made her queen instead of Vashti. Then the king gave a great feast to all his officials and servants in honor of Esther.

In those days while Mordecai was sitting in the king's gate, two of the king's servants, who guarded the entrance of the palace, became enraged and tried to kill King Xerxes. But Mordecai learned of the plot and told it to Queen Esther, and she told the king in Mordecai's name. When the truth was known, the men who plotted against the king were both hanged on a tree; and it was written down in the daily record of events that was kept before the king.

After these events King Xerxes promoted Haman, the Agagite, and gave him a place above all the officials who were with him. All the king's servants who were in the king's gate used to bow down before Haman, for so the king had commanded. But Mordecai did not bow down before Haman.

Then the king's servants, who were in the king's gate, said to Mordecai, "Why do you disobey the king's command?" When they had spoken to him day after day without his listening to them, they told Haman, so as to find out whether Mordecai's acts would be permitted, for he had told them that he was a Jew. When Haman saw that Mordecai did not bow down before him, he was very angry; but as they had told him that Mordecai was a Jew, he decided not to lay hands on him alone but to plot to destroy all the Jews in the whole kingdom of Xerxes.

So Haman said to King Xerxes, "There is a certain people scattered among the peoples in all the provinces of your kingdom, whose laws differ from those of every other and who do not keep the king's laws. Therefore it is not right for the king to leave them alone. If it seems best to the king, let an order be given to destroy them, and I will pay ten thousand silver talents into the royal treasury."

So the king took off his ring from his hand and gave it to Haman, "The money is yours and the people also to do with them as you wish." So messages were sent by men on horses to all the king's provinces, to destroy, to kill, and to put an end to all the Jews, young and old, little children and women, on the thirteenth day of the twelfth month, and to rob them of all that they had. Then the king and Haman sat down to drink, but the people of Susa were troubled.

When Mordecai learned all that had been done, he tore his clothes and put on sackcloth and put ashes on his head, and went out into the city and raised a loud and bitter cry of sorrow. And he went as far as the king's gate, for no one could enter the gate clothed with sackcloth. In every province, wherever the king's command went, there was great mourning, fasting, weeping, and wailing among the Jews; and many of them sat in sackcloth and ashes.

When Esther's maids and servants told her about it, she was greatly troubled. She sent garments for Mordecai to put on, that he might take off his sackcloth; but he would not accept them. So Esther called Hathach, one of the king's servants whom he had appointed to wait on her, and ordered him to go to Mordecai to learn what this meant and how it had happened.

So Hathach went to Mordecai at the city square in front of the king's gate. And Mordecai told him all that had happened to him and the exact sum of money that Haman had promised to pay into the king's treasury. Also he gave him a copy of the order to destroy them, that had been given out in Susa, to show to Esther that she might know about it. He also urged her to go to the king and ask his mercy and plead with him for her people.

When Hathach came and told Esther what Mordecai had said, she commanded Hathach to go and say to Mordecai, "All the king's servants and the people of the king's provinces know that death is the punishment for every man or woman who goes to the king into the inner court without being called, except for the one to whom the king may hold out the golden sceptre, which means that he may live. But now for thirty days I have not been called to go in to the king."

When Mordecai was told what Esther had said, he sent back this answer to Esther, "Do not think that you alone of all the Jews will escape because you belong to the king's household. If you keep silent at this time, help will come to the Jews from somewhere else, but you and your family will perish. Who knows but that you have been raised to the throne for a time like this?"

Then Esther sent this message to Mordecai: "Go, gather all the Jews in Susa and fast for me; do not eat nor drink anything for three days and nights. I and my maids will fast also, and so I will go in to the king, although it is against the law. And if I perish I perish." So Mordecai went away and did as Esther directed.

On the third day, Esther put on her royal garments and stood in the inner court of the royal palace opposite the king's house. The king was sitting on his throne in the palace, opposite the entrance. When he saw Esther, the queen, standing in the court, she won his favor, and he held out to her the golden sceptre that was in his hand. So Esther went up and touched the top of the sceptre. Then the king said to her, "Whatever you wish, Queen Esther, and whatever you ask, it shall be granted, even if it is the half of the kingdom." Esther said, "If it seems best to the king, let the king and Haman come to-day to the feast that I have prepared for him." Then the king said, "Bring Haman quickly, that Esther's wish may be granted."

So the king and Haman went to the feast that Esther had prepared. While they were drinking wine, the king said to Esther, "Whatever you ask shall be granted, even if it takes the half of my kingdom." Esther answered, "If I have won the king's favor and if it seems best to the king to grant what I ask, let the king and Haman come to the feast which I shall prepare for them; and to-morrow I will do as the king wishes."

So Haman went out that day joyful and happy, but when he saw Mordecai in the king's gate and noticed that he neither stood up nor moved for him, he was furiously angry with Mordecai. But Haman controlled his temper and went home. Then he called together his friends and Zeresh, his wife, and told them the greatness of his wealth, how many children he had, and all the ways in which the king had honored him, and how he had given him a place above the officials and the royal servants. Haman said, "Queen Esther brought no one in with the king to the feast which she had prepared but me, and to-morrow also I am invited by her along with the king. Yet all this does not satisfy me as long as I see Mordecai, the Jew, sitting at the king's gate."

Then Zeresh, his wife, and all his friends said to him, "Let a gallows seventy-five feet high be built and in the morning speak to the king and let Mordecai be hanged on it. Then go merrily with the king to the feast." The advice pleased Haman, and so he had the gallows built.

On that night the king was unable to sleep; so he gave orders to bring the books that told of great deeds; and they were read before the king. And it was written how Mordecai had told about the two servants of the king who had tried to kill King Xerxes. Then the king said, "How has Mordecai been honored and rewarded for this?" When the king's pages who waited on him replied, "Nothing has been done for him," the king said, "Who is in the court?" Now Haman had just entered the outer court of the king's house to speak to the king about hanging Mordecai on the gallows that he had prepared for him. So the king's pages said to him, "Haman is standing there in the court." The king said, "Let him enter."

So Haman entered, and the king said to him, "What shall be done for the man whom the king wishes to honor?" Haman said to himself, "Whom besides me does the king wish to honor?" So Haman said to the king, "For the man whom the king wishes to honor let a royal garment be brought, which the king has worn, and the horse on which the king has ridden and on whose head a royal crown has been placed. Then let the garment and the horse be placed in charge of one of the king's noble officials and let him clothe the man whom the king longs to honor and make him ride on the horse through the city square and proclaim before him, 'This is what is done for the man whom the king wishes to honor.'"

Then the king said to Haman, "Make haste and take the garment and the horse, as you have said, and do thus to Mordecai, the Jew, who sits in the king's gate. Do not fail to do all you have said." So Haman took the garment and the horse and clothed Mordecai, and made him ride through the city square and proclaimed before him, "This is what is done for the man whom the king wishes to honor."

Mordecai returned to the king's gate, but Haman hurried to his house, mourning, with his head covered. And Haman told Zeresh, his wife, and all his friends everything that had happened to him. Then his wise men and Zeresh, his wife, said to him, "If Mordecai before whom you have already been disgraced is of the Jewish race, you can do nothing against him, but you will surely fall before him."

While they were still talking with him, the king's servants came and quickly took Haman to the feast that Esther had prepared. So the king and Haman went to drink with Queen Esther. And the king said to Esther, as they were drinking wine, "Whatever you ask, Queen Esther, it shall be granted you, even if it takes half of the kingdom." Then Queen Esther answered, "If I have won your favor, O king, and if it seems best to the king, let my life and my people be given me at my request, for I and my people have been sold to be destroyed, to be killed, and to perish!"

The King Xerxes said to Queen Esther, "Who is he and where is he who dares to do so?" Esther answered, "A foe, an enemy, this wicked Haman." Then Haman shrank in terror before the king and the queen, and Harbonah, one of those who waited on the king, said, "There, standing in the house of Haman, are the gallows, seventy-five feet high, which Haman built for Mordecai, who spoke a good word for the king." The king said, "Hang him on them." So they hanged Haman on the gallows that he had prepared for Mordecai. Then the wrath of the king was quieted.

At that time King Xerxes gave the property of Haman, the Jews' enemy, to Queen Esther. And Mordecai was made one of the king's advisers, for Esther had told of his relationship to her. The king also drew off his signet-ring, which he had taken from Haman, and gave it to Mordecai; and Esther placed Mordecai in charge of Haman's property.

Then Esther came again before the king and fell at his feet and with tears begged him to prevent the evil that Haman had planned against the Jews. The king held out to her the golden sceptre, and she arose and stood before him. Then King Xerxes said to Queen Esther and to Mordecai, the Jew, "Write in behalf of the Jews, as seems best to you, in the king's name and seal it with the king's ring; for what is written in the king's name and sealed with the king's ring no one may disobey."

So Mordecai wrote in the name of King Xerxes and sealed it with the king's ring. And he sent by messengers, who rode the king's swift horses, mules, and camels, the king's command that the Jews who were in every city should gather together and protect their lives.

The command had also been given out in the royal palace at Susa; and Mordecai had gone out from the presence of the king in royal garments of violet and white and with a great crown of gold and with a robe of fine linen and purple. The people of Susa shouted and were glad. To the Jews there came light and gladness and joy and honor. And in every country and city, where the king's command came, there was gladness and joy among the Jews, and a holiday.

On the fourteenth day of the month Adar, the Jews rested and made it a day of feasting and rejoicing. Therefore the Jews who live in the country villages keep the fourteenth day of the month Adar as a day of rejoicing and feasting and a holiday, and as a day on which they send gifts to one another. But the Jews in Susa rested on the fifteenth day of the same month and made it a day of feasting and rejoicing.

The Jews made it a custom for them, and for their children, and for all who should join them, so that it might not be changed, that they should observe these two days as feasts each year. For Haman had plotted to destroy the Jews completely, and he cast pur, that is, the lot, to destroy them. For this reason these days are called Purim.

Esther Denouncing Haman
Painted by Ernest Normand

REBUILDING THE TEMPLE

That the promise made by Jehovah through the mouth of Jeremiah might be fulfilled, Jehovah influenced Cyrus, king of Persia, in the first year of his reign to make this written law throughout all his kingdom, "Thus commands Cyrus, king of Persia: 'Jehovah, the God of heaven, has given me all the kingdoms of the earth and has charged me to build him a temple in Jerusalem in Judah. Whoever among you of all his people wishes to return, may his God be with him, and let him go up to Jerusalem, in Judah, and rebuild the temple of Jehovah, the God of Israel. (He is the God who lives at Jerusalem.) In every place where any who are left of Jehovah's people now live, let the men of that place help with silver, with gold, with goods, and with animals, in addition to the offering each man wishes to give for the house of God at Jerusalem.'"

Then the heads of the families of Judah and Benjamin and the priests and the Levites, including all whom God had influenced to build the temple of Jehovah at Jerusalem, started to return. And all their neighbors supplied them with silver, with gold, with goods, with animals, and with precious things in addition to all that each man wished to give.

Cyrus, king of Persia, had the vessels of the temple of Jehovah, which Nebuchadrezzar had carried from Jerusalem, brought out under the direction of Mithredath, the treasurer, and given to Sheshbazzar, the prince of Judah; and he carried them to Jerusalem, with the people who returned from captivity in Babylon. And Jehovah commanded them, through Haggai, the prophet, "Go up to the mountains and bring wood and rebuild the temple, then I will be pleased with it and I will show my glory."

Then Zerubbabel and Joshua, the high priest, with all the rest of the people obeyed the command of Jehovah their God; and they came and worked on the temple of Jehovah their God. They finished the building as the God of Israel commanded.

NEHEMIAH'S ANSWER TO A CALL FOR HELP

In the twentieth year of Artaxerxes' reign, in the month of November, I (Nehemiah) was in Shushan, the royal palace, when Hanani, one of my brothers, and certain men came from Judah. I asked them about Jerusalem and about the Jews who were left from the captivity. They told me, "Those still living there in the province are in great trouble and disgrace. The wall of Jerusalem is broken down and its gates have been destroyed by fire."

When I heard these words I sat down and wept and mourned several days. Then I fasted and offered this prayer to the God of heaven, "I pray thee, O Jehovah, the God of heaven, who showest kindness to those who love and follow thy commands, let thine ears now be open to hear the prayers of thy servant which I am now making before thee day and night for the Israelites, thy servants, while I confess the sins which we have committed. These are thy servants and thy people, whom thou hast saved by thy great power and by thy strong hand. O Lord, I pray thee, let thine ear be open to the petition of thy servant and to the petitions of thy servants who take pleasure in worshipping thee, and give success to thy servant this day, and grant that he may win this man's sympathy."

Now I was cupbearer to the king, and in the month of March in the twentieth year of the reign of Artaxerxes, the king, I had charge of the wine offered to the king. Up to this time I had not been sad; so the king said to me, "Why is your face sad, for you are not sick? This is nothing else but sorrow of heart." Then I was greatly afraid, and I said to the king, "Let the king live forever! Why should not my face be sad, when the city, the place where my fathers are buried, lies in ruins and its gates are destroyed by fire?" Then the king said to me, "What do you wish?" So I prayed to the God of heaven and said to the king, "If it please the king and if your servant has won your favor, then send me to Judah, to the city where my fathers lie buried, that I may rebuild it." The king said to me (and the queen was also sitting by him), "How long will your journey take, and when will you return?" Then I told him when I would return, so that the king was willing to let me go.

I also said to the king, "If the king is willing, let letters be given me to the governors of the province west of the Euphrates, that they may let me pass through until I come to Judah, and a letter to Asaph, the keeper of the king's park, that he may give me timber to make beams for the gates of the castle which guards the temple and for the wall of the city and for the house in which I shall live." The king granted me all this, for my God kindly cared for me.

Then I went to the governors of the province and gave them the king's letters. The king had sent with me officers and horsemen; and when Sanballat, the Horonite, and Tobiah, the Ammonite slave, heard of it, it troubled them greatly, that one had come to look out for the welfare of the Israelites.

So I arrived at Jerusalem. After I had been there three days I rose in the night, together with a few of my followers. I told no one what my God had put into my mind to do for Jerusalem, and I had no animal with me except the one upon which I rode. I went out by night through the Valley Gate, toward the Dragon's Well and to the Dung Gate; and I examined carefully the walls of Jerusalem which were broken down and the places where its gates had been destroyed by fire. Then I went on to the Fountain Gate and to the King's Pool, but there was no place for the animal on which I rode to pass.

I also went up in the night along the Brook Kidron and examined the wall; then I turned back and entered by the Valley Gate and so returned. The rulers did not know where I went or what I did, and I had not as yet told my plan to the Jews or to the priests or to the nobles or to the rulers or to the others who did the work.

Then I said to them, "You see the bad condition in which we are, how Jerusalem lies in ruins and its gates are destroyed by fire. Come and let us rebuild the wall of Jerusalem, that we may no longer be in disgrace." I told them too how my God had kindly cared for me and the words which the king had spoken to me. They said, "Let us go to work and build?" So they entered heartily into the good work.

OVERCOMING GREAT DIFFICULTIES

Now when Sanballat heard that we were rebuilding the wall, he was so angry and indignant that he mocked the Jews. He spoke before his tribesmen and the army of Samaria and said, "What are these feeble Jews doing? Will they leave it to God? Will they offer a sacrifice? Will they finish the work in a day? Will they recover the stones from the heaps of rubbish even after they have been destroyed by fire?"

Tobiah, the Ammonite, was with him, and he said, "This stone wall which they are building—if a fox should go up on it, he would break it down!"

But we went on rebuilding the wall; and all the wall was joined together to half its height, for the people were eager to work. But when Sanballat and Tobiah and the Arabians and the Ammonites and the Ashdodites heard that the rebuilding of the walls of Jerusalem was going on, so that the broken places began to be closed, they were very angry. And they all planned together to come and fight against Jerusalem and frighten the people there. But we prayed to our God and set a watch as a protection against them day and night.

When our enemies heard that their plan was known to us and that God had not let them carry it out, we all returned to the wall, each to his own work. From that time on, while half of my servants were at work, half of them held the lances, the shields, the bows and the coats of mail; and the rulers stood behind all the people of Judah. Those who built the wall and those who carried burdens were also armed, each using one of his hands for the work, and was ready with the other to grasp his spear. And each builder worked with his sword fastened at his side. The man who sounded the alarm was by me; and I said to the nobles and to the rulers and to the rest of the people, "The work is great and spread out, and we on the wall are far from each other. Wherever you hear the sound of the trumpet, gather about us; our God will fight for us."

So we worked hard, while half of them held the lances from early in the morning until the stars came out. And I said at that time to the people, "Let each man with his servant stay in Jerusalem, that they may protect us at night and work during the day." So neither I, nor any of my relatives, nor my servants, nor the men of the guard who accompanied me took off our clothes, but each kept his spear in his right hand.

After fifty-two days the wall was finished. When our enemies heard of it, all the nations around us were afraid, and it seemed very wonderful to them, and they knew that this work had been done by our God.

After the wall had been built and I had set up the doors, and the porters and the singers and the Levites had been appointed, I placed my brother Hanani, the commander of the castle, in charge of Jerusalem, for he was a faithful man and more God-fearing than many. And I said to them, "Let not the gates of Jerusalem be opened until after sunrise; and at night, while the watchmen are still on guard, let them shut the doors and bar them. Also let the people who live in Jerusalem be on guard, each at his post opposite his own house."

Now the city was wide and large, but there were few people in it, and the houses had not been rebuilt. So my God put it into my mind to gather together the nobles and the officials and the people. The officials lived in Jerusalem. The rest of the people drew lots that one out of every ten should live in Jerusalem, the sacred city, while the others stayed in the villages.

Then I had the officials of Judah take their place on the wall, and I formed two great processions. The first marched to the right upon the wall toward the Dung Gate; and behind them went Hoshaiah and half of the officials of Judah. At the Fountain Gate they went straight up the stairs of the City of David by the ascent along the wall above the House of David to the Water Gate on the east of the city.

The other procession went to the left on the wall above the Tower of the Furnaces, and I after them, with half of the people, to the broad wall and above the Gate of Ephraim and past the Old Gate, the Fish Gate, the Tower of Hananel, and the Tower of the Hundred to the Sheep Gate. Then they stood in the Gate of the Guard. So the two processions took their position in the temple and I and half of the rulers who were with me.

Then the singers sang loudly, and the people offered many sacrifices that day and rejoiced, for God had given them great cause for joy. The women and children rejoiced, too, so that the cries of joy at Jerusalem were heard far away.

A BRAVE KNIGHT

Then the common people and their wives raised a loud cry against their fellow Jews. Some said, "We must give up our sons and our daughters in pledge to get grain that we may eat and live." Others said, "We must give up our fields and our vineyards and our houses, that we may get grain because there is so little." Others said, "We have borrowed money to pay the king's taxes. Although our flesh is as the flesh of our brothers, our children as their children; yet we must sell our sons and our daughters as slaves. Some of our daughters have already been made slaves, and it is not in our power to stop it, for our fields and our vineyards belong to the nobles."

When I heard their cry and these words, I was very angry. After I had thought about it, I rebuked the nobles and the rulers and said to them, "You make each of your fellow Jews pay what you loan him."

Then I called a great meeting to protest against what they were doing. And I said to them, "We ourselves have, as far as we could, bought back our fellow Jews who have been sold to foreigners. Would you sell your fellow Jews, and should they be sold to us?" Then they were silent and could not find a word to say. So I said, "What you are doing is not good. Ought you not to live in the fear of God, so as not to be an object of shame to our foreign foes? I, too, my relatives, and my servants lend the people money and grain. Let us stop taking anything for what we lend. Give back to them at once their fields, their vineyards, their olive-yards, and their houses, and whatever you have made them pay for the money, the grain, the new wine and the oil."

Then they said, "We will give them back and will ask nothing from them; we will do even as you say." Then I called the priests and made them solemnly promise that they would do as they had said.

For twelve years from the time that I was appointed to be their governor in the land of Judah, I and my relatives did not eat the food which was my right as governor. But the governors who were before me were an expense to the people and took from them bread and wine and forty pieces of silver each day. Their servants also were cruel to the people. But I did not do so, for I feared God. I also gave myself to the work on the wall, and we did not buy any land, but all my servants were gathered there for work. Also a hundred and fifty of the Jews and rulers, beside those who came to us from other nations, were fed at my table. Each day one ox and six choice sheep and fowls were prepared at my expense, and once in ten days plenty of wine for all. Yet with all this expense, I did not demand the food which was due me as governor, because the public work was a heavy burden upon this people. Remember to my credit, O my God, all that I have done for them!

JONAH THE NARROW-MINDED PATRIOT

This message from Jehovah came to Jonah, the son of Amittai: "Arise, go to that great city, Nineveh, and preach against it; for their wickedness is known to me." But Jonah started to flee to Tarshish from the presence of Jehovah. He went down to Joppa and found a ship going to Tarshish. So he paid the fare and went aboard to go with them to Tarshish from the presence of Jehovah.

But Jehovah made a furious wind blow over the sea, and there was such a great storm that the ship was in danger of breaking to pieces. Then the sailors were afraid and each cried for help to his own god. They threw into the sea the things that were in the ship, in order to make it lighter. But Jonah had gone down into the bottom of the ship and lay fast asleep. Then the captain of the ship went and said to him, "How is it that you are asleep? Call on your god; perhaps that god will think of us, so that we may not be lost."

And they said to one another, "Come, let us cast lots, that we may know on whose account this evil has come upon us." So they cast lots, and the lot fell upon Jonah. Then they said to him, "Tell us, what is your business, and where do you come from? What is your country and to what race do you belong?" He said to them, "I am a Hebrew, and a worshipper of Jehovah, the God of heaven, who made the sea and the dry land." Then the men were greatly frightened and said to him, "What is this you have done?" For they knew that he was fleeing from the presence of Jehovah, because he had told them.

Then they said to him, "What shall we do to you, that the sea may be calm for us?" for the sea grew more and more stormy. He said to them, "Take me up and throw me into the sea, and the sea will be calm for you, for I know that on account of me this great storm has overtaken you." But the men rowed hard to get back to the land; they could not, however, for the sea grew more and more stormy ahead.

Therefore they cried to Jehovah and said, "We pray thee, O Jehovah, we pray thee, let us not die for this man's life, nor let us be guilty of shedding innocent blood, for thou art Jehovah; thou hast done as it pleases thee." So they took up Jonah, and threw him into the sea; and the sea became calm. Then the men greatly feared Jehovah, and they offered a sacrifice and made promises to him.

But Jehovah prepared a great fish to swallow Jonah, and Jonah was inside the fish three days and three nights. There Jonah prayed to Jehovah his God; and Jehovah spoke to the fish, and it threw Jonah out upon the dry land.

This message from Jehovah came to Jonah the second time, "Arise, go to that great city, Nineveh, and give to it the message that I tell you." So Jonah started for Nineveh, as Jehovah commanded. Now Nineveh was so large a city, that it took three days' journey to cross it. And Jonah began by going through the city a day's journey, and he said, "Forty days more and Nineveh shall be overthrown."

And the people of Nineveh believed God; and they ordered a fast and put on sackcloth, from the greatest to the least of them. And when word came to the king of Nineveh, he rose from his throne, took off his robe, dressed in sackcloth, and sat in ashes. And he gave this order: "By the order of the king and his nobles: Man, beast, herd, and flock shall not taste anything; let them not eat nor drink water. Let both man and beast put on sackcloth and let them cry earnestly to God; let them turn each from his evil way and from the deeds of violence which they are doing. Who knows but God may be sorry for us and turn away his fierce anger, that we may not die."

When God saw that they turned from their evil way, he was sorry for the evil which he said he would do to them, and did not do it.

But this displeased Jonah very much and he was angry. And he prayed to Jehovah and said, "Ah, Jehovah, was not this what I said when I was still in my own country? That was why I fled at once to Tarshish; for I knew that thou art a God, gracious and merciful, patient, and loving and ready to forgive. Therefore, O Jehovah, take now, I beg of thee, my life from me; for it is better for me to die than to live!" But Jehovah said, "Are you doing right in being angry?"

Then Jonah went out of the city and sat down on the east side, and there made a hut for himself and sat under it, until he might see what would become of the city. And Jehovah prepared a gourd and made it grow up over Jonah as a shade for his head. So the gourd gave Jonah great pleasure; but at dawn the next day God prepared a worm which injured the gourd, so that it wilted. And when the sun rose, God prepared a hot east wind. And the sun beat upon Jonah's head, so that he was faint and begged that he might die, saying, "It is better for me to die than to live." But God said to Jonah, "Are you doing right in being angry about the gourd?" He replied, "It is well for one to be angry, even to death!" Jehovah said, "You care for a gourd which has cost you no trouble and which you have not made grow, which came up in a night and wilted in a night. Should I not care for the great city Nineveh, in which there are one hundred and twenty thousand people who do not know their right hand from their left; besides much cattle?"

THE STORY OF JOB

In the land of Uz there lived a man named Job; and he was blameless and upright, one who revered God and avoided evil. He had seven sons and three daughters. He owned seven thousand sheep, three thousand camels, five hundred yoke of oxen, five hundred asses; and he had many servants, so that he was the richest man among all the peoples of the East.

One day when the sons of God came before Jehovah, Satan came with them. Jehovah said to Satan, "From where do you come?" Satan answered, "From going back and forth on the earth, and walking up and down on it." And Jehovah said to Satan, "Have you seen my servant Job? For there is no man like him on the earth, blameless and upright, who reveres God and avoids evil." Satan answered, "But is it for nothing that Job reveres God? Have you not yourself made a hedge all about him, about his household, and about all that he has? You have blessed whatever he does, and his possessions have greatly increased. But just put out your hand now and take away all he has; he certainly will curse you to your face." Then Jehovah said to Satan, "See, everything that he has is in your power; only do not lay hands on Job himself." So Satan left the presence of Jehovah.

One day, as Job's sons and daughters were eating and drinking in the oldest brother's house, a messenger came to Job and said, "The oxen were ploughing and the asses were grazing near them when Sabeans suddenly attacked and seized them; the servants were put to the sword, and I alone have escaped to tell you."

While he was still speaking, another messenger came and said, "Lightning has fallen from heaven and has completely burned up the sheep and the servants, and I alone have escaped to tell you."

While this man was still speaking, another messenger came and said, "The Chaldeans, attacking in three bands, raided the camels and drove them away; the servants were put to the sword, and I alone have escaped to tell you."

While this one was still speaking, another messenger came and said, "Your sons and daughters were eating and drinking in their oldest brother's house when a great wind came from across the wilderness, struck the four corners of the house, and it fell upon the young men and killed them. I alone have escaped to tell you."

Then Job rose, tore his robe, shaved his head, threw himself on the ground and worshipped, saying:

> "Jehovah gave, Jehovah has taken away;
> Blessed be the name of Jehovah!"

In all this Job did not sin nor blame God.

On another day when the sons of God came before Jehovah, Satan came with them. And Jehovah said to Satan, "From where do you come?"

Satan answered, "From going back and forth on the earth, and from walking up and down on it." Jehovah said to Satan, "Have you seen my servant Job? For there is no man like him on the earth, blameless and upright, one who reveres God and avoids evil; he still is faithful, although you led me to ruin him without cause." Satan answered Jehovah, "Skin for skin, yes, a man will give all that he has for his life. But just put out your hand now, and touch his bone and his flesh; he certainly will curse you to your face." Jehovah said to Satan, "See, he is in your power; only spare his life."

So Satan left the presence of Jehovah, and afflicted Job from the sole of his foot to the crown of his head with leprosy so terrible that Job took a piece of broken pottery with which to scrape himself.

As he sat among the ashes, his wife said to him, "Are you still holding to your piety? Curse God and die." But he said to her, "You speak like a senseless woman. We accept prosperity from God, shall we not also accept misfortune?" In all this Job said nothing that was wrong.

When Job's three friends heard of all this trouble that had befallen him, they came each from his own home: Eliphaz the Temanite, Bildad the Shuhite, and Zophar the Naamathite, for they had arranged to go together and show their sympathy for him and comfort him. But when they saw him in the distance, they did not at first know him. Then they all wept aloud and tore their robes and threw dust upon their heads.

And they sat down with him on the ground seven days and seven nights without any one saying a word to him, for they saw that he was in great trouble.

Then Job began to speak and said:

"Why did I not die at birth,
Breathe my last when I was born?
I should then have lain down in quiet,
Should have slept and been at rest
With kings and counsellors of earth,
Who built themselves great pyramids;
With princes rich in gold,
Who filled their houses with silver.

"There the wicked cease from troubling,
There the weary are at rest;
Captives too at ease together,
Hearing not the voice of masters.
There the small and great are gathered,
There the slave is free at last."

Then Eliphaz, the Temanite, answered:

"If one dares to speak, will it vex you?
But who can keep from speaking?
See! you have instructed many,
And strengthened the drooping hands.
Your words have upheld the fallen,
Giving strength to tottering knees.
But now that trouble comes, you are impatient,
Now that it touches you, you lose courage.

"Is not your religion your confidence;
Your blameless life, your hope?
Remember! What innocent man ever perished?
Or where were the upright ever destroyed?
Happy the man whom God corrects;
Therefore, spurn not the Almighty's chastening.
For he causes pain but to comfort,
And wounds, that his hands may heal."

Then Job answered:

"What strength have I, that I should endure?
And what is my future, that I should be patient?
Is my strength the strength of stones,
Or is my body made of brass?
A friend should be kind to one fainting,
Though he lose his faith in the Almighty.
Teach me, and I will keep silent.
Show me how I have sinned."

Then Bildad, the Shuhite, answered:

"Is God a God of injustice?
Or can the Almighty do wrong?
If your children sinned against him,
He has let them suffer the penalty;
But you should earnestly seek him,
And devoutly beseech the Almighty.
If you are pure and upright,
He will surely answer your prayer,
And will prosper your righteous abode."

Then Job answered:

"To be sure, I know that it is so;
    But how can a man be just before God?
    He is wise in mind and mighty in strength,
    Who has ever defied him and prospered,
    Blameless I am! I regard not myself;
    I hate my life; it is all one to me.
    Therefore, I openly declare:
    He destroys the blameless as well as the wicked."

Then Zophar, the Naamathite, answered:

"If you would cleanse your heart,
    And stretch out your hands to God,
    And put away sin from your hand,
    And let no wrong dwell in your tent,
    You would then lift your face without spot,
    You would then be steadfast and fearless."

Then Job answered:

"Verily you are the people,
    And with you wisdom shall die!
    But I have a mind as well as you,
    And who does not know all this?
    Oh, that my words were now written,
    That they were inscribed in a book,
    That with an iron pen and with lead
    In rock they were carved forever!

"For I know that my Defender lives,
That at last he shall stand upon earth;
And after this skin is destroyed.
Freed from my flesh, I shall see him,
Whom I shall behold for myself;
My own eyes shall see, and no stranger's."

Job again spoke and said:

"Oh, to be as in months of old,
As in days when God guarded my steps,
When his lamp shone above my head,
And I walked by his light through the darkness;
As I was in my prosperous days,
When God protected my tent;
When still the Almighty was with me,
And my children were all about me!

"When I went to the gate of the city,
And took my seat in the open,
The youths, when they saw me, retired,
And the aged rose up and stood;
The princes refrained from talking,
And laid their hands on their mouths;
The voices of nobles were hushed,
And their tongues stuck fast to their palates.

"He who heard of me called me happy,
He who saw me bore me witness,
For I saved the poor who cried,
And the orphan with none to help him.

The suffering gave me their blessing,
And I made the widow's heart glad.

"Eyes was I to the blind,
Feet was I to the lame,
And a father to those who were needy.
I defended the cause of the stranger,
I shattered the jaws of the wicked,
And wrested the prey from his teeth.

"Men listened to me eagerly,
And in silence awaited my counsel.
After my words they spoke not,
And my speech fell as rain-drops upon them.
But they sing of me now in derision,
And my name is a by-word among them.

"Oh, for some one to hear me!
Behold my defense all signed!
Let now the Almighty answer,
Let Jehovah write the charge!
On my shoulder I would bear it,
As a crown I would bind it round me;
I would tell him my every act;
Like a prince I would enter his presence!"

Then out of the whirlwind Jehovah answered Job:

"Where were you when I founded the earth?
You have knowledge and insight, so tell me.
You must know! Who determined its measures?
Or who measured it off with a line?

On what were its foundations placed?
Or who laid its corner-stone,
When the morning stars all sang together,
And the sons of God shouted for joy?

"Can you lift up your voice to the clouds,
That abundance of water may answer you?
Can you send on their missions the lightnings;
To you do they say, 'Here we are'?

"Does the hawk soar because of your wisdom,
And stretch her wings to the south wind?
Does the eagle mount up at your bidding,
And build her nest on high?

"Will the fault-finder strive with Almighty?
He who argues with God, let him answer.
Will you set aside my judgment,
And condemn me, that you may be justified?"

Then Job answered the Lord:

"How small I am! what can I answer?
I lay my hand on my mouth.
I spoke once, but will do so no more;
Yes, twice, but will go no further.

"I know thou canst do all things,
And that nothing with thee is impossible.
I spoke, therefore, without sense,
Of wonders beyond my knowledge.
I had heard of thee but by hearsay,

But now my eye has seen thee;
Therefore I despise my words,
And repent in dust and ashes."

Then Jehovah gave back to Job, twice as much as he had before. And Jehovah blessed the last part of Job's life more than the first part; and he had fourteen thousand sheep, six thousand camels, a thousand yoke of oxen, and a thousand asses. He also had seven sons and three daughters. And after this Job lived an hundred and forty years.

* * * * *

PSALMS

THE KING OF GLORY

The earth is the Lord's in its fulness,
The world and those who live in it;
He founded it upon the seas,
And established it upon the floods.

Who may go up to the hill of the Lord?
Who may stand in his holy place?
The man with clean hands and pure heart,
Who plans no evil purpose,
Nor promises in order to deceive.
He shall win from the Lord a blessing,
And approval from God his Saviour.
Such is the man who may worship him,
Who may enter thy presence, O God of Jacob.

Lift up your heads, O gates,
Be lifted up, O everlasting doors,
Let the King of Glory come in!

Who is this King of Glory?
The Lord, strong and mighty,
The Lord, mighty in battle!

Lift up your heads, O gates,
Be lifted up, O everlasting doors,
That the King of Glory may come in.

Who is this King of Glory?
The Lord, the God of hosts,
He is the King of Glory!

GOD THE LOVING CREATOR

Bless the Lord, O my soul!
O Lord, my God, thou art great;
Thou art clothed with glory and majesty,
Thou hast put on light as a mantle;
Thou hast stretched the heavens like a tent,
Thou framest thy upper stories in the waters,
Thou makest the clouds thy chariot,
Thou ridest on the wings of the wind,
Thou makest winds thy messengers,
Flames of fire are thy servants.

Thou didst fix the earth on its foundations,
That it should not be moved forever.
Thou didst cover it with the sea as with a garment.
The waters stood far above the mountains,
But at thy reproof they fled,
At the sound of thy thunder they hastened away,
Not to pass the bound thou hadst set,
Not to return to cover the earth.
Mountains rose, valleys sank,
To the place which thou hadst prepared for them.

Thou sendest the springs to the valleys,
They run down between the mountains,
They give drink to every wild beast,
The wild asses quench their thirst.
The birds make their home beside them,
They sing from among the branches.

Thou waterest the mountains from thine upper stories;
The earth is filled with the fruit of thy works.
Thou makest grass spring up for the cattle,
And green herbs for the service of man,
Causing food to spring from the earth,
Wine to gladden man's heart,
Oil that makes his face shine,
And bread to strengthen his heart.
The trees of the Lord are full of sap,
The cedars of Lebanon, which he has planted,
Where the birds build their nests;
The stork has her home in the fir-trees.
The high mountains are for the wild goats,
The rocks are a hiding-place for the marmots.

Thou createst the moon to divide the year,
The sun knows when it should set.
Thou makest darkness, and it is night,
In which wild beasts creep forth;
The young lions roar for their prey,
And seek their food from God.
When the sun arises they disappear,
And lay themselves down in their dens.
Man goes out to his work,
To toil until evening comes.

O Lord, how many are thy works!
Wisely thou madest them all;
The earth is full of thy creatures.
There is the sea, great and wide,
With its crawling things innumerable,
Living things both small and great;
There go the monsters of the sea,
And the dragon thou madest to play.

These all wait for thee,
To give them their food in due season.
When thou givest to them, they gather it;
Thou openest thy hand, they are satisfied.
Thou hidest thy face, they are frightened;
Thou takest their breath, they die,
And return to the dust from which they came.
Thou sendest thy spirit, and they are created;
Thou refillest the earth with living things.

May the glory of the Lord be eternal,
Let the Lord rejoice in his works.
He looks at the earth, and it trembles,
He touches the mountains, and they smoke.
I will sing to the Lord as long as I live,
I will sing praise to my God while I exist.
May my thoughts be pleasing unto him;
I myself find my joy in the Lord.

GOD THE LOVING FATHER

Bless the Lord, O my soul,
And all that is within me, bless his holy name.
Bless the Lord, O my soul,
And forget not all his benefits,
Who forgives all your iniquities,
And heals all your diseases,
Who redeems your life from the grave,
And crowns you with love and tender mercy,
Who satisfies your mouth with good things,
So that your youth is renewed like the eagle's.

The Lord is a doer of righteous acts,
And of justice to all the oppressed.
He made known his laws to Moses,
His deeds to the people of Israel.

The Lord is merciful and gracious,
Patient and full of love.
He will not always chide,
Nor keep his anger forever.

He has not dealt with us according to our sins,
Nor rewarded us according to our iniquities.
For as high as the heavens are above the earth,
So great is his love toward those who revere him.
As far as the east is from the west,
So far has he removed our wrong deeds from us.

As a father loves his children,
So the Lord loves those who revere him,

For he understands our nature,
He remembers that we are dust.

Frail man—his days are as grass;
As a flower of the field he flourishes,
For the wind passes over it, and it is gone,
And its place knows it no more.

But the love of the Lord is eternal,
And his righteousness to children's children,
To those who keep their covenant with him,
And remember to obey his commands.

He has established his throne in the heavens,
And his rule extends over all.
Bless the Lord, his angels,
You strong ones who do his bidding.

Bless the Lord all his hosts,
You servants who do his will,
Bless the Lord, all his works,
In every place where he rules,
Bless the Lord, O my soul.

"Lo, Children are a Heritage of the Lord"
Painted by W. L. Taylor

GOD FROM WHOM ALL GOOD THINGS COME

Unless the Lord builds the house, its builders labor in vain.
Unless the Lord guards the city, the watchman wakens in vain.
It is vain for you to rise up early, to sit down at your meal late,
And so eat the bread of toil; for he gives to his loved ones sleep.

Children too are a gift from the Lord, they are a reward.
As arrows in the hand of a warrior, so are the children of youth.
Happy indeed is the man whose quiver is full of them,
He shall not be put to shame when he argues with foes in the court.

GOD'S GOODNESS AND MERCY

The Lord is gracious and merciful,
Patient, and full of loving-kindness.
The Lord is good to all,
Showing mercy to all his creatures.
All thy works give thee thanks, O Lord,
And those who love thee praise thee,
They speak of thy glorious rule,
And proclaim thy mighty power,
That men may know thy great deeds,
And the glorious splendor of thy rule.
Thy rule is an everlasting rule,
Thy dominion endures forever.

The Lord lifts up all who fall,
And raises up all who are bowed down.
The eyes of all wait for thee,
And thou givest them food in due season.
Thou it is who openest thy hand,
And satisfiest the desires of all creatures.

The Lord is righteous in all his ways,
And gracious in all his acts.
He is near all who call upon him,
To all who call upon him in truth.
He fulfils the desire of his worshippers,
He hears their cry and saves them.
He takes care of all who love him,
But destroys all those who do wrong.

My mouth shall speak the praise of the Lord.
Let all flesh praise his holy name forever.

GOD THE ALL-SEEING

O Lord, thou searchest and knowest me,
Whether I sit or stand, thou knowest,
Thou readest my thought afar off,
When I walk or lie down thou dost know it.

Thou knowest all my ways.
There is not a word on my tongue
That thou, O Lord, dost not know!
Behind and before thou enfoldest me,
Over me thou dost lay thy hand.
Such knowledge for me is too wonderful!
Too high, I cannot attain it.

Where shall I go from thy spirit,
Where shall I flee from thy presence?
If I climb into heaven, thou art there,
If I lie down in the grave, thou art there.
Should I take the wings of the morning,
And dwell on the most distant sea,
Even there thy hand would grasp me,
Thy right hand would hold me fast.

If I say, "The darkness will hide me,
And the night throw its curtain about me,"
Even darkness for thee is not dark,
But the night shines clear as the day.
Thou didst form my vital parts,

Thou didst make me from the beginning,
I thank thee, for I am wonderfully made;
Fearful and marvellous are thy works.

How precious to me are thy thoughts, O God!
How great is the sum of them all!
Should I count them, they would be more than the sand;
When I awake, I am still with thee.

Search me, O God, and know my heart,
Try me, and know my secret thoughts,
And see if I have any evil in me,
And lead me in the way to eternal life.

GOD WHO ALWAYS WATCHES OVER HIS PEOPLE

I will lift up my eyes to the hills; from whence comes my help?
My help comes from the Lord, who made heaven and earth.
He will not let your foot be moved; he who keeps you does not slumber;
Behold, he who keeps Israel neither slumbers nor sleeps!

The Lord is your protector; the Lord is your shade upon your right hand;
The sun shall not smite you by day, nor the moon by night!
The Lord will keep you from all evil; he will preserve your life;
The Lord will protect your going out and your coming in forevermore!

"I will Lift up mine Eyes unto the Hills"
Painted by W. L. Taylor

GOD WHO PROTECTS FROM ALL DANGER

Give thanks to the Lord, for his goodness,
For his love endures forever.
Let those he has redeemed say so,
Whom he has set free from the hand of the foe,
And gathered together from many lands,
From the east, from the west,
From the north and the south.

Some strayed in the barren wilderness,
Finding no inhabited city,
Hungry, indeed, and thirsty,
Their very life ebbing away.
Then they cried to the Lord in their trouble,
And he saved them from their distresses.
He led them along the right way,
Till they reached an inhabited city.
Let them praise the Lord for his love,
And his wonderful works unto men!
For he satisfies the longing soul,
And the hungry he fills with good things.

Some dwelt in darkness and gloom,
Being bound in affliction and iron,
Because they had rebelled against God,
And despised the counsel of the Most High.
He humbled their heart with sorrow;
When they fell, there was none to help them.
Then they cried to the Lord in their trouble,
And he saved them from their distresses.
Out of darkness and gloom he brought them,
And broke their bonds in pieces.
Let them praise the Lord for his love,
And his wonderful works unto men!
For he shattered the gates of brass,
And hewed bars of iron asunder.

Fools because of their wrong-doing,
And because of their sins were afflicted;
They hated all kinds of food,
And drew near to the gates of death.

Then they cried to the Lord in their trouble,
And he saved them from all their distresses.
He sent his command to heal them,
And saved their life from destruction.
Let them praise the Lord for his love,
And his wonderful works unto men!
Let them sacrifice to him a thank-offering,
And with joy recount his deeds.

Those who go to the sea in ships,
Who do business in great waters,
They see the works of the Lord,
And his wonders in the great deep.
When he speaks, the tempest rises,
And tosses the waves on high.
Up to heaven, then down they go,
Their courage melts at the danger,
They stagger and reel like drunkards,
And their skill is all exhausted.
Then they cry to the Lord in their trouble,
And he saves them from their distresses.
He makes the tempest a calm,
And the waves of the sea are still.
They are glad when the waves go down;
To the haven they long for he brings them.
Let them praise the Lord for his love,
For his wonderful works unto men;
In the popular assembly extol him,
In the council of elders praise him.

GOD'S PROTECTION OF THOSE WHO TRUST IN HIM

I will bless the Lord at all times,
His praise is continually in my mouth,
My soul glories in the Lord,
Let the afflicted hear and rejoice.
O exalt the Lord with me,
Let us praise his name together.

I sought the Lord and he answered me,
From all my fears he delivered me.
He who looks to him, becomes radiant,
And his face is not covered with shame.
This afflicted man cried and he heard him,
And from all his distresses delivered him.
The angel of the Lord encamps
About those who revere him, and saves them.

Taste and see that the Lord is good;
Happy the man who seeks refuge with him.
Revere the Lord, O holy ones,
For those who revere him lack nothing.
Though young lions feel want and suffer hunger,
Those who seek the Lord shall not lack any good thing.

Come, children, listen to me;
I will teach you true religion:
Who of you desires to live,
Loves long life that he may enjoy happiness?
Then keep your tongue from evil,
And your lips from speaking falsehood;

Turn from evil and do good,
Seek for peace and pursue it.

The Lord is against evil-doers,
To cut off their memory from the earth.
The Lord watches over the upright,
His ear is open to their cry.
When they cry to the Lord, he hears,
And saves them from all their troubles.

The Lord is near those who are broken-hearted,
He delivers those whose spirits are crushed.
The misfortunes of the upright are many,
But the Lord delivers him from them all.
The Lord guards all his bones,
Not one of them is broken.
Misfortune shall slay the wicked,
Those who hate the upright shall be condemned;
But the Lord redeems his servants,
And none who takes refuge in him shall be condemned.

GOD'S LOVING CARE

The Lord is my shepherd; I shall not want.
He makes me lie down in green pastures,
He leads me to the still waters,
He restores my soul.

He guides me in straight paths for his name's sake;
Though I walk through the valley of death,
I will fear no evil, for thou art with me,
Thy rod and thy staff—they comfort me.

Thou preparest a table before me in the presence of my enemies,
Thou anointest my head with oil, my cup runs over;
Surely goodness and love will follow me all the days of my life,
And I shall dwell in the house of the Lord forever.

TRUSTING IN GOD'S CARE

Be not disturbed because of the wicked,
Nor be envious of those who do wrong;
For like grass they shall quickly wither,
And fade like the green herbs.

Trust in the Lord and do right,
Live in the land and act faithfully.
Then the Lord shall be your delight,
He will grant you your heart's desire.

Commit your way to the Lord,
Trust in him, and he will work with you,
He will bring to light your honesty,
And make it as clear as the noonday.

A PRAYER OF TRUST

To thee, O God, I lift up my soul,
All the day long do I wait for thee.
I trust in thee, O God, let me not be ashamed;
Let not my enemies exult over me,
And let none who hope in thee be ashamed;
But let wicked traitors be disgraced.

Show me thy ways, O Lord,
Teach me thy way to live.
Lead me in thy truth and teach me,
For thou art the God who saves me,
And in thee do I hope continually.

Remember thy tender mercies, O Lord,
And thy loving deeds, for they are eternal.
Do not recall the sins of my youth,
But in thy love remember thou me,
Because of thy goodness, O Lord.

Good and upright is the Lord,
So he teaches sinners the way,
He guides the humble aright,
And teaches the meek his way,
All his rules are loving and true,
To those who follow his law and commands.
For thy name's sake, O Lord,
Pardon my guilt, for it is great.

Who is the man that reveres the Lord?
He will teach him the way to choose.
That man shall continue to prosper,
And his children inherit the land.
He is friendly with those who revere him,
And with his covenant he makes them acquainted.

My eyes are ever turned toward the Lord,
For he saves my feet from the net.
Turn to me and be gracious,
For I am alone and afflicted;

Relieve the troubles of my heart,
And deliver me from my distresses;
Look on my affliction and suffering,
And pardon all my sins.

Consider my enemies, for they are many,
And they hate me with violent hatred;
Oh save my life and deliver me,
Let me not be ashamed, for I trust thee.
Let innocence and uprightness preserve me,
For I wait for thee, O Lord.

SAFETY IN GOD'S CARE

You who dwell in the shelter of the Most High,
Who abide in the shadow of the Almighty,
Who say to the Lord, "Thou art my refuge,
And my fortress, my God in whom I trust,"
He will surely deliver you from the snare,
When entrapped from the destructive pit.
With his pinions he will cover you,
And under his wings you may hide.

His faithfulness is a shield and defense,
You shall not be afraid of the terror by night,
Nor of the arrow that flies by day,
Of the pestilence that stalks in darkness,
Nor the destruction that wastes at noonday.
A thousand may fall at your side,
And ten thousand at your right hand,
But it shall not come near unto you.

You need but look with your eyes,
To see how the wicked are punished.

Because the Lord is your refuge,
And you have made the Most High your abode,
There shall no evil befall you,
No plague come near your tent;
For he will give his angels charge over you,
To keep you in all your ways;
They shall bear you up on their hands,
Lest you strike your foot on a stone.
You shall tread on the lion and adder,
You shall trample on the young lion and dragon.

"Because of his love for me I will deliver him,
I will exalt him, for he knows my name.
He shall call upon me and I will answer him,
In time of trouble I will be with him,
I will deliver him and bring him honor,
With long life will I satisfy him,
And show him my power to save."

GOD OUR REFUGE

God is our refuge and strength,
An ever-present help in trouble.
So we fear not, though the earth trembles,
And mountains tumble into the heart of the sea;
Though its waters roar and foam,
Though mountains quake at its uproar.
The Lord of hosts is with us,
The God of Jacob is our refuge.

As the brooks refresh the city of God,
So the Most High makes holy his abiding-place;
God is in her midst, she cannot be moved,
God will help her at the turn of the morn.

Nations were in tumult, kingdoms fell,
He uttered his voice, the earth melted.
The Lord of hosts is with us,
The God of Jacob is our refuge.

Come, see the mighty works of the Lord,
Who makes wars cease to the end of the earth
He snaps the bow, and breaks the spear,
And burns up the chariots with fire.
"Be still, and know that I am God,
Exalted over the nations, exalted on earth."
The Lord of hosts is with us,
The God of Jacob is our refuge.

THE JOY OF WORSHIPPING GOD

Oh come, let us sing to the Lord,
Let us shout to the Rock who saves us,
Let us come before him with thanksgiving,
Let us sing to him joyful songs;
For the Lord is indeed a great God,
A great King above all gods,
In whose hand are the depths of the earth,
The heights of the mountains are his,
The sea is his, for he made it,
And his hands prepared the dry land.

Oh come, let us worship and bow down,
Let us kneel before the Lord, our Maker;
For he is the Lord our God,
And we are his people, the sheep of his pasture.

Shout with joy to the Lord, all the earth,
Serve the Lord with gladness,
Come into his presence with singing,
Know that the Lord is God,
He has made us and we are his,
His people, the flock that he tends.

Enter his gates with thanksgiving,
His courts with songs of rejoicing,
Give thanks to him, praise his name,
He is good, his kindness eternal,
And his faithfulness unto all generations.

WHAT GOD ASKS OF THOSE WHO WORSHIP HIM

O Lord, who may be a guest in thy tent?
Who may dwell on thy holy hill?

He who lives blamelessly and does right,
And speaks the truth in his heart,
Who utters no slander with his tongue,
Who does no wrong to his friend,
Who makes no charge against his neighbor;
In whose sight the vile are despised,
But he honors those who revere the Lord.
He keeps his oath at all costs,

His money he puts not out to usury,
And cannot be bribed to injure the innocent.

He who does this can never be moved.

A CALL TO PRAISE GOD

Oh, sing to the Lord a new song;
Sing to the Lord, all the earth,
Sing to the Lord, praise his name,
Proclaim his salvation each day;
Tell his glory among the heathen,
His wonders among all peoples.

God is great, and worthy of praise,
Above all gods should he be revered,
For all the gods of the peoples are idols,
But it is the Lord who made the heavens.
Honor and majesty are in his presence,
Strength and beauty are in his sanctuary.

Give to the Lord, you tribes of the nations,
Give to the Lord glory and strength.
Give to the Lord the glory that is due him;
Bring an offering, and enter his courts.
Oh, worship the Lord in holy attire,
Tremble before him, all the earth.
Say to the nations, "The Lord reigns,
And he will rule the peoples justly."

Let the heavens be glad, and the earth rejoice,
Let the sea roar and all of its inhabitants,

Let the fields exult, and all that is in them,
Let the trees of the forest sing with joy
Before the Lord, for he has come,
For he has come to rule the earth;
He will rule the world with justice,
He will rule the nations with faithfulness.

THE UNITED SONG OF PRAISE

Praise the Lord from the heavens,
Praise him on the heights.
Praise him, all his angels,
Praise him, all his host!

Praise him, sun and moon,
Praise him, all stars of light!
Praise him, heavens of heavens,
And waters above the heavens!

Let them praise the name of the Lord,
For at his command they were made;
He fixed them forever and ever,
Set a bound they must not pass.

Praise the Lord from the earth,
Sea-monsters and all deeps!
Fire, hail, snow, and vapor,
Storm wind, fulfilling his word!

Mountains and all hills,
Fruit-trees and all cedars!

Wild beasts and all cattle,
Creeping things and winged birds!

Kings of earth and all peoples,
All rulers and judges of earth,
Young men and maidens too,
Old men and children together!

Let them praise the name of the Lord,
For his name alone is exalted.
Over heaven and earth is his majesty,
He has strengthened the might of his people;
He is praised by all who are faithful,
By the Israelites, who are near him.

Praise God in his holy place,
Praise him for his mighty firmament,
Praise him for his deeds of power,
Praise him for his infinite greatness.

Praise him with the blast of the horn,
Praise him with lyre and harp,
Praise him with timbrel and dance,
Praise him with strings and pipe,
Praise him with clanging cymbals,
Praise him with clashing cymbals.
Let all that breathes praise the Lord!

MAN'S PLACE IN GOD'S WORLD

O Lord, our God, how glorious
Is thy name in all the earth!

Thou hast spread thy splendor over the heavens;
At the cry of babes and infants
Thou hast set up a bulwark, because of thine enemies,
To silence the foe and avenger.

When I see thy heavens, the work of thy fingers,
The moon and stars which thou hast made;
What is man that thou art mindful of him;
Or the son of man that thou visitest him?

Yet thou hast made him little less than divine,
And hast crowned him with glory and honor,
Making him lord of creation,
So that all things are subject to him.

The sheep and the oxen, all of them,
Yes, and the beasts of the field,
The birds of the air and the fish,
That dart through the paths of the sea.

O Lord, our God, how glorious
Is thy name in all the earth!

THE REWARD OF DOING RIGHT

Happy is the man
Who follows not the counsel of the wicked,
Nor takes his stand with sinners,
Nor sits among the scoffers,
But delights in the law of the Lord,
And day and night meditates on it.
For he is like a tree planted by streams of water,

Which yields its fruit in due season,
Whose leaf never withers,
And all that he does prospers.

Not so the wicked!
They are like the chaff driven by the wind.
So the wicked shall not rise up at the judgment,
Nor sinners where the righteous are gathered;
For the Lord directs the way of the righteous,
But the way of the wicked leads to ruin.

A PRAYER FOR FORGIVENESS

Have mercy upon me, O God,
According to thy loving-kindness,
According to the multitude of thy tender mercies,
Blot out all my transgressions,
Wash me thoroughly from mine iniquity,
And cleanse me from my sin.
For well do I know my misdeeds,
And my sin is always before me.
Against thee, thee only have I sinned,
And done what is wrong in thy sight;
Therefore thou art right when thou speakest,
And just when thou pronouncest thy judgment.

Verily I was born in iniquity,
And in sin did my mother conceive me.
Yet thou desirest truth in the heart,
In my inner soul thou wouldst teach me wisdom.
Cleanse me with hyssop that I may be clean,
Wash me whiter than snow.

Fill me with joy and gladness,
That the bones which thou hast broken may rejoice.
Hide thy face from my sins,
And blot out all mine iniquities.

Create in me a clean heart, O God,
And renew a right spirit within me.
Cast me not away from thy presence,
Withdraw not thy holy spirit from me.
Give me back the glad sense of thy help,
And with a willing spirit sustain me.

Then I will teach sinners thy ways,
And wrong-doers shall turn unto thee.
Save me from bloodshed, O God,
That my tongue may sing of thy righteousness.
O Lord, open thou my lips,
That my mouth may declare thy praise!

For thou takest no pleasure in sacrifice,
No delight in gifts of burnt-offering.
The sacrifices pleasing to thee
Are a broken and a contrite spirit.

* * * * *

THE SAYINGS OF THE WISE

THE REWARDS OF LISTENING TO THE ADVICE OF THE WISE

My son, if you heed my words,
And store my commands in your mind,
Pay close attention to wisdom,
And give careful heed to reason.
If you will but seek her as silver,
And search for her as for hid treasures,
You shall then understand true religion,
And gain a knowledge of God.
For wisdom shall enter your mind,
And knowledge shall be pleasant to you,
Discretion shall watch over you,
And understanding shall guard you,
To keep you from doing wrong,
From men whose words are evil,
Who leave the paths of right
To walk in ways that are dark,
Who rejoice in doing wrong,
And take pleasure in evil deeds.

Happy the man who finds wisdom,
And he who gains understanding.

In her right hand is long life,
In her left are riches and honor.
Her ways are pleasant ways,
And all her paths are peaceful.
She gives life to those who seek her,
They are happy who hold her fast.
You shall then go on your way securely,
And your foot shall never stumble.
When you sit down, you shall not be afraid,
When you lie down, your sleep shall be sweet.

WHAT GOD LIKES AND DISLIKES

The eyes of the Lord are all-seeing,
Keeping watch on both wicked and good.
A man thinks all that he does is right,
But the Lord tests the motive.
A man plans the way in his mind,
But the Lord directs his steps.

The Lord detests a false balance,
But a just balance is his delight.
To do what is just and right
Is more acceptable to the Lord than sacrifice.
The conduct of the wicked is hateful to him,
But he loves the man eager to do right.
The Lord detests the evil-minded,
But is well pleased with him who lives uprightly.

The sacrifice of the wicked is hateful to the Lord,
But the prayer of the upright is a delight to him!
The Lord holds aloof from the wicked,

But hears the prayer of the upright.
Lying lips are hateful to the Lord,
But they who act honestly are his delight.

There are six things that the Lord hates,
Yes, seven are detestable to him:
Haughty eyes and a lying tongue,
And hands that shed innocent blood,
A mind that plans wicked schemes,
Feet that make haste to do evil,
A false witness who utters lies,
And he who sows strife between brothers.

GOD'S CARE FOR THOSE WHO TRY TO DO RIGHT

The curse of the Lord is on the house of the wicked,
But he blesses the home of him who does right.
Surely he scoffs at the scoffers,
But to the modest he ever shows favor.

The Lord does not let the righteous go hungry,
But he disappoints the desire of the wicked.
The Lord is a stronghold to him who lives rightly,
But he brings destruction to those who do wrong.

The name of the Lord is a strong tower,
To which the righteous runs and is safe.
Every word of God is true;
He is a shield to those who trust him.

Say not, "I will be revenged for a wrong";
Wait for the Lord, he will save you.

For the Lord gives wisdom,
From his mouth come knowledge and understanding;
He stores up sound wisdom for the upright,
He is a shield to those who live clean lives,
That he may guard the course of justice,
And protect the way of his faithful ones.

Reverence for the Lord is the beginning of knowledge,
But the foolish despise wisdom and discipline.
Reverence comes through wise instruction,
And before honor goes modesty.

Trust in the Lord with all your heart,
Depend not on your own understanding;
In all you do make him your friend,
And he will direct your paths.

Be not wise in your own eyes.
Revere the Lord, and avoid sin.
Then you will have health of body
And your bones will be refreshed.

Honor the Lord with your wealth,
With the best of all you receive,
Then your barns will be filled with grain,
And your vats overflow with wine.

A greedy man stirs up strife,
But he who trusts in the Lord will prosper.
Intrust what you do to the Lord,
Then your plans will succeed.

THE WAY TO BE WELL AND HAPPY

Many a man tells of his own kindness.
But a trustworthy man who can find?
A child is known by his acts,
Whether his work is pure and right.

Worry in a man's mind makes it sad,
But a kind word makes it happy.
A man's spirit upholds him in sickness,
But who can raise up a broken spirit?

A calm mind is the life of the body,
But jealousy rots the bones.
A joyful heart makes a cheerful face,
But by inward sorrow the spirit is broken.
A joyful heart is good medicine,
But a broken spirit dries up the bones.

THE IMPORTANCE OF BEING WILLING TO LEARN

The lips of the wise speak knowledge,
But the fool does not understand.
A fool's way seems right in his sight,
But a wise man listens to advice.
A fool despises his father's correction,
But he who regards reproof acts wisely.

Listen to advice and receive instruction,
That you may be wise in your later life.
Advice in a man's mind is like deep water,
But a man of sense will draw it out.

Hold fast instruction, let it not go;
Keep it, for it is your life.

My son, reject not the discipline of the Lord,
And do not spurn his reproof,
For whom he loves he reproves,
Even as a father the son of whom he is fond.
He who rejects correction despises his own self,
But he who listens to reproof gains understanding.

HOW TO HONOR YOUR PARENTS

My son, hear the instruction of your father,
And forsake not the teaching of your mother;
They shall be a crown of beauty for your head,
And a necklace about your neck.
Listen to your father who begat you,
And despise not your mother when she is old.
He who does what he is told is a wise son.
But he who makes friends of spendthrifts,
Brings disgrace on his father.

He who robs father or mother,
Saying, "There is no wrong in it,"
Is like him who is a destroyer.
He who curses his father or mother,
His lamp shall go out in the blackest of darkness.
A wise son makes a glad father,
But a foolish son despises his mother.
A foolish son is a grief to his father,
And brings bitterness to her who bore him.

Be wise, my son, and make glad my heart,
That I may answer the one who reproaches me.
Let your father be filled with joy,
And let her who bore you rejoice.

THE TROUBLES OF THOSE WHO ARE LAZY

The lazy man says, "A lion is outside!
I shall be killed in the streets!"
As the door turns on its hinges,
So the lazy man turns on his bed.
He dips his hand in the dish,
But does not bring it to his mouth!
The lazy man is wiser in his own mind,
Than seven who can answer intelligently.
The way of the lazy is hedged in with thorns,
But the path of the diligent is a well-built highway.

I went by the field of the lazy man,
By the vineyard of him who lacked sense,
It was all overgrown with thorns,
Its surface was covered with nettles,
And its stone wall was broken down.
Then I beheld and reflected,
I saw and received instruction:
A little sleep, a little slumber,
A little folding of the hands to rest,
And your poverty comes as a robber,
And your want as a well-armed man.

THINGS THAT ARE BETTER THAN RICHES

Better is a poor man who lives uprightly
Than one who is dishonest, though he be rich.
Better is a little with righteousness
Than great abundance with injustice.

Better is a modest spirit with the humble,
Than to divide spoil with the proud.
A good name is better than great riches,
More highly valued than silver and gold.
He who trusts in riches shall fail,
But the upright flourish like a green leaf.

Toil not that you may become rich;
Cease through your own understanding.
Should you set your eyes upon it, it is gone!
For riches fly away,
Like an eagle that flies toward heaven.
Better is little with reverence for the Lord
Than great treasure and trouble as well.

Two things I ask of thee, O God,
Deny me them not ere I die:
Put far from me deceit and lying,
Give me neither poverty nor riches;
Provide me with the food that I need,
That I may not be filled to the full and deny thee,
And say, "Who is the Lord?"
Or else be poor and steal,
And disgrace the name of my God.

RIGHT EATING AND DRINKING

If you find honey, eat only what you need,
That you may not be too full and be ill.

Wine is a mocker, strong drink makes one quarrelsome,
And whoever is misled by it is not wise.
Who cries, "Woe"? who, "Alas"?
Who has quarrels? Who complains?
Who has wounds without cause?
Who has redness of eyes?
They who linger long over wine,
They who go in to taste mixed wine.

So look not on wine when it is red,
When it sparkles in the cup,
And glides down smoothly.
At last it bites like a snake,
And stings like an adder.

Then you will see strange things,
And your mind will be confused.
You will be like one sleeping at sea,
Like one asleep in a violent storm.
"I have been struck, but I feel no pain;
I have been beaten, but I know it not.
When shall I awake from my wine?
I will seek it yet again."

THE RIGHT USE OF THE TONGUE

Do you see a man who speaks before he thinks?
There is more hope for a fool than for him.
He who answers before he hears
Covers himself with confusion.

He who is sparing of words has knowledge,
And he who has a cool spirit is a man of sense.
Even a fool, if he keeps still, is considered wise;
Prudent, if he keeps his lips shut.

He who guards his mouth and tongue
Guards himself against trouble.
Life and death are in the power of the tongue;
They who are fond of using it must eat its fruit.

A man has joy from the utterance of his mouth,
And a word in season, how good it is!
A word fitly spoken
Is like golden fruit in silver settings.
Pleasant words are like honeycomb,
Sweet to the taste and healing to the body.

THE CONTROL OF THE TEMPER

A mild answer turns away wrath,
But a harsh word stirs up anger.

A man without self-control
Is a ruined city whose wall is broken.
A fool gives way to his wrath,

But a wise man restrains his anger.
A fool's anger is known at once,
But a sensible man heeds not an insult.

A man's wisdom makes him patient,
It is his glory to overlook faults.
He who is patient is better than a warrior,
And he who rules his temper than he who takes a city.

WHAT IT MEANS TO BE MODEST

Do not boast what you will do to-morrow,
For you know not what a day may bring forth.
Do you see a man wise in his own opinion?
There is more hope for a fool than for him!

Pride goes before destruction,
And a haughty spirit before a fall.
When pride comes, then comes disgrace,
But with the modest is wisdom.

It is not good to eat much honey;
But to seek the glory of others is glorious.
Let another man praise you, not your own mouth;
Some other, and not your own lips.

BEING GENEROUS AND LOVING

He who returns evil for good,
From his house evil shall not depart.

It is an honor for a man to avoid strife;
Only a fool is quarrelsome.
Charcoal for embers, and wood for fire,
And a quarrelsome man to kindle strife!

Strive not with a man without cause,
If he has done you no harm.

The beginning of strife is as when one lets out water;
Therefore leave off strife before quarrelling begins.
Better a dry crust with quietness
Than a house full of feasting with strife.

A just man regards the life of his beast,
But the heart of the wicked is cruel.

He who oppresses the poor reviles his Maker,
But he who has pity on the needy honors him.
He who listens not to the cry of the poor,
He also shall call and not be answered.
He who pities the poor, lends to the Lord
And he will repay him for his good deed.

If your enemy hungers, give him food;
If he thirsts, give him water to drink;
For you will heap coals of fire on his head,
And the Lord will reward you.

Hatred stirs up strife,
But love overlooks faults.
Better a meal of herbs where love is,
Than a fatted ox with hate.

Let not love and truth leave you,
Bind them about your neck;
So you will enjoy favor and a good reputation
In the sight of God and man.

* * * * *

THE NEW TESTAMENT

JESUS IS BORN AT BETHLEHEM

The Nativity
Painted by W. L. Taylor

The angel Gabriel was sent from God to a young woman named Mary in Nazareth, a town of Galilee. She was to be married to a man named Joseph of the family of David. When he came to her the angel said: "Hail, highly honored one! God is with you!"

She was startled by his words and wondered what such a greeting might mean. But the angel said to her, "Fear not, Mary, for you have found favor with God. You will have a son and will name him Jesus. He will be great and will be called the Son of the Most High."

Then Mary said to the angel, "How can this be, for I am not yet married." The angel answered her, "The Holy Spirit will come upon you and the power of the Most High will cover you; therefore your child will be called holy, the Son of God." Mary said: "I am God's servant. May it be with me as you say." Then the angel left her.

In those days the Emperor Augustus commanded that every one should be registered. So all went to be registered, each to his own town. Joseph, because he was of the family of David, went to be registered with Mary, his wife, from the town of Nazareth in Galilee to Bethlehem in Judea where David was born. While they were there Mary's first son was born. And she wrapped him in swaddling-clothes and laid him in a manger, because there was no room for them in the inn.

In that country there were shepherds living in the fields and keeping watch over their flocks by night. And an angel from God stood by them and a heavenly light shone around them, and they were frightened. But the angel said to them:

"Fear not, for behold I bring you good news
Of great joy which shall be for all the people.
For to you is born this day in the town of David
A Saviour who is God's Anointed.
This will be a sign to guide you:
You will find a baby in swaddling-clothes lying in a manger."

Then suddenly there was with the angel a great number of the heavenly ones singing praise to God and saying:

"Glory to God on high,
And on earth peace, good-will among men."

When the angels had gone away from them into heaven, the shepherds said to one another, "Let us go now to Bethlehem to see this which God has made known to us." So they went quickly and found Mary and Joseph; and the baby was lying in a manger.

When they had seen him, they made known what had been told them about this child. All who heard the words of the shepherds wondered, but Mary kept these things to herself and often thought about them. And the shepherds returned, thanking and praising God for what they had heard and seen, as it had been foretold.

THE WISE MEN BRING GIFTS TO THE YOUNG CHILD

The Three Wise Men
Painted by W. L. Taylor

When Jesus was born in Bethlehem, wise men from the east came to Jerusalem and asked, "Where is the newly born King of the Jews? For we saw his star in the east and have come to worship him."

When Herod heard these things, he and every one else in Jerusalem were greatly troubled. So when he had gathered all the high priests and scribes together, he asked them where the Christ was to be born. They said to him, "In Bethlehem of Judea."

Then Herod privately called the wise men and asked them exactly how long the star had been seen since it appeared in the east. And he sent them to Bethlehem with the command, "Go and search carefully for the young child, and when you have found him, come and let me know, that I also may go and worship him." When they had heard the king, they went away, and the star which they had seen in the east went before them until it stood over the place where the young child was. They were overjoyed at the sight; and when they came into the house and saw the child with Mary, his mother, they knelt down and worshipped him. Opening their treasures they presented to him gifts of gold, frankincense and myrrh. But being warned in a dream not to return to Herod, they went back to their own country by another way.

THE BOY JESUS ASKS QUESTIONS

After Joseph and Mary had done all that the law commanded, they returned to Galilee to their own town of Nazareth. And the boy Jesus grew and became strong in body and mind. And the blessing of God was upon him.

Now his parents went every year to Jerusalem to the Feast of the Passover, and when he was twelve years old they went up as usual. After they had stayed the full number of days and were returning, the boy Jesus remained behind in Jerusalem. His parents did not know this; but, supposing him to be in the caravan, they travelled on for a whole day. Then they searched for him among their relatives and friends. When they did not find him, they returned to Jerusalem, still looking for him. After three days they found him in the Temple, sitting with the teachers, listening to them and asking them questions. All who heard him were amazed at his intelligence and his answers.

When his parents saw him, they were astonished; and his mother said to him, "Son, why have you treated us like this? Your father and I have been anxiously looking for you." He said to them, "Why did you look for me? Did you not know that I must be in my Father's house?" But they did not understand what he meant.

Then he went down with them and came to Nazareth; and he was obedient to them; but his mother kept all these sayings in her heart. And Jesus grew in wisdom and body and in favor with God and man.

JOHN THE BAPTIST TELLS OF JESUS' WORK

"O Little Town of Bethlehem"
Painted by W. L. Taylor

While Pontius Pilate was governor of Judea and Herod was ruler of Galilee, a man named John, the son of Zachariah, lived in the desert country. And God commanded him and he went into all the country around the river Jordan calling upon men to be baptized to show that they were sorry for their sins and wished to be forgiven. Those who were truly sorry for their sins, he baptized in the river Jordan.

This John wore a garment of camel's hair and a leather belt, and his food was locusts and wild honey.

Then the people of Jerusalem and all Judea and the country around the Jordan began to go out to him to confess their sins and to be baptized by him in the Jordan.

To the crowds that went out to be baptized by him he said, "You children of vipers! Who warned you to flee from the coming wrath? Bear fruits, then, that will prove that you are truly sorry for what you have done. Do not say to yourselves, 'We are children of Abraham'; for I tell you, God can raise up children for Abraham from these stones. Already the axe lies at the root of the trees. Every tree, therefore, that does not bear good fruit is cut down and thrown into the fire."

The crowds kept asking him, "What must we do?" He answered them, "Let him who has two coats share with him who has none; and let him who has food do the same."

When the tax-gatherers came to be baptized, they said to him, "Teacher, what must we do?" He said to them, "Do not take more from any one than rightfully belongs to you." Soldiers also asked him, "And what must we do?" To them he said, "Do not take money from anybody by force, nor make false charges, but be content with your wages."

Now as the people were wondering whether John might possibly be the Christ, John said to them all, "I indeed baptize you with water; but One is coming mightier than I, whose shoe-strings I am not worthy to untie. He will baptize you with the Holy Spirit and with fire. His fan is in his hand, and he will thoroughly cleanse his threshing-floor, and will gather the wheat into his storehouse; but the chaff he will burn up with fire that cannot be put out." In this way, and with many other earnest words, he told the good news to the people.

JESUS DECIDES HOW HE WILL DO HIS WORK

At this time Jesus came from Nazareth in Galilee and was baptized by John in the Jordan. And as he was coming up from the water, he saw the heavens opening and the Spirit, like a dove, coming down upon him. And a voice from heaven said,

"Thou art my beloved Son,
In thee I am well pleased."

Then Jesus was led by the Spirit into the wilderness to be tempted by the devil. And after he had fasted forty days and forty nights he was hungry. Then the tempter came and said to him, "If you are the Son of God, command these stones to become bread." But Jesus answered, "It is written,

"'Man is not to live on bread alone,
But on every word that comes from God.'"

Then the devil took him to the holy city and, setting him on the highest point of the Temple, said to him, "If you are the Son of God, throw yourself down; for it is written,

"'He will give his angels charge of you,
And on their hands they will bear you up,
Lest you strike your foot against a stone.'"

Jesus said to him, "It is also written,

"'You shall not tempt the Lord your God.'"

Once more the devil took him to a high mountain and showed him all the kingdoms of the world and their glory, and he said to him, "All these things I will give you if you will fall down and worship me." Jesus said to him, "Away with you, Satan! for it is written,

"'You shall worship the Lord your God,
And him only shall you serve.'"

JESUS WINS DEVOTED FRIENDS

Herod seized John the Baptist and bound him, and put him in prison because of Herodias, his brother Philip's wife, for John said to him, "It is not right for you to have her." And although Herod wanted to put him to death, he was afraid of the people, for they believed John to be a prophet.

Now after John was put in prison, Jesus came into Galilee, preaching God's good news: "The time has come; repent of your sins and believe in the good news, for the kingdom of God is at hand."

Leaving Nazareth, Jesus went to live in Capernaum, which is on the Sea of Galilee. As he was passing along the shore of the Sea of Galilee, he saw Simon and Andrew his brother casting their nets into the sea, for they were fishermen. Jesus said to them, "Come with me, and I will make you fishers of men." And they at once left their nets and followed him. And going a little farther on, he saw James, the son of Zebedee, with John his brother, who were in their boat mending their nets. He called them, and they at once left their father, Zebedee, in the boat with the hired men, and went with him.

Then Jesus found Philip and said to him, "Come with me." Now Philip was from Bethsaida, the home of Andrew and Peter. Philip, finding Nathanael, said to him, "We have found him of whom Moses in the law and also the prophets wrote: Jesus of Nazareth, the son of Joseph." But

Nathanael said to him, "Can anything good come out of Nazareth?" Philip replied, "Come and see."

Jesus saw Nathanael coming to him and said to him, "Here is a true Israelite, in whom there is no deceit." Nathanael said to him, "How do you know me?" Jesus answered, "Before Philip called you, when you were under the fig-tree, I saw you." Nathanael answered him, "Rabbi, you are the Son of God, you are the King of Israel." Jesus replied, "Do you believe because I said to you, 'I saw you under the fig-tree'? You shall see greater things than these!"

Christ and the Fishermen
Painted by E. Zimmerman

THE WEDDING AT CANA

Two days later there was a wedding at Cana in Galilee; and the mother of Jesus was there. Jesus and his disciples had also been invited. When the wine had all been used, Jesus' mother said to him, "They have no wine." Jesus answered, "What is that to me? My time has not yet come." His mother said to the servants, "Do whatever he tells you." Six stone water-jars (such as the Jews used in washing) were there; each jar would hold about twenty gallons. Jesus said, "Fill up the jars with water." So they filled them to the brim. Then Jesus said, "Pour some out, and take it to the one in charge of the feast." And they did so. When the one in charge of the feast tasted the water which had become wine, he did not know where it came from (although the servants who had poured out the water knew), so he called the bridegroom and said to him, "Every one serves the good wine first, and the wine that is not so good after men have drunk freely; but you have kept the good wine until now." This the first of his wonderful signs, showing his power, Jesus did at Cana in Galilee; and his disciples believed in him.

THE HEALING OF THE TEN LEPERS

On their way to Jerusalem, Jesus and his disciples passed through Samaria and Galilee. When he entered a certain village, he was met by ten lepers, who cried to him from a distance, "Jesus, Master, have pity on us." When Jesus saw them he said to them, "Go, and show yourselves to the priests." And as they went, they were made clean.

One of them, when he saw that he was healed, turned back, and with a loud voice praised God; and he fell down at the feet of Jesus with his face to the ground and thanked him; and this man was a Samaritan. Jesus said to him, "Were not ten made clean? Where are the other nine? Was there no one who returned to give praise to God except this stranger?" And Jesus said to him, "Arise, and go on your way, your faith has made you well."

HEALING THE MAN AT THE POOL

There was a festival of the Jews in Jerusalem, and Jesus went there. In Jerusalem there is a pool beside the sheep gate. In Hebrew it is called, Bethesda. It has five porches, and a crowd of people who were sick, blind, lame or helpless were lying there, waiting for the water to move, for an angel of the Lord went down into the pool at certain times and stirred the water; and the first person who stepped into the water after it was stirred was made well, no matter what disease he had.

One man was there who had been ill for thirty-eight years. Jesus saw him lying there, and knew that he had been ill for a long time; and he said to him, "Do you want to be made well?" The sick man answered, "Sir, I have no one to put me in the pool when the water is stirred, and while I am getting in, some one else steps in before me." Jesus said to him, "Arise, take up your bed, and walk." Immediately the man was made well, and he took up his bed and walked.

JESUS TALKS WITH A SAMARITAN WOMAN

When Jesus left Judea and went back into Galilee, he had to pass through Samaria; and he came to a city of Samaria called Sychar, near the piece of ground that Jacob gave his son Joseph. Now Jacob's well was there. Jesus, therefore, being wearied by the journey, sat down by the well. It was about noon and a woman of Samaria came to draw water. Jesus said to her, "Give me a drink." (For his disciples had gone away into the city to buy food.)

The Samaritan woman said to him, "How is it that you, a Jew, ask a drink of me who am a Samaritan?" for the Jews have nothing to do with Samaritans. Jesus answered her, "If you knew the gift of God and who it is who says to you, 'Give me a drink,' you would have asked him and he would have given you living water." The woman said to him, "Sir, you have nothing with which to draw and the well is deep; where then do you get that living water? Are you greater than our father Jacob who gave us the well and himself drank from it, together with his children and his cattle?" Jesus answered her, "Whoever drinks of this water will thirst again; but whoever drinks of the water that I will give shall never thirst. The water that I give him will become in him a well of water springing up into eternal life." The woman said to him, "Sir, give me this water, that I may not thirst again nor have to come here to draw."

Jesus said to her, "Go, call your husband, then come back here." The woman answered, "I have no husband." Jesus said to her, "You are right in saying, 'I have no husband,' for you have had five husbands, and he whom you now have is not your husband; in saying that, you spoke the truth."

The woman said to him, "Sir, I see that you are a prophet. Our fathers worshipped in this mountain; and you Jews say that Jerusalem is the place where men ought to worship." Jesus said to her, "Woman, believe me, the time will come when you will worship the Father neither on this mountain nor at Jerusalem. The time is coming, yes, has already come, when the true worshippers will worship the Father in spirit and in truth; for such worshippers the Father seeks. God is a spirit, and they who worship him must worship him in spirit and in truth." The woman said to him, "I know that the Messiah (which means Christ) is coming. When he comes he will explain all things to us." Jesus said to her, "I who am talking to you am he."

At this point the disciples came up and were astonished that he was talking with a woman; but none of them said, "What do you want?" or, "Why are you talking to her?"

Then the woman left her water-pot and going into the city said to the men, "Come, see a man who told me all that I ever did. Is not this the Messiah?" And they set out from the town on their way to him.

Meanwhile Jesus' disciples urged him, saying, "Master, take some food"; but he said to them, "I have food to eat of which you know not."

So they said to one another, "Has any one brought him something to eat?" Jesus said to them, "My food is to do the will of him who sent me and to carry out his work. Do not say, 'Four months and then comes the harvest'; I say to you, lift up your eyes and see these fields white for the harvest! Already the reaper is receiving his wages and gathering in a crop for eternal life, that the sower and reaper may rejoice together. For here the proverb holds true, 'One sows and another reaps.' I sent you to reap a harvest for which you had not toiled; other men have toiled and you are sharing the results of their toil."

Because of the words of the woman who had said, "He told me everything that I ever did," many Samaritans from the town believed in Jesus; and when they came to him, they begged him to stay with them. And he stayed there two days, and many more believed because of what he himself said. To the woman they said, "Now we believe, not because of your words but because we have heard for ourselves and know that this is indeed the Saviour of the world."

GIVING LIFE TO A WIDOW'S SON

Jesus went to a town called Nain; and his disciples went with him followed by a large crowd. Just as Jesus came to the gate of the town, he saw one who was dead being carried out. He was the only son of his mother who was a widow. Many people of the town were with her.

When Jesus saw her, he had sympathy for her and said to her, "Do not weep." And he came and touched the coffin, and those who carried it stood still. Jesus said: "Young man, I say to you, arise." And he who had been dead sat up and began to speak. And Jesus gave him back to his mother. And all the people were filled with fear and praised God, saying, "A great prophet has appeared among us, and God has visited his people." And the story of what Jesus had done was told in all of Judea and the country around there.

JESUS HEALS THE SICK

Jesus and his disciples entered Capernaum; and on the next Sabbath he went into the synagogue and began to teach. And the people were astonished at his teaching, for he taught them as one who had authority, and not as the scribes.

In their synagogue that day was a man under the power of an unclean spirit, who cried out, "What have you to do with us, Jesus of Nazareth? Have you come to destroy us? I know you are God's Holy One." But Jesus reproved the unclean spirit, saying, "Be still, and come out of him." Then the unclean spirit, after convulsing the man, came out of him with a loud cry. The people were so astonished that they began to ask one another, "What is this? Is it a new teaching? With authority he commands even the unclean spirits and they obey him." So the news about Jesus spread at once in every direction all through the country about Galilee.

After leaving the synagogue they went straight to the house of Simon and Andrew; and James and John went with them. The mother of Simon's wife was ill in bed with a fever; so at once they told Jesus about her. He went to her and, taking her by the hand, lifted her up. Then the fever left her, and she began to wait upon them.

In the evening, after the sun had set, they brought to him all who were sick or under the control of evil spirits, until all the people of the city were gathered at the door. He healed many who were sick with different kinds of diseases, and cast out many evil spirits, but would not let them speak, because they knew who he was.

One day a leper came to him and on bended knees begged him: "If you will, you can make me clean." Feeling sorry for him, Jesus stretched out his hand and touched him, and said, "I will; be cleansed!" At once the leprosy left him and he was cleansed. Then Jesus, after strictly warning him, sent him away with the command, "See that you do not say a word to any one, but go, show yourself to the priest and offer what Moses commanded as proof to them that you are clean." But the man went away and began to tell every one about it, so that Jesus could no longer enter a city openly, but had to stay outside in lonely places; and people from everywhere came to him.

JESUS CURES A MAN WHO CANNOT WALK

When Jesus entered Capernaum again, after some days, it was reported that he was at home, and so many people gathered about him that there was no longer room for them, not even at the door. While Jesus was preaching to them, four men came, carrying a man who was paralyzed and could not move. As they could not get near to Jesus on account of the crowd, they tore up the roof over his head. When they had made a hole, they let down the bed on which the man who could not move was lying. Seeing their faith, Jesus said to him, "Son, your sins are forgiven." But some of the scribes sitting there said to themselves, "Why should this man say such a thing? He is blaspheming! Who can forgive sins except God alone?"

Knowing at once what they were saying, Jesus said to them, "Why do you say these things to yourselves? Which is easier: to say to the man who cannot move, 'Your sins are forgiven'; or to say, 'Get up, take your bed, and walk'? But that you may know that the Son of Man has the power on earth to forgive sins" (he said to the man who could not walk) "I say to you, Rise, take up your bed, and go to your home." Then the man rose and at once took up his bed and went out in the presence of them all, so that they were all filled with wonder and praised God, saying, "We have never seen anything like this."

JESUS MAKES EVEN WRONG-DOERS HIS FRIENDS

Then Jesus went out again beside the Sea of Galilee; and all the crowd came to him, and he taught them. As he passed along he saw Levi, the son of Alphæus, sitting at the house where taxes were collected, and he said to him, "Come with me." So Levi arose and followed him.

Now while Jesus was eating dinner in Levi's house, many tax-gatherers and sinners sat down with Jesus and his disciples. The scribes and Pharisees, seeing this, said to his disciples, "Does he eat with tax-gatherers and sinners?" On hearing this, Jesus said to them, "Not those who are well, but those who are sick have need of a physician. I did not come to call the righteous but sinners to repentance."

At another time one of the Pharisees invited Jesus to dine with him. So Jesus entered the Pharisee's house and sat down at the table. In the town was a wicked woman who, when she heard that Jesus was sitting at the table in the Pharisee's house, brought an alabaster jar of perfume. She stood behind at his feet, weeping; and as her tears began to wet his feet, she wiped them with her hair. And she tenderly kissed his feet and poured the perfume over them.

When the Pharisee who had invited him saw it, he said to himself, "If this man were a prophet, he would know about the woman who is touching him, for she is a sinner."

Jesus answered him, "Simon, I have a word to say to you." He replied, "Say it, Master." "There were two men who owed a certain money-lender some silver: one owed him five hundred silver pieces and the other fifty. Neither of them was able to pay anything; so he forgave them both. Now which of them will love him the more?" Simon answered, "I suppose the man who owed the most." Jesus said to him, "You have decided rightly."

Turning to the woman, Jesus said to Simon, "You see this woman? When I came into your house, you gave me no water for my feet; but she has wet my feet with her tears and wiped them with her hair. You gave me no kiss, but she, since I came in, has not ceased tenderly to kiss my feet. You did not pour any oil on my head, but she has poured perfume on my feet. Therefore, I say to you, her sins, though they be many, are forgiven, for she has loved much. He to whom little is forgiven, loves little."

Then Jesus said to her, "Your sins are forgiven." And the other guests began to say to themselves, "Who is this man who even forgives sins?" But he said to the woman, "Your faith has saved you; go and be at peace."

JESUS FINDS JOY IN ALL HIS WORK

Once when John's disciples and the Pharisees were keeping a fast, people came to Jesus and said, "Why do the disciples of John and the disciples of the Pharisees fast, but your disciples do not fast?"

Jesus said to them, "Can guests fast at a wedding while the bridegroom is with them? As long as they have the bridegroom with them they cannot fast. But the time will come when the bridegroom is taken away from them; then they will fast. No one sews a piece of new cloth on an old coat; otherwise the patch breaks away from it, the new from the old, and the tear is made worse. No man pours new wine into old wine-skins; otherwise the new wine bursts the skins, and both the wine and the wine-skins are lost. Instead new wine is poured into fresh wine-skins."

One Sabbath Jesus was walking through the grain-fields; and his disciples, as they made their way through, began to pull off the heads of the grain. The Pharisees said to him, "Sir, why are they doing things that on the Sabbath are unlawful?" He said to them, "Have you never read what David did when he and his followers were in need and hungry? how he went into the house of God, when Abiathar was high priest, and ate the holy bread which only the priests are allowed to eat, and gave it also to those who were with him?"

And Jesus said to them, "The Sabbath was made for man, and not man for the Sabbath; so that the Son of Man is master even of the Sabbath."

At another time he went into a synagogue. A man was there whose hand was shrivelled. And they watched Jesus to see whether he would heal him on the Sabbath day, that they might bring a charge against him. Jesus said to the man whose hand was shrivelled, "Rise and come forward."

Then he said to them, "Is it lawful on the Sabbath day to do good or to do harm? To save life or to kill? Who of you, if he has but one sheep and it falls into a hole on the Sabbath, will not take hold of it and lift it out? Is not a man of much greater value than a sheep?" But they did not answer. Then looking around upon them with sorrow and indignation because they had no sympathy, he said to the man, "Stretch out your hand." He stretched it out, and his hand was entirely cured. But the Pharisees went out and at once began to plot with the Herodians against him, how they might put him out of the way.

JESUS CALMS THE STORM

Jesus withdrew to the sea with his disciples, and a crowd followed him from Galilee. Also from Judea, Jerusalem, Idumea the other side of the Jordan, and from the country about Tyre and Sidon a great number, having heard what he was doing, came to him. So he told his disciples to have a small boat ready for him to keep him from being crushed by the crowd; for he had healed so many that all who were sick and in trouble were pressing forward to touch him. And whenever those who had evil spirits saw him, they fell down before him and cried, "You are the Son of God." But again and again he commanded them not to tell who he was.

In the evening Jesus said to his disciples, "Let us cross to the other side." So, leaving the crowd, they took him with them in the boat just as he was; and there were other boats with his. A heavy wind-storm arose and the waves began to break into the boat so that it was filling; but Jesus was in the stern asleep on the cushion. So they woke him and said to him, "Master, is it nothing to you that we are lost?" And he awoke and reproved the wind, and said to the sea, "Peace, be still!" And immediately the wind ceased and the sea was calm; and he said to them, "Why are you afraid? Why do you not have faith?" But they were filled with wonder and said to one another, "Who then is he, that even the wind and the sea obey him?"

JESUS HEALS A LITTLE GIRL

Raising the Daughter of Jairus
Painted by Léon Gérôme

When Jesus again crossed the Sea of Galilee in a boat to the other side, a large crowd had gathered to meet him; so he stayed beside the sea. One of the rulers of the synagogue, Jairus by name, came up, and, on seeing Jesus, fell at his feet and earnestly begged him, saying, "My little daughter is dying; come, I beg of you, and place your hands on her that she may be cured and live." So Jesus went with him, and a great crowd followed and pressed about him.

In the crowd was a woman who had suffered from hemorrhage for twelve years and had been treated by many physicians, spending all that she had, yet was none the better, but rather had grown worse. Having heard about Jesus, she came up behind him in the crowd and touched his robe, for she said to herself, "If I can but touch his garments, I shall be cured."

Immediately the hemorrhage stopped, and she knew that she was cured of her disease. Jesus, knowing at once that healing power had gone from him, turned around in the crowd and said, "Who touched my garments?" His disciples said to him, "You see the crowd pressing around you, and yet do you ask, 'Who touched me?'" But still he looked for her who had done this, until the woman, frightened and trembling, knowing what had happened to her, came forward and fell down before him and told him the truth. He said to her, "Daughter, your faith has cured you. Go and live in peace, and be healed of your disease."

While Jesus was still speaking, messengers came from the house of the ruler of the synagogue, saying, "Your daughter is dead. Why trouble the Master further?" But Jesus, overhearing the message, said to the ruler of the synagogue, "Have no fear, only trust."

Jesus would allow no one to go with him except Peter and James and John the brother of James. When they came to the house of the ruler of the synagogue, he found a crowd of people weeping aloud and wailing. Entering, Jesus said to them, "Why are you making an uproar and weeping? The child is not dead, but asleep." And they laughed at him scornfully. But he sent them out and took the father and mother of the child and those who were with him into the room where she was. Then, taking her by the hand, he said to her, "Talitha koumi," which means, "Little girl, arise." To the astonishment of all, the little girl (who was twelve years of age) got up at once and walked about. But Jesus charged them strictly to let no one know of this, and told them to give the little girl something to eat.

JESUS VISITS HIS OLD HOME

Jesus went to Nazareth where he had been brought up. As was his custom, he went into the synagogue on the Sabbath, and stood up to read the lesson. And he was given the scroll of the prophet Isaiah, and on unrolling it he found the place where it is written:

"The Spirit of the Lord is upon me,
For he has called me to preach good news to the poor,
He has sent me to proclaim release to captives,
And recovery of sight to the blind,
To set free those who have been crushed by cruelty,
To proclaim the year when the Lord will show favor."

Then, having rolled up the scroll, he handed it back to the attendant and sat down. The eyes of all in the synagogue were fixed on him, and he said to them, "To-day what is here written is fulfilled in your sight."

As he went on to teach in the synagogue, many who heard him were astonished and said: "Where did he get these teachings? What is this wisdom which has been given him? and what are these wonderful acts of healing that he does? Is he not the carpenter, the son of Mary and the brother of James and Joses and Judas and Simon? Are not his sisters living here among us?" And they would not believe in him. Jesus said to them, "A prophet is not without honor except in his own country and among his relatives and in his own home."

In that place he could do no wonderful acts except laying his hands on a few sick people and healing them; and he was astonished at their lack of faith. So he went about the near-by villages teaching.

JESUS CALLS TOGETHER HIS FRIENDS AND HELPERS

Jesus went up on the hillside near Capernaum and called to him the men whom he wanted, and they came to him. He appointed twelve to be with him and to go out to preach, with power to cast out evil spirits. These were the twelve disciples: Simon to whom he gave also the name Peter, James the son of Zebedee and John his brother, whom he called "Sons of Thunder," Andrew, Philip, Bartholomew, Matthew, Thomas, James the son of Alphæus, Thaddeus, Simon the Zealot, and Judas Iscariot, who at last betrayed him.

Then Jesus went into a house and the crowd gathered again so that it was impossible even to eat a meal. When his relatives heard of this, they set out to get hold of him, for they said, "He is out of his mind." Standing outside, his mother and his brothers sent word to him to come out to them. He was in the midst of a crowd seated about him when some one said to him, "Here are your mother and your brothers and sisters outside hunting for you." He answered, "Who are my mother and my brothers?" Then looking around at those who sat in a circle about him, he said, "Here are my mother and my brothers. Whoever does the will of God is my brother and sister and mother."

Christ with Mary and Martha
Painted by H. Siemiradzki

WHAT JESUS ASKS OF HIS FRIENDS AND HELPERS

Once Jesus entered a certain village where a woman named Martha invited him to her house. She had a sister named Mary who seated herself at Jesus' feet and listened to his words. But Martha was worried by her desire to wait on him, and came and said to him, "Lord, do you not care that my sister has left me to do all the work alone? Tell her to help me." But Jesus said to her, "Martha, Martha, you are anxious and troubled about many things, but few things are necessary, really only one. Mary has chosen the better part, which shall not be taken away from her."

Once when Jesus and his disciples were walking along the road, some one said to him, "I will follow you wherever you go." Jesus said to him, "The foxes have holes and the wild birds their nests, but the Son of Man has no place to lay his head." He said to another, "Follow me"; but the man said, "Let me first go and bury my father." Jesus said to him, "Let the dead bury their dead, but you go and tell about the Kingdom of God." Still another said, "I will follow you, Lord, but let me first say good-by to my people at home." Jesus said to him, "No one who looks back after having put his hand to the plough is fit for the Kingdom of God."

Once, when crowds were following him, he turned and said to them, "If any one who comes to me is not willing to give up his father and mother and wife and children and brothers and sisters, yes, and his very life, he cannot be my disciple. Whoever does not carry his own cross, as he follows me, cannot be my disciple.

"Who of you, if he wishes to build a tower, does not first sit down and count the cost, to see whether he has money enough to finish it? Otherwise, if he has laid the foundation and is unable to finish the building, all who see it make fun of him and say, 'This man began to build but could not finish!'"

THE WAY TO LEARN FROM JESUS

Jesus taught his disciples, saying, "Do not think that I came to set aside the old law or the teachings of the prophets. I did not come to set them aside but to complete them.

"Come to me, all you who labor and are heavily burdened, and I will give you rest. Take my yoke upon you and learn of me, for I am kind and sympathetic, and you will find rest, for my yoke is easy and my burden light.

"He who hears these words of mine and keeps them in mind will be like a wise man who built his house upon the rock. The rain fell, the floods came, the winds blew and beat upon that house; yet it did not fall, for its foundation was built on the rock.

"He who hears these words of mine but does not keep them in mind will be like a foolish man who built his house upon sand. The rain fell, the floods came, the winds blew and beat upon that house, and it fell, and great was its downfall."

The Sower
Painted by Herbert Moore

At another time when Jesus was teaching beside the lake, such a large crowd gathered about him that he entered a boat and sat in it, while the crowd stayed on the shore. He then taught them many truths by means of stories, and said, "Listen to me. The sower went out to sow, and as he sowed, some of the seed fell on the road where birds came and ate it up. Some fell on rocky ground, where it had but little soil, and because there was no depth of earth it began to grow at once; but when the sun rose, it was scorched with the heat, and having no root it withered away. Some of the seed fell among thorns, and the thorns grew up and choked it so that it bore nothing. Other seed fell on good soil, and sprouted and grew and bore at the rate of thirty, sixty, and a hundredfold." And he said to them, "Let him who has ears to hear, remember this."

When Jesus was alone, those who were with him and the twelve disciples asked him what this story meant. He said to them, "Do you not see the meaning of this? How then will you understand all my other stories? The sower sows his teaching. The teaching that is sown along the road is like some people who hear but immediately Satan comes and takes away the teaching which has been sown in them.

"And the seed that has been sown on rocky places, is like those people who hear the teaching and receive it at once with joy, but it takes no root in them and they remember it only for a short time.

"The seed sown among thorns is like those who hear the teaching but the pleasures of this life, the desire for wealth and other things makes them forget the teaching, and so it bears no fruit.

"But the seed sown on good soil is like those people who hear the teaching and remember it, and it bears fruit; some thirty, some sixty, and some a hundredfold.

"Can a blind man guide a blind man? Will not both fall into a ditch? A disciple is not above his teacher; but every pupil when perfectly trained will be like his teacher.

"No good tree bears rotten fruit; neither does a rotten tree bear good fruit; for each tree is known by its own fruit. Figs are not gathered from thorns, nor grapes picked from a bramble-bush. From the good stored in his heart the good man brings forth goodness, but the evil man from his evil store brings forth evil; for the mouth speaks that with which the heart is filled.

"You are the light of the world. A city on a hill cannot be hidden. One does not light a candle to put it under a basket but on a stand, where it shall give light to all who are in the house. So let your light shine before men that they may see your good deeds and praise your heavenly Father."

THE REWARDS FOR FOLLOWING JESUS' TEACHINGS

James and John, the sons of Zebedee, once came to Jesus and said, "Master, we want you to do for us what we shall ask." So he said, "What do you want me to do for you?" They answered, "When you enter into your kingly glory, let one of us sit on your right hand and one on your left." But Jesus said to them, "You do not know what you are asking. Can you drink the cup of woe that I am to drink, or be baptized with the baptism of suffering with which I am to be baptized?" They said to him, "We can." Jesus said, "You will drink the cup that I am to drink and be baptized with my baptism, but to sit on my right hand and on my left is not mine to give; for it is for those for whom it has been prepared."

When the ten other disciples heard this request, they were at first angry with James and John, but Jesus called them to him and said, "You know that those who are rulers in foreign countries lord it over those under them, and their great men have authority over them; but it is not so among you. Whoever wishes to be great among you must serve you, and whoever wishes to be first among you must be ready to be the servant of all. For I did not come to be served but to be of service to others, and to give my life so as to secure freedom for many."

Then he took a little child and set him in their midst. And taking him in his arms, he said to them, "Whoever receives a little child like this, in my name, receives me; and whoever receives me receives not only me, but God who sent me. Whoever gives one of these little ones even a cup of cold water to drink because he is my disciple will, I tell you, not lose his reward.

"When the Son of Man comes in his glory and with him all the angels, he will sit upon his glorious throne, and all people shall be gathered before him. And he will separate them one from another as a shepherd separates the sheep from the goats, placing the sheep on his right hand and the goats on his left.

"Then the King will say to those on his right, 'Come, you whom my Father has blessed, enter into possession of the kingdom prepared for you since the creation of the world; for I was hungry and you gave me food, I was thirsty and you gave me drink, I was a stranger and you welcomed me, I was naked and you clothed me, I was sick and you cared for me, I was in prison and you came to me.'

"Then the upright will answer him, 'Lord, when did we see you hungry and feed you? Or thirsty and give you drink? When did we see you a stranger and welcome you? Or naked and clothe you? Or when did we see you sick or in prison and come to you?' The King will answer them, 'Truly, I say to you, as you have done it even to the least of these my brothers, you have done it to me.'"

GOD'S LOVE EVEN FOR SINNERS

Seeking the Lost Sheep
Painted by Herbert Moore

Because tax-gathers and sinners kept coming to Jesus to hear him, the Pharisees and scribes complained, "This man welcomes sinners and even eats with them!" So he told them this story: "What man of you, if he has a hundred sheep and loses one, does not leave the ninety-nine in the wilderness and go and hunt for the lost sheep until he finds it? And when he has found it, he joyfully puts it on his shoulders and when he gets home calls together his friends and says, 'Rejoice with me, for I have found the sheep that I lost.' So, I tell you, there will be more joy in heaven over one sinner who is truly sorry and promises to do right than over ninety-nine upright men who have no need to do so.

"Or which one of you women, if she has ten silver coins but has lost one, does not light a lamp, sweep the house thoroughly, and search carefully until she finds it? After finding it she calls together her friends and neighbors and says, 'Rejoice with me, for I have found the coin that I lost.' So, I tell you, there is rejoicing among the angels of God over one sinner who is truly sorry and promises to do right."

Jesus said, "There was a man who had two sons. The younger said to his father, 'Father, give me the part of your property that belongs to me.' So the Father divided his property between his two sons. A few days later, the younger son got together all that he had and went into a distant country where he wasted his money in reckless living. After he had spent it all, there was a great famine in the land, and he began to be in want. So he agreed to work for a man of that country, who sent him into his fields to feed swine; and he was ready to eat even the pods that the swine were eating, for no one gave him food. But when he came to himself he said, 'How many of my father's hired servants have more than enough to eat while I die here of hunger! I will go to my father and say, 'Father, I have sinned against God and against you. I am no longer worthy to be called your son. Treat me as one of your hired servants.'

The Prodigal Son
Painted by Herbert Moore

"So he went to his father. But while he was still a long way off, his father saw him and felt pity for him, and ran and threw his arms about his neck and tenderly kissed him. Then his son said to him, 'Father, I have sinned against God and against you. I am no longer worthy to be called your son.' But the father said to his servants, 'Quick, bring a coat, the best, and put it on him and put a ring on his finger and sandals on his feet. And bring the fatted calf, kill it, and let us eat and be merry; for this son of mine was dead but has come back to life, he was lost but has been found.' So they began to make merry.

"Now the elder son was out in the fields, and as he came near the house he heard music and dancing. And he called one of the servants and asked what all this meant. The servant said to him, 'Your brother has come, and your father has killed the fatted calf because he has him back safe and sound.' And he was angry and would not go in so his father came out to reason with him, but he answered, 'See all these many years I have worked for you and never disobeyed one of your commands, yet you never gave me so much as a young goat that I might have a feast with my friends. But now when this son of yours comes, who has wasted your money with wicked women, you kill the fatted calf for him!' His father answered, 'Son, you are with me always and all that I have is yours; but it was right to make merry and rejoice because of your brother, for he was dead but has come back to life, he was lost but has been found.'"

GOD'S READINESS TO ANSWER PRAYER

Jesus said: "Ask and you will receive, seek and you will find, knock and the door will be opened to you; for every one who asks receives, and he who seeks finds, and to him who knocks the door will be opened.

"What man is there among you, who if his son asks him for a loaf of bread, will give him a stone? Or if he asks for a fish, will give him a snake? Then if you, evil as you are, know how to give good gifts to your children, how much more will your Father in heaven give good things to those who ask him.

"Also I tell you: if two of you on earth agree about that for which you ask, it will be granted to you by my Father in heaven. For where two or three have gathered together in my name, I am there with them."

HOW TO PRAY

The apostles said to Jesus, "Help us to have greater faith." But he said, "If you had faith even the size of a mustard-seed and said to this mulberry-tree, 'Be rooted up and be planted in the sea,' it would obey you."

Again he said to them, "Have faith in God. Indeed I tell you that if any one will say to this hill, 'Throw yourself into the sea,' and has no doubt in his heart but believes that what he says will come to pass, it shall be done for him. Therefore, I say to you, believe that whatever you ask for in prayer you have received, and it shall be yours. And whenever you stand up to pray, if any one has done wrong to you, forgive him, that your Father in heaven may also forgive you your wrong-doing."

When Jesus was praying at a certain place and had finished, one of his disciples said to him, "Lord, teach us to pray as John taught his disciples." So he said to them, "When you pray, say: 'Our Father who art in heaven, hallowed be thy name, thy kingdom come, thy will be done on earth as it is in heaven. Give us this day our daily bread, and forgive us our wrong-doings as we have forgiven those who have wronged us. Help us to resist temptation and deliver us from evil.'

"When you pray, do not do as the hypocrites who like to stand and pray in the synagogues and on the corners of the main streets so as to be seen by men. I tell you, they have received their full reward! But when you pray, go into your room, close the door, and pray to your Father who is found in secret, and your Father who sees what is done in secret will give you your reward.

"When you pray do not say the same things over and over as do the heathen, who believe that they will be heard because of their many words. Do not do as they do. Your Father knows what things you need before you ask him."

WHY WE SHOULD TRUST GOD

"Do not be anxious about your life, what you shall eat, or what you shall wear. Does not life mean more than food, and the body more than clothing? Consider how the birds of the air neither sow nor reap nor gather into barns, and yet your heavenly Father feeds them. Are you not worth far more than they? Are not two sparrows sold for a penny? Yet not one of them falls to the ground without your Father's knowledge. As for you, the very hairs of your head are numbered. Then have no fear, for you are worth far more than the sparrows.

"Which of you by being anxious can add a single foot to his height? And why be anxious about what you wear? Consider the lilies of the field, how they grow! They neither toil nor spin, and yet I tell you, not even Solomon in all his splendor was clothed like one of these. Now if God so clothes the grass of the field which is alive to-day but to-morrow is thrown into the oven, is it not far more certain that he will clothe you, O men of little faith?

"Do not be anxious then and say, 'What shall we eat or what shall we drink or with what shall we be clothed?' For all these things the heathen are seeking, but your heavenly Father knows that you need all these things. Seek first to do right as he would have you do, and all these other things will be given to you. Therefore, do not be anxious about to-morrow, for to-morrow will take care of itself."

THE KINGDOM OF GOD

Once when little children were brought to Jesus that he might touch them, the disciples found fault with those who brought them. When Jesus saw it, he was displeased and said to his disciples, "Allow the little children to come to me; and do not forbid them, for of such as these is the Kingdom of God. I tell you, whoever will not accept the Kingdom of God like a little child, will never enter it." Then he took the children in his arms, laid his hands on them, and lovingly blessed them.

One Sabbath day Jesus went to dine at the house of a leading Pharisee. One of the guests said to him, "Fortunate is he who will have a share in the Kingdom of God."

But Jesus said to him, "A man once gave a great dinner and invited many guests. At dinner-time he sent out his servant to say to those who had been invited, 'Come, for everything is now ready.' But all of them began to make excuses. The first said, 'I have bought a field and must go and look at it. I must ask you to excuse me.' Another said, 'I have bought five yoke of oxen and am on my way to try them. I must ask you to excuse me.' Another said, 'I have just married and so I cannot come.'

"The servant returned and reported these answers to his master. Then the master of the house was angry and said to his servant, 'Go out at once into the streets and alleys of the city, and bring in the poor, the crippled, the blind, and the lame.' When the servant reported, 'Sir, your order has been carried out, yet there is still room,' the master said to him, 'Go out into the highways and the country lanes and compel people to come, so that my house may be filled; for I tell you, that not one of those who were first invited shall taste of my dinner.'"

Once when Jesus was walking along the road, a man ran up and knelt before him and asked, "Good Master, what must I do that I may be sure of eternal life?" Jesus said to him, "Why do you call me good? No one is good except one only: God. You know the commandments: 'Do not commit adultery. Do not murder. Do not steal. Do not bear false witness. Do not be dishonest. Honor your father and mother.'" He said to him, "Master, I have kept all these commands from my youth." Looking upon him, Jesus loved him and said, "One thing you lack; go, sell all that you have and give to the poor, and you will have treasure in heaven. Then come with me." But when the man heard this, he looked sad, and he went away in sorrow, for he had great wealth. Then Jesus looked around and said to his disciples, "How hard it is for those who have wealth to enter the Kingdom of God!" They were surprised at his words, but again he said, "Children, how hard it is for those who trust in wealth to enter the Kingdom of God. It is easier for a camel to go through a needle's eye than for a rich man to enter the Kingdom of God." And they were so astonished that they said,

"Then who can be saved?" Jesus looked at them and said, "With men it is impossible, but not with God, for with God everything is possible."

THE TWO GREAT COMMANDMENTS

Once a lawyer asked Jesus, "What is the most important of all the commandments?" Jesus answered, "The most important is: 'The Lord our God is one Lord; and you shall love the Lord your God with your whole heart, with your whole soul, with your whole mind and with your whole strength.'

"The second is this: 'You shall love your neighbor as yourself.' There is no other commandment greater than these."

The lawyer said to him, "Teacher, you have rightly and truly said, 'There is one God and there is none other. Also to love him, with all one's heart, and with all one's understanding, and with all one's strength, and to love one's neighbor as one loves himself is far more than all whole-burnt offerings and sacrifices.'"

When Jesus saw that the lawyer had answered wisely, he said to him, "You are not far from the Kingdom of God."

THE REWARDS OF MODESTY AND UNSELFISHNESS

Once Jesus went into the house of a leading Pharisee to dine. When he saw how the guests chose the best places, he gave them this advice: "When any one invites you to a marriage feast, do not sit down in the best place, for perhaps the host has invited some one of higher rank than yourself. Then the host will come to you and say, 'Make room for this man,' and with shame you will take the lowest place.

"Instead, when you are invited, go and sit down in the lowest place, so that when your host comes he may say to you, 'Friend, come up higher.' Then you will be honored in the sight of all your fellow guests. For every one who puts himself forward will be humbled, but he who does not put himself forward will be honored."

Then Jesus said to his host, "When you give a dinner or a supper, do not invite your friends or brothers or relatives or rich neighbors, for they will invite you in return and you be repaid. But when you give a feast, invite the poor, the crippled, the lame and the blind. Then you will be blessed. For they have no way of repaying you, and you will be rewarded when the upright rise from the dead."

Peter said to him, "But we have left everything and have followed you." Jesus answered, "I tell you, there is no one who has left home or brothers or sisters or mother or father or children or lands for my sake and for the good cause, who does not receive a hundredfold as much at this present time: houses, brothers, sisters, mothers, children, and lands, along with persecution, and in the time to come eternal life. But many who are first now will be last, and the last will be first."

HOW TO USE MONEY

A man from the crowd once said to Jesus, "Master, tell my brother to give me my share of the property that belongs to us." Jesus answered, "Man, who made me your judge to divide between you?" Then to the people he said, "Take care that you do not become greedy for wealth, for life does not consist in having more things than you need."

And he told them this story: "The land of a certain rich man bore large crops; so he thought to himself, 'What am I to do, for I have no place to store my crops.' Then he said, 'This is what I will do: I will pull down my barns and build larger ones in which I can store all my grain and goods. Then I will say to myself, Now you have plenty of things laid up for many years to come; take your ease, eat, drink and be happy.'

"But God said to him, 'Foolish man! This very night your life is required of you, and who will have all the things that you have gathered?'

So it is with the man who lays up wealth for himself instead of that which in the sight of God is the true wealth.

"Do not store up for yourselves treasures on earth where moth and rust destroy, and where thieves break in and steal; but store up for yourselves treasures in heaven where neither moth nor rust destroys, and where thieves do not break in and steal. For where your treasure is, there will your heart be also.

"No man can serve two masters: either he will hate one and love the other, or else he will be loyal to one and untrue to the other. You cannot worship both God and wealth."

Once as Jesus was sitting opposite the treasury of the Temple, he watched the way in which the people put in their money. Many rich men were putting in large sums, but a poor woman came and dropped in two small coins worth less than a penny. He called his disciples and said to them, "I tell you, this poor widow has given more than all the rest who have put their money into the treasury, for they have given out of their plenty, but she out of her poverty has given all that she has, even that which is needed to keep her alive."

DIFFERENT WAYS OF USING TALENTS

"The Kingdom of Heaven is like a man who before going abroad called his servants and gave what he had into their charge. To one he gave five talents, to another two, and to another one, each according to what he was able to do. Then the man went on his journey.

"The servant who had received five talents went at once and traded with them and gained five more talents. In the same way the one who had received two gained two more. But he who had received one talent went away and dug a hole in the ground and hid his master's money.

"After a long time the master of those servants came back and settled his accounts with them. When the one who had received five talents came bringing five more, he said, 'Master, you gave me five talents. See,

I have gained five more.' His master said to him 'Well done, good and faithful servant! You have been faithful over a few things, I will put you in charge of many things. Share your master's happiness.'

"The one who had received the two talents also came and said, 'Master, you gave me two talents. See, I have gained two more.' His master said to him, 'Well done, good and faithful servant! You have been faithful over a few things, I will put you in charge of many things. Share your master's happiness.'

"Then he who had received one talent came and said, 'Master, I knew that you are a hard man, reaping where you have not sown and gathering where you have not winnowed; so I was afraid and hid your talent in the ground. There you have what belongs to you.'

"But his master answered, 'Idle, worthless servant! You knew that I reap where I have not sown and gather where I have not winnowed. You ought therefore to have put my money in the hands of bankers and on my return I would have received it with interest. Take my talent away from him and give it to the servant who has the ten talents; for to every one who has shall more be given and he shall have plenty; but from him who has only a little, even what he has shall be taken away. Throw this worthless servant into the outer darkness where men shall wail and grind their teeth.'"

THE GOOD SAMARITAN

The Good Samaritan
Painted by Herbert Moore

Once a lawyer stood up to test Jesus with this question, "Master, what shall I do to receive eternal life?" Jesus said to him, "What is written in the law? How does it read?" He answered, "You shall love the Lord your God with all your heart, with all your soul, and with all your strength and with all your mind; also your neighbor as yourself." Jesus said to him, "You have answered correctly; do this and you will live."

But wishing to justify himself he said to Jesus, "Who is my neighbor?" Jesus answered, "A certain man going down from Jerusalem to Jericho fell in with robbers who after stripping and beating him went away, leaving him half dead. Now it happened that a certain priest was going by the same road, but when he saw the man, he passed by on the other side.

"In the same way a Levite, when he came to the place, looked at the man and passed by on the other side. But a Samaritan, travelling along, came near to where the man was, and when he saw him he was filled with pity. He came to him and bound up his wounds, pouring on them oil and wine. Then he set him on his own beast, brought him to an inn, and took care of him. The next day he took out two pieces of money and gave them to the inn-keeper, saying, 'Take care of him, and whatever more you spend I will pay you when I return.'

"Which of these three do you think proved neighbor to the man who fell in with robbers?" He said, "The man who took pity on him." Jesus said to him, "Then go and do likewise."

THE WAY TO TREAT THOSE WHO WRONG US

"If your brother wrongs you, go, show him his fault when you and he are alone. If he listens to you, you have won over your brother. Even though he wrongs you seven times in a day, if he turns to you seven times and says, 'I am sorry,' you shall forgive him."

Peter came and said to Jesus, "Master, how often am I to let my brother wrong me and forgive him? Seven times?" Jesus said to him, "I tell you, not seven times but seventy times seven.

"That is why the Kingdom of Heaven may be compared to a king who wished to settle his accounts with his servants. When he had begun to settle them, a man was brought to him who owed him ten thousand talents; but as he was unable to pay, the master ordered that he be sold, together with his wife and children and all that he had, in payment of the debt. At this the servant threw himself on the ground and begged of him, 'Master, have patience with me and I will pay you all I owe you.' Then the master out of pity for him let him go and forgave him his debt.

"But as soon as the servant went out, he found one of his fellow servants who owed him one-sixtieth of a talent, and he seized him by the throat and said, 'Pay me what you owe me.' The man fell down and begged him, 'Have patience with me and I will pay you.' But he would not and had him imprisoned until he should pay what was due.

"Now when his fellow servants saw what had been done, they were troubled and came and told their master what had happened. Then the master called him and said, 'You wicked servant! When you begged of me, I forgave you all your debt. Should you not then show the same mercy to your fellow that I showed to you?' And in anger his master turned him over to the jailers until he should pay all that was due. So also will my heavenly Father do to you unless each of you sincerely forgives his brother."

THE GOLDEN RULE

"You have heard the saying, 'You shall love your neighbor and hate your enemy.' But I say to you, love your enemies, bless those who curse you, do good to those who hate you, and pray for those who persecute you, that you may become sons of your Father in heaven; for he makes his sun to rise on the wicked and the good alike, and sends rain on both those who do right and those who do wrong. For if you love only those who love you, what reward have you earned? Do not even the tax-gatherers as much? And if you show courtesy only to your friends, what more are you doing than others? Do not even the heathen do as much? You must therefore become perfect, even as your heavenly Father is perfect.

"Therefore, whatever you wish that men should do to you, do even so to them."

Christ on the Hilltop
Painted by C. A. Slade

THE PEOPLE WHO ARE REALLY HAPPY

Jesus said to his disciples:

"Blessed are the poor in spirit,
For theirs is the Kingdom of Heaven.
Blessed are the meek,
For they shall inherit the earth.
Blessed are they who mourn,
For they shall be comforted.
Blessed are they who hunger and thirst for righteousness,
For they shall be satisfied.
Blessed are the merciful,

For they shall receive mercy.
Blessed are the pure in heart,
For they shall see God.
Blessed are the peacemakers,
For they shall be called the sons of God.
Blessed are they who are persecuted because of their righteousness,
For theirs is the Kingdom of Heaven.
Blessed are you when you are reviled, persecuted, and falsely maligned because of loyalty to me;
Rejoice and be glad, for great is your reward in heaven, for so the prophets were persecuted who came before you."

JESUS SENDS OUT THE FIRST MISSIONARIES

Jesus went through all the towns and villages, teaching in their synagogues, preaching the good news about the Kingdom of God, and healing all kinds of diseases and weaknesses. At sight of the crowds, troubled and scattered like sheep without a shepherd, he was filled with pity, and said to his disciples, "This is a large harvest, but the laborers are few. Pray to the lord of the harvest to send laborers into his fields."

Then calling the twelve disciples, he sent them out two by two; and he gave them power over evil spirits. He told them to take nothing for their journey but a staff. Also he said, "Go your way. Remember that I send you out as lambs among wolves. Take with you neither purse nor bag nor an extra pair of shoes, and do not stop to greet any one on the road. Whatever household you first enter, say, 'Peace to this house!' And if the man living there is worthy, your peace will rest upon him; but if not, it shall return to you. Stay at the same house, eating and drinking what they give you, for the laborer deserves his wages. Do not go from one house to another.

"Also in whatever town you enter, if the people receive you, eat what they set before you. Heal those in that town who are ill, and tell them, 'The Kingdom of God is near you.' But if you enter any town where the people do not receive you, go out into its streets and say, 'Even the dust of your town which clings to our feet, we wipe off in protest against you.' But know this: that the Kingdom of God is at hand. I tell you, on that day it will be better for Sodom than for that city.

"Do not give to the dogs that which is sacred, nor throw your pearls before swine, for fear that they trample them under their feet and then turn back to attack you. He who hears you, hears me; he who rejects you, rejects me; he who rejects me, rejects him who sent me."

So Jesus' disciples went out and preached so as to lead men to be sorry for their sins and live as they should. They also cast out many evil spirits and cured many sick by pouring oil upon them. Then returning to Jesus they told him what they had done and taught.

JESUS PRAISES JOHN THE BAPTIST

When John heard in prison what Jesus was doing, he sent his disciples to ask him, "Are you the Promised One who is coming, or are we to look for some one else?" Jesus answered them, "Go and tell John what you see and hear: the blind see, the lame walk, the lepers are made clean, the deaf hear, the dead are brought back to life, and the poor have the good news told to them. Blessed is the man who does not lose faith in me."

As the disciples of John went away, Jesus talked to the people about John: "What did you go into the wilderness to see? A reed shaken by the wind? Then what did you go out to see? A man wearing fine clothes? Men dressed like that live in palaces. But why did you go out? To see a prophet? Yes, I tell you, and more than a prophet! This is he of whom it is written:

"'Behold, I send my messenger before you,
Who shall make the way ready for you.'

"I tell you, no man has appeared who is greater than John the Baptist; and yet he who is least in the Kingdom of God is greater than he.

"To what shall I compare the people of to-day? They are like children sitting in the market-places, who call to their playmates and say:

"'We played the pipes for you but you would not dance;
We cried but you would not lament.'

For John came neither eating nor drinking, and men said, 'He has an evil spirit!' The Son of Man came eating and drinking, and men say, 'He is a great eater and drinker, a friend of tax-gatherers and sinners!' But what I do shows that I am wise and right."

Now when Herod's birthday came, the daughter of Herodias danced in public and delighted him. Thereupon he promised with an oath that he would give her whatever she might ask. Prompted by her mother, she said to him, "Give me here on a dish the head of John the Baptist." Although the king did not wish to do it, yet because of his oath and his guests he ordered that it be given her. So he commanded that John be beheaded in prison, and his head was brought on a dish and given to the girl, and she brought it to her mother. Then John's disciples came and carried away the body to bury it.

JESUS FEEDS THE HUNGRY

When Herod the ruler of Galilee heard what Jesus was doing, he was greatly puzzled, for some said that John had come back from the dead, some that Elijah had appeared, and others that one of the old prophets had come to life again. Herod said, "I have beheaded John; but who is this of whom I hear these stories?" And he tried to find him.

Then Jesus said to his disciples, "Come by yourselves to some quiet place and rest a while"; for so many people were coming and going that the disciples could not find time even to eat. So they went in a boat by themselves to a quiet place; but many people saw and knew them as they went, and, running from all the towns, they arrived before them. When Jesus landed he found a large crowd waiting for him. Feeling sorry for them because they were like sheep without a shepherd, he began to teach them many things.

As it was already late in the day, his disciples came to him and said, "This place is far away from any town and it is now late. Send the people away to the neighboring farms and villages to buy food for themselves." But he answered "Give them some food." They replied, "Are we to go and buy two hundred silver pieces' worth of food for them?" He said, "Go and see how many loaves you have." When they found out, they said, "Five, and two fishes." Then he commanded them to make the people sit down in groups on the green grass.

So they sat down in companies of a hundred and of fifty. Then Jesus took the five loaves and the two fishes, and, looking up to heaven, he blessed the loaves, and broke them in pieces; and he gave to the disciples to set before the people. He also divided the two fishes among them, and all ate and had enough. Then they picked up twelve baskets full of broken pieces of the bread and fish, although the number of the people who had shared them was five thousand.

Then Jesus had his disciples enter the boat and cross before him to Bethsaida, while he himself sent away the crowd. After sending them away, he climbed a hill to pray. When evening came the boat was in the middle of the sea and he alone on the land. Seeing that they were having trouble as they rowed, for the wind was against them, he went to them at about three o'clock in the early morning, walking on the sea as if he intended to pass them. When they saw him walking on the sea, they believed that he was a ghost and cried out, for all saw him and were frightened; but he spoke to them at once, saying, "Have courage, it is I; do not be afraid."

Then he went on board the boat and the wind dropped, but they were greatly astonished for they had not learned the lesson of the loaves, for they were slow to understand its meaning.

After crossing the sea they landed at Gennesaret and fastened the boat. As soon as they had gone ashore, the people knew Jesus and searched all that part of the country, and whenever they heard that he had come to a certain place, they brought to him the sick on their beds. In every city or town or village to which he went people would lay their sick in the market-place and beg him to let them touch even the edge of his robe. And all who touched him were made well.

JESUS TELLS WHAT IT MEANS TO BE CLEAN

Among the Lowly
Painted by L. L'hermitte. In the Metropolitan Museum of Art

The Pharisees and some of the scribes who had come from Jerusalem went together to Jesus, because they had seen that some of his disciples ate their food without washing their hands as the scribes thought necessary. For the Pharisees and all the Jews always wash their hands up to the wrists before eating. So the Pharisees and scribes asked him, "Why do not your disciples obey the old custom instead of eating food with unwashed hands?" Jesus said to them, "Well did Isaiah prophesy about you hypocrites: 'This people honors me with their lips, but their heart is not with me; their worship is worthless, for they teach what are only commands of men.' You set aside the command of God and follow that of men.

"Moses said, 'Honor your father and your mother,' and, 'He who speaks evil of father or mother shall die.' But you say, 'If a man says to his father or to his mother, What you were to have received from me is given to God,' you hold that he need not do anything for his father or mother. In this way you set aside the command of God in favor of the teaching which you have handed down; and you do many other things like that."

Then calling the crowd to him again, he said to them, "Hear me, all of you, and understand. Nothing can make a man unclean by going into him from outside. It is what comes from him that makes him unclean, for from within, from the heart of man, come evil thoughts, acts of theft, murder, greed, wickedness, deceit, impure thoughts, envy, slander, pride, and recklessness. All these evil things come from within, and they make a man unclean."

JESUS IS KIND TO A STRANGER

Certain Pharisees came to Jesus and said to him, "Go away from here; for Herod wishes to kill you." He said to them, "Go and tell that fox, 'See, I cast out evil spirits and cure the sick to-day and to-morrow, but on the third day I must go on my way; for it cannot be that a prophet will be put to death anywhere except in Jerusalem.'"

Jesus left Capernaum and went into the land of Tyre and Sidon. Going into a house, he wished that no one should know that he was there, but he could not escape notice. Soon a woman whose little daughter had an evil spirit heard of him and came and knelt at his feet. Now the woman was a heathen of the Phœnician race. She begged him to drive the evil spirit out of her daughter, but he said to her, "Let the children of Israel first be fed, for it is not fair to take their bread and throw it to the dogs!" She answered him, "True, sir, yet the little dogs under the table do eat the children's crumbs." He said to her, "Because of this answer go to your home; the evil spirit has gone out of your daughter." On returning home she found the child lying on the bed and the evil spirit gone from her.

Jesus again left the land of Tyre and passed through Sidon to the Sea of Galilee, crossing the land of Decapolis. The people brought to him a deaf man, who also stammered; and they begged Jesus to lay his hand on him.

Jesus took the man away from the crowd, put his fingers into the man's ears, touched his tongue with saliva, and looking up to heaven, sighed, and said to him, "Ephphatha" (which means "Open"). And at once, the man could hear and could talk without stammering.

Then Jesus told them to tell no one, but in spite of what he said the people kept telling about it, saying: "How well he has done everything! He even makes the deaf hear, and the dumb speak."

JESUS MAKES AN HEROIC CHOICE

On their way to the villages of Cæsarea Philippi Jesus asked his disciples, "Who do people say I am?" They told him, "John the Baptist; others say, 'Elijah'; some say, 'One of the prophets.'" Then he said to them, "But you yourselves, who do you say that I am?" Peter answered him, "You are the Christ." But he strictly charged them to tell no one that he was the Christ.

Then Jesus began to explain to his disciples that he must suffer many things and be rejected by the elders and high priests and scribes and be killed, but that after three days he would rise from the dead. This he said openly; and Peter tried to reprove him. But Jesus turned and, looking upon his disciples, reproved Peter, saying, "Away with you, Satan, for your mind is not on the things of God but of men."

Then Jesus called the crowd and his disciples to him, and said to them, "If any one wishes to follow me, let him forget himself, take up his cross, and come with me. For any one who is thinking only of saving his life, will lose it; but whoever loses his life for my sake and for the sake of the good news, will save it. What does it profit a man to gain the whole world and lose his soul? For what could a man give in exchange for his soul? Whoever is ashamed of me and my teachings in this sinful world, of him I will be ashamed when I come in the glory of my Father with the holy angels."

JESUS IS GLORIFIED

Six days later Jesus took Peter, James and John up a high mountain where they were alone, and in their presence he was transfigured. His clothes glistened with a dazzling whiteness such as no bleaching could give on earth. And there appeared to them Elijah and Moses, who talked with Jesus. Then Peter said, "Master, it is fortunate that we are here. Let us make three tabernacles, one for you, one for Moses, and one for Elijah." (For in his terror he did not know what to say.) Then a cloud came and overshadowed them, and a voice from the cloud said, "This is my Beloved Son; give heed to him." And suddenly, looking around, they saw no one with them but Jesus.

As they came down from the mountain, he commanded them to tell no one what they had seen until after he had risen from the dead. And they obeyed the command but discussed among themselves what "rising from the dead" meant. Therefore they asked him, "How is it that the scribes say, 'Elijah must first come'?" He answered, "Elijah is to come first to restore everything. And what is written about the Son of Man? Is it not that he is to endure great suffering and be despised? But I tell you, Elijah has come, and they have done to him what they pleased, even as it is written of him."

JESUS TELLS HOW ONE MAY BECOME GREAT

Leaving Cæsarea Philippi, Jesus and his disciples passed through Galilee; but he wished no one to know of this, for he was teaching his disciples. He said to them, "The Son of Man will be betrayed and men will put him to death, but in three days he will rise from the dead." But they did not understand his meaning and were afraid to ask.

When they had reached Capernaum and were in the house, he asked them, "What were you arguing about on the way?" But they made no reply, for they had been disputing on the way about which of them was greatest. Sitting down, he called the twelve disciples, and said, "If any one wishes to be first, he will be last of all and servant of all." Then he took a little child and set him by his side and with his arm around him said to them, "Whoever receives a little child like this in my name, receives me, and whoever receives me, receives not only me, but God who sent me."

JESUS MAKES THE WICKED ZACCHEUS HIS FRIEND

As Jesus passed through Jericho a man named Zaccheus, who was the chief tax-gatherer and rich, tried to see what Jesus was like, but could not on account of the crowd and because he was short. So he ran ahead and climbed into a sycamore-tree to see Jesus, for he was to pass that way. When Jesus came to the place, he looked up and said to him, "Zaccheus, come down, for to-day I must stay at your house." And Zaccheus came down quickly and welcomed him joyfully.

Then all who saw this began to find fault, saying, "He has gone to eat with a man who is a sinner." But Zaccheus stood up and said to Jesus, "Lord, I will give half of all that I have to the poor; and to every man whom I have cheated out of anything I will give back four times as much." And Jesus said to him, "To-day salvation has come to this house, for you have proved yourself to be a true son of Abraham. For the Son of Man came to seek and to save the lost."

JESUS IS GLADLY WELCOMED BY THE PEOPLE

As Jesus was leaving Jericho with his disciples, followed by a large crowd, there sat by the road a blind beggar, Bartimæus (the son of Timæus). When he heard that it was Jesus of Nazareth, he cried out, "Jesus, son of David, have pity on me!" Many reproved him, saying, "Keep still," but he cried out the more, "Son of David, have pity on me!" Jesus stopped and said, "Call him." So they called the blind man and said, "Have courage! Get up, he has sent for you." Throwing off his cloak, he sprang up and came to Jesus. Jesus said to him, "What do you want me to do for you?" The blind man answered, "Master, let me receive my sight." Then Jesus said to him, "Go your way, your faith has healed you." And at once he received his sight, and followed Jesus along the road.

When Jesus and those with him were drawing near to Jerusalem and had reached Bethpage and Bethany, near the Mount of Olives, he sent two of his disciples ahead, saying, "Go into the village over there. As soon as you enter it, you will find a colt tied, which no one has ever ridden. Untie it and bring it here. If any one asks you, 'Why are you doing that?' say, 'The Master needs it and will immediately send it back.'"

So they left him and found a colt tied, outside a door, on the street. As they untied it, some of the men standing there said, "What are you doing, untying the colt?" The disciples answered as Jesus had told them, and the men let them take it. When they had brought it to Jesus, they threw their cloaks upon it, and he mounted it. Many also spread their clothes on the road, while others strewed leafy branches cut from the fields; and people in front and behind kept shouting:

"God save him!
Blessed is he who comes in the name of the Lord!
Blessed is the coming Kingdom of our father David!
God on high, save him!"

Jesus entered Jerusalem and went into the Temple. And when he had looked about, because it was already late in the day, he went out to Bethany with his twelve disciples.

Christ in the Temple
Painted by C. A. Slade

JESUS FIGHTS WRONG IN THE TEMPLE

About this time certain people came to tell Jesus of the Galileans whom Pilate had killed while they were offering sacrifices. He said to them, "Do you believe that these Galileans were worse sinners than the rest? No, I tell you; and unless you are sorry for your sins and do right, you too will all likewise perish. Or those eighteen men who were killed by the fall of the tower of Siloam—do you suppose that they were worse sinners than the rest of the people of Jerusalem? No, I tell you; and unless you are sorry for your sins and do right, you too will all perish."

Then Jesus went into the Temple, and drove out those who were buying and selling there. He upset the tables of the money-changers, and the seats of those who sold doves, and would allow no one to carry any goods through the Temple. For he said to them, "Is it not written, 'My house shall be called a house of prayer for all nations'? But you have made it a den of robbers!" When the chief priests and scribes heard of it, they began to look for some way of putting him to death, for they feared him because all the people were deeply stirred by his teachings. But each evening he and his disciples left the city.

Then once more Jesus and his disciples entered Jerusalem, and as he was walking about the Temple, some high priests and scribes and elders came and asked him, "By what right are you doing these things, and who gave you this right?" Jesus answered, "I will ask you a question; answer me, and I will tell you by what right I do such things. What about John's baptism? Was it from God or from men? Answer me." They argued among themselves, saying, "If we answer, 'From God,' he will ask, 'Why then did you not believe in him?' But if we say, 'From men'"—they were afraid of the people, for the people believed that John was truly a prophet. So they answered Jesus, "We do not know." He said to them, "Then I will not tell you by what right I do these things.

"But give me your opinion. A man who had two sons went to one of them and said, 'Son, go and work in the vineyard to-day.' And the young man answered, 'I will not'; but afterward changed his mind and went. Then the man went with the same request to the other son, who said, 'I will go, sir'; but he did not go. Which of the two did as his father wished?" They answered, "The first." Jesus said to them, "I tell you that tax-gatherers and sinners will enter the Kingdom of God before you; for John showed you the way to an upright life, and you did not believe him. But the tax-gatherers and sinners believed him; and even when you saw, you would not say that you were wrong and believe in him.

"Listen to this: There was a landowner who planted a vineyard, and set a hedge around it, dug a pit for the wine-press, and built a watch-tower. Then he leased it to tenants and went to another country. At vintage time he sent his servants to the tenants to collect the fruits of the vineyard, but they took the servants and flogged one, stoned another, and killed another. Then he sent other servants, more than at first, but they did the same to these. Finally he sent his son, saying to himself, 'They will respect my son.' But the tenants said to one another, 'This is the heir. Come, let us kill him and get his inheritance.' So they threw him out of the vineyard and killed him. Now, when the owner of the vineyard comes, what will he do to these tenants?" They said, "He will destroy the wretches and lease the vineyard to others who will give him the fruits in their season."

Jesus said to them, "Have you never read in the scriptures:

> "'The stone which the builders rejected
> Has been made the chief corner-stone;
> This is the Lord's doing,
> And marvellous in our sight.'"

When the high priests and the Pharisees heard these stories, they knew that he was speaking about them, and they wished to seize him but were afraid of the common people who regarded him as a prophet.

JESUS CONDEMNS THOSE WHO PRETEND TO BE GOOD

The common people were listening to Jesus eagerly. As he taught he said, "Be on your guard against the scribes, who like to walk about in long robes and to have the people bow to them in the market-places. They like to sit in the front seats in the synagogue and in the best places at feasts. These, who use up the property of widows and then to cover their guilt make long prayers, will receive the greater condemnation."

He also said, "Woe to you scribes! For you load men with burdens heavy to bear, which you yourselves do not touch with one of your fingers. Woe to you, scribes and Pharisees, hypocrites! You shut in men's faces the door to the Kingdom of God; for you neither enter yourselves nor let those enter who wish to come in.

"Woe to you, scribes and Pharisees, hypocrites! For you carefully pay to the Temple the tenth part of what grows in your garden, but you do not show justice, mercy, and faithfulness. Blind guides, who strain out the gnat and swallow the camel!

"Woe to you, scribes and Pharisees, hypocrites! For you make clean the outside of the cup and the plate, and then fill them with your greed and selfishness. Blind Pharisee! first make clean the inside of the cup, that the outside as well may become clean.

"Woe to you, scribes and Pharisees, hypocrites! For you are like whitewashed tombs, beautiful outside, but inside full of dead men's bones and filth. So you yourselves appear upright, but inside you are full of hypocrisy and sin."

JESUS WARNS HIS DISCIPLES

As Jesus went out of the Temple, one of his disciples said to him, "Master, see what great stones and what a beautiful building!" Then Jesus answered, "This Temple, made by man's hands, shall be destroyed. But another will soon arise, made without hands." And as he sat on the Mount of Olives opposite the Temple, Peter and James and John and Andrew asked him privately, "Tell us, when shall these things happen, and what is to be the sign to show when all these things are about to happen?" Jesus said to them, "No one knows the day or the hour when this will happen, not even the angels in heaven, nor the Son, but only the Father."

"The Kingdom of God shall be like ten maidens who took their torches and went out to meet the bridegroom. Five of them were foolish and five were wise. For the foolish ones, when they took their torches, took no oil with them; but the wise took oil in their vessels with their torches.

"Now while the bridegroom delayed, they all slumbered and slept. And at midnight a cry was raised: 'Look! The bridegroom! Come out to meet him!' Then all those maidens rose, and trimmed their torches. And the foolish ones said to the wise, 'Give us some of your oil; for our torches are going out.' But the wise maidens answered, 'There may not be enough for us and for you. Go rather to those who sell, and buy for yourselves.' Now while they went away to buy, the bridegroom came and those who were ready went in with him to the marriage feast; and the door was shut. Afterward the other maidens came also and said, 'Sir, open to us.' But he answered, 'I tell you truly, I do not know you.'

"Watch, therefore, for you do not know the day nor the hour when the Kingdom of God shall come."

JESUS CURES A BLIND MAN

As Jesus was passing along the road he saw a man who was born blind, and the disciples asked him, "Master, for whose sin, his own or his parents', was this man born blind?" Jesus answered, "Neither for his own sin nor his parents', but that God's power to heal may be shown in him. We must do the work of him who sent me while day lasts; night is coming when no man can work. While I am in the world, I am the light of the world."

When he had said this, he spat on the ground and made clay with the saliva, put the clay on the eyes of the blind man, and said to him, "Go, wash in the Pool of Siloam." So he went off and washed, and returned able to see.

Then the neighbors and those who before had seen him begging said, "Is not this the man who used to sit and beg?" Some said, "It is he." Others said, "No, but he is like him." He said, "I am the man." So they said to him, "How then were your eyes opened?" He answered, "The man who is called Jesus made clay and put it upon my eyes, and said to me, 'Go to the Pool of Siloam and wash.' So I went away and washed, and I received my sight." They asked him, "Where is he?" He answered, "I do not know."

Then they brought the man who had once been blind to the Pharisees. Now it was on the Sabbath that Jesus had made the clay and opened his eyes. Therefore the Pharisees asked him again how he had received his sight, and he told them, "Jesus put clay on my eyes and I washed them and can see." Then some of the Pharisees said, "This man does not come from God, for he does not keep the Sabbath." Others said, "How can a sinner do such wonderful deeds of healing?" And they could not agree among themselves. So they asked the blind man once more, "What have you to say about him, for it was your eyes that he opened?" The man replied, "He is a prophet."

Now the Jews would not believe that he had been born blind and had received his sight until they called his parents and asked them, "Is this your son who you say was born blind? How is it that he now can see?" His parents answered them, "We know that this is our son and that he was born blind, but we do not know why he can now see nor who opened his eyes. He is of age; ask him, he can speak for himself." His parents said this because they were afraid of the Jews; for the Jews had already agreed that any one who said that Jesus was the Christ should be put out of the synagogue. That was why his parents said, "He is of age, ask him."

So the Jews again called the man who had been born blind, and said to him, "Give God the praise; we know that this man Jesus is a sinner." He answered and said, "I do not know whether he is a sinner; one thing I do know, that, although I was blind, I now see." So they said to him, "What did he do to you? How did he give you your sight?" He replied, "I have told you already, but you would not listen to me. Why do you want to hear it again? Do you also wish to become his disciples?" Then they reviled him and said, "You are his disciple, but we are disciples of Moses. We know that God spoke to Moses, but we do not know where this man came from." The man answered, "This is strange! You do not know where he comes from, and yet he gave me my sight! We know that God does not listen to sinners but that he does listen to him who worships him and does his will. Since the world began no one has ever heard of sight being given to a man born blind. If this man were not from God, he could do nothing." They answered, "You were born wholly bad, and yet you would teach us?" Then they put him out of the synagogue.

Jesus heard that they had put him out, and meeting him said, "Do you believe in the Son of God?" He answered, "Who is he, sir? Tell me that I may believe." Jesus said to him, "Not only have you seen him but he is now talking to you." The man said, "Then I do believe, Master," and he worshipped him, and Jesus said to him, "It is to right wrongs that I have come to this world, that the blind may see and that those who see may become blind." Hearing this, some of the Pharisees who were with him said, "And are we blind?" Jesus replied, "If you were blind you would not be guilty; but you say, 'We can see,' and so your sin remains."

JESUS TELLS WHAT HE CAME TO DO

Jesus said to the people, "I am the light of the world; he who follows me shall not walk in darkness, but shall have the light which gives life."

As Jesus spoke these words many believed in him. Then he said to the Jews who had believed in him, "If you faithfully do what I say, you are truly my disciples, and you shall know the truth and the truth shall set you free." They answered him, "We are Abraham's descendants and have never been slaves to any man. What do you mean by saying, 'You shall be set free'?" Jesus answered them, "Truly, I tell you, every one who sins is a slave of sin. The slave does not remain in the household forever, but the Son remains forever. If therefore the Son sets you free, you shall be free indeed.

"I am the Door; if any man enters by me he shall be saved and shall go in and go out and find pasture. The thief comes only to steal and kill and destroy. I have come that they may have life, and that they may have it more abundantly.

"I am the Good Shepherd; the good shepherd lays down his life for the sheep. But a hired man, who is not a shepherd and does not own the sheep, leaves them and runs away when he sees the wolf coming, and the wolf snatches the sheep and scatters them. The hired man runs away because he is only a hired man and does not care for the sheep.

"I am the Good Shepherd and know my own, and my own know me, just as the Father knows me and I know the Father, and I lay down my life for the sheep. I have other sheep which do not belong to this fold; I must lead them also, and they will hear my voice, and they will be one flock and one shepherd."

JESUS BRINGS LAZARUS BACK TO LIFE

Now a certain man, Lazarus of Bethany, was sick. He was the brother of Martha and of the Mary who anointed the Master with perfume and wiped his feet with her hair. Jesus loved Martha, and her sister, and Lazarus. So the sisters sent word to him, "Master, he whom you love is sick." But when Jesus heard it he said, "This sickness is not to end in death, but it is for the glory of God, that the Son of God may be glorified by it."

So when he heard that Lazarus was sick, he stayed where he was two days. After that he said to the disciples, "Let us go again into Judea. Our friend Lazarus has fallen asleep, but I am going to waken him." The disciples said to him, "Master, if he has fallen asleep he will get well." Now Jesus had spoken of his death, but they thought that he meant taking rest in sleep. So Jesus said to them plainly, "Lazarus is dead, and for your sakes I am glad that I was not there, so that you may learn to believe. But let us go to him."

When Jesus came he found that Lazarus had been in the tomb four days. Now Bethany was only about two miles from Jerusalem, and many of the Jews had come to comfort Mary and Martha about their brother.

When Martha heard that Jesus was coming, she went out to meet him, while Mary stayed at home. Martha said to Jesus, "Master, if you had been here my brother would not have died, but I know that even now God will give you whatever you ask him." Jesus said to her, "Your brother shall rise again." Martha said to him, "I know that he shall rise again, at the resurrection on the last day." Jesus said to her, "I am the resurrection and the life. He who believes in me shall live even though he die; and whoever lives and believes in me shall never die. Do you believe this?" She said to him, "Yes, Master, I do believe that you are the Christ, the Son of God who was to come into the world."

When Martha had said this she went away to call Mary, her sister, telling her secretly, "The Master is here and is calling you." When Mary heard this she rose quickly and went to him. Jesus had not yet come into the village but was still in the place where Martha met him. When the Jews who were trying to comfort Mary in the house saw her rise up quickly and go out, they followed her, supposing that she was going to weep at the tomb. But when Mary reached the place where Jesus was and saw him, she fell at his feet, saying to him, "Master, if you had been here, my brother would not have died."

When Jesus saw her and the Jews who came with her weeping, he was deeply moved, and said in great distress, "Where have you laid him?"

They said to him, "Master, come and see." Jesus wept. The Jews therefore said, "See how he loved him!" Some of them said, "Could not this man who gave sight to the blind have also kept Lazarus from dying?"

Jesus was again deeply moved, as he came to the tomb. It was a cave, and a stone lay against it. Jesus said, "Take away the stone." Martha, the dead man's sister, said to him, "Master, by this time his body has begun to decay, for he has been dead four days." Jesus said to her, "Did I not tell you that if you only would believe you should see the glory of God?" So they removed the stone, and Jesus lifted up his eyes and said, "Father, I thank thee that thou hast heard me. I knew that thou always dost listen to me, but I spoke for the sake of the people standing near, that they may believe that thou hast sent me." When he had said this, he cried in a loud voice, "Lazarus, come forth." Then he who was dead came forth with his hands and feet wrapped in bandages and his face bound with a cloth. Jesus said to them, "Untie him and let him go."

Then many of the Jews who had come with Mary and had seen what Jesus did, believed in him.

JESUS PRAISES A WOMAN WHO GAVE HER BEST

While Jesus was at dinner at Bethany in the house of Simon, the jar-maker, a woman came in with an alabaster jar of pure perfume, which was very costly. Breaking the jar she poured the perfume over his head. Some said to each other in indignation, "Why this waste of perfume? It might have been sold for more than three hundred silver pieces and the money given to the poor."

But because they found fault with her, Jesus said, "Let her alone, why do you trouble her? She has done me a beautiful service. The poor are with you always; to them you can do good whenever you wish, but me you will not always have. She has done what she could; she has poured oil on my body beforehand for burial. I tell you, wherever through all the world the good news is told, this deed of hers will be told in memory of her."

JESUS EATS THE LAST SUPPER WITH HIS DISCIPLES

Judas Iscariot, one of the twelve disciples, went to the high priests with the intention of betraying Jesus. And when they heard, they rejoiced, promising to give him money; and he began to look for an opportunity to betray him.

On the first day of the Feast of Unleavened Bread, when the Jews kill the lambs that are sacrificed at the Passover Feast, Jesus' disciples said to him, "Where do you wish us to make ready for your passover meal?"

The Last Supper

So Jesus sent two of his disciples, saying to them, "Go into the city, where you will meet a man carrying a jar of water. Follow him and say to the owner of whatever house he enters, 'The Master says, Where is my room in which I may eat the passover meal with my disciples?' He will show you a large upper room already furnished. There make ready for us." So the disciples went into the city and found things as he had said they would; and they prepared for the Passover.

When it was evening Jesus came with his twelve disciples; and while they were eating at the table, he said, "I know surely that one of you now eating with me will betray me." In deep sorrow the disciples said to him, one after the other, "Surely it is not I?" He said to them, "It is one of the twelve, one who is dipping his fingers into the dish with me. The Son of Man will depart as it has been foretold of him, but woe to that man by whom the Son of Man is betrayed! It would be better for that man if he had never been born!"

Then Jesus took the bread and, when he had given thanks to God, he broke it and said, "This is my body which is broken for you; do this in remembrance of me."

In the same way, after he had eaten, Jesus took the cup, and when he had given thanks to God, he gave it to his disciples and they drank of it. Then he said, "This is the new covenant made by my blood which is shed for many. As often as you drink this cup, do it in remembrance of me." Then after singing a hymn they went out to the Mount of Olives.

There Jesus said to them, "You will all desert me, for it is written in the scriptures: 'I will smite the shepherd and the sheep will be scattered.' But after I have risen, I will go before you into Galilee." Peter said to him, "Though all others should desert you, I will not." Jesus said to him, "Indeed I tell you, this very night before the cock crows you will deny three times that you know me." But Peter said more emphatically, "Even if I have to die with you, I will never deny you." And all of them said the same.

JESUS ENCOURAGES HIS FRIENDS AND HELPERS

Jesus said, "Let not your heart be troubled; you believe in God, believe also in me. In my Father's house are many homes; if it were not so, I would have told you, for I go to prepare a place for you. And if I go and prepare a place for you, I will return and take you to be with me that where I am, you may be also; and you know the way to the place where I am going."

Thomas said to him, "Master, we do not know where you are going; how then can we know the way?" Jesus said to him, "I am the way, the truth, and the life; no man comes to the Father except through me. If you had learned to know me, you would have known my Father also; from now on you know him and have seen him."

Philip said to him, "Master, let us see the Father and we will be satisfied." Jesus said to him, "Have I been all this time with you and yet you do not know me, Philip? He who has seen me has seen the Father; then how can you say, 'Let us see the Father'? Do you not believe that I am in the Father and the Father in me? The words that I speak do not come from me but from the Father who lives in me. Believe me, that I am in the Father and the Father in me, or else believe me because of the work itself. I say to you, he who believes in me will do the work which I do and still greater works than these, for I go to the Father. And whatever you shall ask in my name I will do, that the Father may be glorified through the Son. If you ask anything in my name, I will do it.

"If you love me you will keep my commands, and I shall ask the Father and he will give you another Helper to be with you forever, even the Spirit of truth.

"In a little while the world will see me no more; but you shall see me, because I live and you shall live also. He who has my commands and obeys them is the one who loves me; and he who loves me will be loved by my Father, and I will love him and will reveal myself to him.

"I have told you all this while I am still with you; but the Helper, the Holy Spirit, whom the Father will send in my name, will teach you everything and remind you of all that I have said to you.

"Peace I leave with you, my own peace I give to you; not as the world gives do I give to you. Let not your heart be troubled nor afraid. You have heard me tell you that I go away and am coming back to you. If you love me you will be glad because I am going to the Father, for the Father is greater than I. I have told you this now, before it takes place, that when it does you may believe.

"I am the true vine and my Father is the vine-dresser. He cuts away each of my branches that does not bear fruit, and cleans every branch that bears fruit so as to make it bear more. You are already clean because of the word which I have spoken to you. Remain united with me and I will remain with you. Just as the branch cannot bear fruit unless it remains united with the vine, neither can you bear fruit unless you remain united with me. I am the vine, you are the branches. He who remains united with me and I with him bears much fruit, but apart from me you can do nothing.

"If you remain united with me and my words remain in you, ask whatever you will and you shall have it. It is by your bearing much fruit and being my true disciples that my Father is glorified. As the Father has loved me, so have I also loved you; continue in my love. If you keep my commands, you will continue in my love, even as I have kept my Father's commands and continue in his love.

"I have told you all this that my joy may be yours, and that your joy may be complete. This is my command: 'Love one another even as I have loved you.' No man has greater love than that which leads him to lay down his life for his friends. You are my friends if you do whatever I command you. I call you servants no longer, for the servant does not know what his master does; but I call you friends, for I have told you everything that I have heard from my Father. You did not choose me, but I chose you and appointed you to bear fruit that will remain, so that whatever you ask of the Father in my name he will give you."

JESUS IS SEIZED BY THE MOB

When Jesus and his disciples came to a certain place called Gethsemane, he said to them, "Sit here while I pray"; but he took with him Peter and James and John. And as he suffered greatly from deep sorrow, he said to them, "My heart is heavy with sadness. Stay here and watch." Then he went forward a short distance and threw himself on the ground and prayed that if possible he might be spared this agony, saying, "Father, with thee all things are possible. Take away this cup of agony from me. Yet not my will, but thy will be done."

When he came back, he found his disciples asleep; and he said to Peter, "Simon, are you asleep? Could you not watch for one hour? Watch and pray that you may overcome temptation. The spirit indeed is willing, but the body is weak." Again he went away and prayed the same prayer. And when he returned, again he found them asleep, for they were very drowsy; and they did not know what to say to him. Then he came the third time and said to them, "Sleep on now and take your rest. It is enough; the hour has come; already the Son of Man has been betrayed into the hands of wicked men. Rise, let us go; for here is the one who has betrayed me."

While Jesus was still speaking, Judas, one of the Twelve, came up, followed by a mob with swords and clubs, who had come from the high priests and the scribes and the elders. Judas had arranged a signal: "He whom I shall kiss," he said, "is the man. Take him, and lead him away without letting him escape." As soon as he came, he went up to Jesus, saying, "Master," and kissed him. Then they seized Jesus and took him; but one of those who were with him drew his sword, and, striking the servant of the high priest, cut off his ear. Jesus turned and said, "Have you come out with swords and clubs to seize me as you would a robber?

Day after day I have been with you teaching in the Temple, yet you never seized me."

Then Jesus' disciples left him and fled. One young man, however, followed him with only a linen sheet thrown about him; but when the men tried to seize him, he left the linen sheet and fled away naked.

The mob led Jesus away and brought him to the house of the high priest. Peter followed at a distance, and when they had kindled a fire in the middle of the courtyard and sat down together, he too sat down among them. A certain maid, seeing him there by the firelight, looked at him closely and said, "This man also was with him." But he denied it, saying, "Woman, I do not know him." After a little while another person who saw Peter said, "You too are one of them"; but he said, "Man, I am not."

About an hour later another man said, "Certainly this fellow also was with Jesus, for he is a Galilean." But Peter said, "Man, I do not know what you are talking about." Immediately while he was still speaking, the cock crowed. And Jesus turned and looked straight at Peter. Then Peter remembered how the Lord had said to him, "Before the cock crows to-day you will deny me three times." And Peter went out and wept bitterly.

JESUS IN THE HANDS OF HIS ENEMIES

The men who seized Jesus mocked him and flogged him. They also blindfolded him and said, "Prophet, tell us who is it that struck you?" And they said many other things, insulting him.

At daybreak they brought him before the council at which were gathered the elders, both the chief priests and the scribes. And they tried to get evidence against him to have him put to death, but could not find any, for though many made false statements, they did not agree. Some men stood up and falsely said, "We heard him say, 'I will destroy this temple made by the hands of men and within three days I will build another made without hands.'" But the statements even of these men did not agree.

Then the high priest arose and asked Jesus, "Do you not answer? What about these statements that these men make against you?" But he was silent and made no answer. And the high priest asked him, "Are you the Christ? If you are, tell us." He said to them, "If I tell you, you will not believe, and if I ask you questions, you will not answer me. But after this the Son of Man will be seated at the right hand of God Almighty." Then they all said to him, "Are you then the Son of God?" He replied, "It is as you say; I am." So they said, "What further need have we of evidence? We have heard it from his own lips."

Then all the high priests and scribes rose and brought Jesus before Pilate, and began to accuse him, saying, "We found this man leading our people astray, forbidding them to pay taxes to the Roman emperor, and saying that he himself is Christ, the King." Pilate asked him, "Are you the King of the Jews?" He answered, "I am." Pilate said to the high priests and the crowd, "I do not find that this man has done anything wrong." But they insisted, saying, "He stirs up the people by teaching through all Judea. He began in Galilee, and now he has come even here." When Pilate heard this he asked whether Jesus was a Galilean, and when he learned that he was and that he came under Herod's rule, he sent him to Herod Antipas, who was also in Jerusalem at this time.

Herod was glad to see Jesus. He had long wished to see him because of what he had heard about him, and because he also hoped to see him do some wonderful deed. Although Herod asked him many questions, Jesus made no answer, and the high priests and the scribes loudly shouted their charges against him. Then Herod, and his soldiers, after mocking him, and dressing him in a bright colored robe, sent him back to Pilate.

Pilate then called together the high priests and other officials and the people, and said, "You brought me this man on the charge that he stirred up the people to rebel. Now I have examined him before you and found no guilt in him of those things of which you accuse him; no, nor has

Herod, for he has sent him back to us. You see that he has done nothing that calls for death. I will therefore have him flogged and then release him" (for it was the custom at this feast to release for them one man). But they all cried out, "Away with him and release for us Barabbas" (a man who had been put into prison because of a riot which had occurred in the city, and on the charge of murder). Pilate spoke to them again, because he wished to release Jesus; but still they shouted, "Crucify him! Crucify him!" He said to them for the third time, "Why, what crime has this man committed? I have found no reason to put him to death. I will therefore have him flogged and then release him." But they shouted and demanded that he should be crucified. And so Pilate, wishing to please the people, released Barabbas, but Jesus he turned over to them to be crucified.

JESUS IS CRUCIFIED BY HIS ENEMIES

The soldiers led Jesus to the courtyard of the governor's palace and called together the whole company. Then they clothed him in a purple robe and, making a crown of thorns, they put it on his head and began to salute him, "Hail, King of the Jews!" They struck him on the head with a reed and spat on him, and on bended knee paid homage to him. After they had made sport of him, they stripped off the purple robe and put on his own clothes, and led him out to be crucified.

They forced a man named Simon, of Cyrene, who was coming in from the country, to carry his cross. So they brought Jesus to the place called Golgotha, which means, the place of the skull. And they offered him wine mixed with myrrh, but he would not take it. Then they crucified him and divided his clothes among them, drawing lots to decide what each should take. It was nine in the morning when they crucified him. The inscription over his head stating the charge against him read:

With him they crucified two robbers, one on his right and one on his left. And those who passed by scoffed at him, shaking their heads in derision and saying, "Ha! you who were to destroy the Temple and rebuild it in three days, save yourself and come down from the cross!" In the same way the high priests and the scribes mocked him among themselves and said, "He saved others, but he cannot save himself. Let the Christ, the 'King of Israel,' now come down from the cross, that we may see and believe!" But Jesus said, "Father, forgive them, for they know not what they do."

One of the criminals who was crucified also scoffed at him, saying, "Are you not the Christ? Save yourself and us!" But the other said in rebuke, "Have you no fear of God even though you are being put to death? We are suffering justly, receiving what we deserve for our crimes, but he has done no wrong." Then he said, "Jesus, remember me when you enter your kingdom." Jesus said to him, "This very day you will be with me in paradise."

Now beside the cross of Jesus stood his mother. Seeing her and the disciple whom he loved standing near, Jesus said to her, "Woman, he is your son!" And to the disciple he said, "She is your mother!" And from that hour the disciple took her into his own home.

Darkness covered the whole land from noon until three o'clock in the afternoon. At that hour Jesus cried aloud, "Eloi, Eloi, lama sabachthani," which means, "My God, my God, why hast thou forsaken me?" When they heard it, some who stood by, said, "He is calling Elijah." And a man ran and, soaking a sponge in vinegar, put it on the end of a reed and was about to give it to him to drink when the others said, "Stop, let us see if Elijah will come to take him down." But Jesus uttered a loud cry and gave up his life. And the curtain of the Temple was torn in two from the top to the bottom. When the Roman captain who stood facing him saw in what way he died, he said, "Surely this man was a son of God."

Looking on from a distance were some women also, among them Mary of Magdala, Mary the mother of James, the younger, and of Joses, and Salome, who had followed him and waited on him when he was in Galilee, and many other women who had come up with him to Jerusalem.

Because it was now evening of the day before the Sabbath, Joseph of Arimathæa, an honorable member of the Jewish national council, who was himself looking for the coming of the Kingdom of God, went to Pilate and had the courage to ask him for the body of Jesus. Pilate, surprised that he was dead, called the captain and asked whether Jesus was already dead, and when he learned this from the captain he gave the body to Joseph. After Joseph had taken Jesus from the cross, he wrapped him in a linen sheet which he had bought, and laid him in a tomb cut out of rock; and he rolled a stone against the door of the tomb. And Mary of Magdala and Mary the mother of Joses, watched to see where Jesus was laid.

JESUS CONQUERS DEATH

When the Sabbath was over, Mary of Magdala, Mary the mother of James, and Salome bought spices to embalm Jesus. Soon after sunrise on the first day of the week they went to the tomb, and they said to one another, "Who will roll away the stone for us from the door?" But they found that the stone, although very large, had been rolled to one side. On entering the tomb they saw a young man in a white robe sitting on the right, and they trembled and were afraid. But he said to them, "Do not be afraid. You are looking for Jesus of Nazareth, who was crucified. He is risen; he is not here. See the place where he was laid! But go and tell his disciples and Peter, 'He is going before you into Galilee; there you will see him, as he told you.'"

Then they remembered Jesus' words, and returning from the tomb they told these things to the eleven disciples and to all the others; but to them, the story seemed to be nonsense, and they were not believed.

Peter, however, ran to the tomb, but when he looked in he saw only the linen bandages; and he went home wondering what had happened.

But Mary of Magdala stood weeping outside the tomb. As she wept, she stooped down and looked into the tomb and saw two angels in white sitting, one at the head and the other at the feet, where the body of Jesus had lain. They said to her, "Woman, why are you weeping?" She said, "Because they have taken away my Master and I do not know where they have laid him!"

When she had said this, she turned around and saw Jesus standing there, but she did not know that it was Jesus. "Woman," said he, "Why are you weeping? For whom are you looking?" Supposing that he was the gardener, she said, "Sir, if you have carried him away, tell me where you have laid him, and I will take him away." Jesus said to her, "Mary!" She turned to him and cried out, "Master!" Jesus said, "Do not touch me, for I have not yet ascended to the Father; but go to my brothers and tell them, 'I am ascending to my Father and to your Father, to my God and your God.'" Mary went to the disciples with the news, "I have seen the Master," and to tell them what he had said to her.

JESUS WALKS AND TALKS WITH TWO OF HIS DISCIPLES

On the same day two of Jesus' disciples were on their way to a village called Emmaus, about seven miles from Jerusalem; and as they talked together about what had happened, Jesus himself drew near and went with them; but their eyes were kept from knowing him.

He said to them, "What are you talking about so earnestly as you walk along?" And they stood still, looking sad, and one of them, named Cleopas, answered, "Are you only a stranger stopping in Jerusalem? Do you not know the things that have happened there within these last few days?" He asked, "What things?" They answered, "Why, about Jesus of Nazareth, who proved himself a prophet, mighty in word and deed before God and all the people, and how our high priests and rulers gave him over to be sentenced to death and had him crucified. But we were hoping that he was the one to save Israel. It is now the third day since these things happened. Yet some of our women who were at the tomb early this morning, amazed us. They told us that they had not found his body but that they had seen a vision of angels who said that he was alive. Then some of those who were with us went to the tomb and found it as the women had said. But him they did not see."

Then Jesus said to them, "O foolish men, so slow of heart to believe in what the prophets have spoken! Was it not necessary for the Christ to suffer and so win his glory?"

When they came to the village to which they were going, he seemed to be going farther on, but they urged him, saying, "Stay with us, for it is almost evening, the day is nearly over." So he went in to stay with them.

As he sat with them at table, he took the bread, blessed it, broke it, and passed it to them. Then their eyes were opened so that they knew him; but he disappeared from their sight. They said to one another, "Did not our hearts glow while he was talking with us on the way!"

At once they started back to Jerusalem, where they found the eleven disciples gathered with their companions, and from them they learned that the Lord had really risen and that he had appeared to Simon. Then they told of their own experience on the road, and how they knew him when he broke the bread.

The Walk to Emmaus
Painted by Eugène Girardet

While the two disciples were speaking, Jesus himself stood among them. And they were frightened and believed that they saw a ghost; but he said to them, "Why are you so frightened? Why do you doubt? See my hands and my feet, that it is I myself. Touch me and see, for a ghost has not flesh and bones as you see that I have." While they were still unable for very joy and wonder to believe, he said to them, "Have you anything to eat here?" And when they gave him a piece of broiled fish, he ate before them.

Then he said to them, "This is what I told you when I was still with you, that everything written about me in the law of Moses and the prophets and the psalms must be fulfilled." Then he helped them to understand the scriptures, and said, "It is written that the Christ must suffer and on the third day rise from the dead, and that in his name all nations must be called upon to turn from their sins and gain God's forgiveness. You yourselves, beginning at Jerusalem, are to tell men about these things."

Now Thomas, one of the twelve disciples, who was called "The Twin," was not with them when Jesus came. The other disciples told him, "We have seen the Master." But he said to them, "Unless I see the marks of the nails in his hands and put my finger where they were and put my hand in his side, I will not believe."

Eight days later Jesus' disciples were again together, and Thomas was with them. Though the doors were closed, Jesus came and stood among them and said, "Peace be with you." Then he said to Thomas, "Put your finger here and look at my hands, and put your hand here in my side. Do not be a doubter but a believer." Thomas answered him, "My Master and my God!" Jesus said to him, "You believe because you have seen me? Blessed are those who believe though they have never seen me!"

Later Jesus appeared to his disciples by the Sea of Galilee, and in this way. As Simon Peter, Thomas, Nathanael from Cana in Galilee, and the sons of Zebedee, were together with two other of his disciples, Simon Peter said to them, "I am going fishing." "We will go too," they said, and they set out and went on board the boat; but that night they caught nothing. At daybreak Jesus stood on the beach, though the disciples did not know that it was he.

He said to them, "Children, have you anything to eat?" They answered, "No." And he said, "Throw your net over on the right side of the boat and you will catch something." So they threw over the net, and now they could not haul it in because of the great number of fish. Then the disciple whom Jesus loved said to Peter, "It is the Master." As soon as Simon Peter heard that it was the Master, he put on his fisherman's coat (for he was stripped for his work), and jumped into the water; but the other disciples, being only about one hundred yards from the shore, came in the small boat dragging the net full of fish.

When they landed, they saw a charcoal fire burning, and over it a fish cooking, and some bread. Jesus said to them, "Bring some of the fish that you have just caught." So Simon Peter went aboard the boat and hauled the net ashore filled with large fish; and although there were so many, the net was not torn. Then Jesus said to them, "Come and eat breakfast." Not one of the disciples had courage to ask, "Who are you?" for they knew that it was the Master. Jesus came and gave them the bread and also the fish. This was the third time he appeared to his disciples after he had risen from the dead.

After breakfast Jesus said to Simon Peter, "Simon, son of John, do you love me more than these?" He said, "Surely, Master, you know I love you." Jesus said to him, "Feed my lambs." Then he asked him a second time, "Simon, son of John, do you love me?" And he answered, "Surely, Master, you know that I love you." Jesus said to him, "Tend my sheep." Jesus said to him a third time, "Simon, son of John, do you love me with all your heart?" Peter was grieved because Jesus asked a third time, "Do you love me?" And he answered, "Master, you know everything, you know that I love you." Jesus said to him, "Feed my sheep."

And Jesus said to them, "All authority has been given to me in heaven and on earth. Go you, therefore, and make disciples of all the nations, baptizing them in the name of the Father and of the Son and of the Holy Spirit, teaching them to observe all things whatsoever I commanded you; and, lo, I am with you always, even to the end of the world."

Jesus showed his disciples, by many proofs, that he still lived, revealing himself to them during forty days and telling them about the Kingdom of God. When he and his disciples were together he told them not to leave Jerusalem but to wait for what the Father had promised—"the promise," he said, "of which you have heard me speak; for John baptized with water, but before many days have passed you will be baptized with the Holy Spirit."

While they were together they asked him, "Master, is this the time when you are going to restore the rulership to Israel?" Jesus said to them, "It is not for you to know the time or the season which the Father has fixed by his own authority; but you will receive power when the Holy Spirit comes upon you, and you will be my witnesses at Jerusalem, throughout all Judea and Samaria and to every part of the earth." When he had said this and while they were still looking at him, he was lifted up, and a cloud took him out of their sight. And while they were staring into heaven, as he went up, two men clothed in white stood beside them, who said, "Men of Galilee, why do you stand looking up into heaven? This Jesus, who has been taken from you into heaven, will come back in the same way as you have seen him go."

On the Day of Pentecost, as they were all together, suddenly, there came from heaven a sound like the rushing blast of a mighty wind which filled the whole house where they were seated. And they were filled with the Holy Spirit and began to speak in a strange way and to cry aloud and shout.

When this was reported a crowd gathered, astonished and perplexed, and asked one another, "What can it mean?" Others with a sneer said, "They are full of new wine!"

But Peter, together with the eleven apostles, stood up and addressed them: "Men of Judea and all who live in Jerusalem, understand this and listen to what I say: these men are not drunk as you suppose, for it is only nine in the morning, but this is what was foretold by the prophet Joel:

"'In the last days,' God declared,
'I will pour out my Spirit on all mankind;
Your sons and your daughters shall prophesy,
Your young men shall see visions.

"'And your old men shall dream dreams,
Even upon my slaves and slave-girls
In those days I will pour out my Spirit,
And they shall prophesy.'"

"Men of Israel, hear these words: By the help of lawless men you nailed to the cross and murdered Jesus of Nazareth, a man who was proved to be from God through the deeds of healing and the wonderful acts which God performed by him among you, as you yourselves know. But God released him from the bonds of death and raised him to life, for death could not hold him. Lifted on high at God's right hand and having received from the Father the promised Holy Spirit, he has poured it upon us as you now see and hear. Let the whole nation of Israel know beyond a doubt that God has made this Jesus, whom you crucified, both Lord and Christ."

When they heard this, their conscience troubled them, and they said to Peter and the rest of the apostles, "Brothers, what are we to do?" Peter answered, "Say that you are sorry for your sins, and let each of you be baptized in the name of Jesus Christ, that your sins may be forgiven; then you will receive the gift of the Holy Spirit, for it is promised to you, and to your children, and to all in distant lands, to any and to all whom the Lord our God shall call."

With many other words he warned and urged them to save themselves from this wicked time. So those who believed what he taught were baptized; and on that day about three thousand were added to the brotherhood.

THE HEALING OF THE LAME MAN AT THE BEAUTIFUL GATE

By agreement the believers met together daily in the Temple. They had their meals from house to house, eating their food with gladness and simple-heartedness, praising God and having the good-will of all the people. Day by day God added many to the number of the saved.

One day Peter and John were on their way to the Temple for the hour of prayer at three in the afternoon. A man who had been lame from birth, and who was placed daily at what was called the Beautiful Gate of the Temple, was being carried there to beg from the people who went in. When he saw that Peter and John were about to go in, he asked them to give him something. But Peter fixed his eyes on him, and John did also, and said, "Look at us." And the man looked attentively, expecting to receive something from them. Peter said, "I have neither silver nor gold, but what I have I give you. In the name of Jesus Christ of Nazareth, walk!" And he took him by the right hand and raised him up. And immediately his feet and his ankles received strength and he leaped up, stood on his feet, walked about and went with them into the Temple, walking, and leaping and praising God.

When the people who saw him walking about and praising God knew that he was the man who used to sit begging at the Beautiful Gate of the Temple, they were filled with wonder and amazement at what had happened to him; and as he still kept close to Peter and John, the astonished crowd rushed to them in what was called Solomon's Porch.

Then Peter said to the people: "Men of Israel, why do you wonder at this? Or why do you stare at us as though we had made him walk by some power or goodness of our own? The God of Abraham and of Isaac and of Jacob, the God of our forefathers, has honored Jesus his servant, whom you delivered up and denied before Pilate when he had decided to let him go. But you denied the Holy and Just One and asked that a murderer be set free and put to death the One who brings life to men! But God brought him back from the dead, as we bear witness. Jesus, through faith in his name, has given strength to this man whom you see and know. Yes, it is faith in him that has made this man perfectly well in the presence of you all.

"And now, brothers, I know that you acted in ignorance, as did also your rulers. Turn then to God and live right lives that your sins may be forgiven, so that God may send you strength. After raising his Servant from the grave, God sent him first to you to bless you by turning each of you from your wickedness."

While they were speaking to the people, they were interrupted by the priests, the officer in charge of the Temple, and the Sadducees, who were angry because they were teaching the people and telling how Jesus rose from the dead. They arrested the apostles and, as it was already evening, put them in prison until the following day.

The next morning a meeting of their rulers, elders and scribes was held in Jerusalem at which the high priest Annas, and Caiaphas, John, Alexander and all the members of the high priest's family were present. They made the apostles stand before them and inquired, "By whose power and in whose name have you done this?"

Then Peter was filled with the Holy Spirit and said to them, "Rulers of the people and elders of Israel, if we are being examined this day for a good deed done to a lame man, to find out how he was healed, you and all the people of Israel should know that this man stands before you completely cured through the name of Jesus Christ of Nazareth, whom you crucified and whom God raised from the dead. He is the stone despised by you builders that has become the chief corner-stone. And salvation comes by none other, for there is no other name under heaven revealed among men through which we can be saved."

When they saw how bold Peter and John were and found out that they were uneducated and ignorant men, they were astonished but they remembered that they had been with Jesus. Ordering them to go out from the council, they said among themselves, "What are we to do with these men? All the people who live in Jerusalem know that a wonderful miracle has been done by them, and we cannot deny it. But to keep this thing from spreading any farther among the people let us stop them by threats from speaking in the future to any one in the name of Jesus." So they called them and ordered them not to teach nor speak a word in the name of Jesus. But Peter and John replied, "Decide for yourselves whether it is right before God to obey you rather than God; for we cannot give up speaking of what we have seen and heard."

Seeing the man who had been healed standing beside them, the rulers could say nothing. So, after further threatening them, they let them go, being unable to find any reason for punishing them on account of the people, for they were all praising God for what had been done.

THE GENEROSITY OF THE EARLY CHRISTIANS

All of the believers were as one in heart and mind; and not one of them called what he had his own, but they all shared with one another. No one among them was in want, for those who owned lands or houses sold them and brought the money that came from the sale to the apostles. The money was then given to whoever needed it. Joseph, whom the apostles called Barnabas, sold his farm and brought the money to the apostles.

But a man named Ananias and his wife Sapphira sold some property, and with her approval kept back part of the price and brought only a part of it to the apostles. "Ananias," said Peter, "why has Satan put into your heart the desire to deceive the Holy Spirit and keep back part of the price of the land? While the land remained unsold, was it not your own? Even after it was sold, was not the money yours to do with as you pleased? How could you plan a thing like this? You have lied not to man but to God." When Ananias heard these words, he fell down and died; and great fear seized all who heard of it. The younger men arose, wrapped up the body, and carried it away to be buried.

About three hours later his wife came in, knowing nothing of what had taken place. Peter said to her, "Tell me, did you sell the land for so much?" And she answered, "Yes, for so much." Peter said to her, "How is it that you two agreed together to test the Spirit of the Lord? The men who have buried your husband are here at the door and they shall carry you out." Instantly she fell dead at his feet; so when the young men came in and found her dead, they carried her out and buried her beside her husband.

Then great fear came upon the whole church and upon all who heard of these things. Many miracles and wonders were done among the people by the apostles. Even from the towns about Jerusalem crowds gathered, bringing sick people, and all were healed.

STEPHEN THE FIRST CHRISTIAN MARTYR

During these days, while the number of the disciples was rapidly increasing, the Jews who came from lands where Greek was spoken began to complain against those who were born and lived in Palestine, because their widows were neglected when the food was given out each day. Therefore the twelve apostles called together all the disciples and said, "It is not right that we should give up our preaching so as to wait on tables. Brothers, choose seven of your own number, men of good reputation, wise and spiritually-minded, whom we will put in charge of this work. But we will continue to give ourselves to prayer and to preaching the good news." This plan pleased all the disciples; so they chose Stephen, a man of strong faith and spiritual power, Philip, Prochorus, Nicanor, Timon, Parmenas, and Nicolaus, who came from Antioch but had become a Jew. These men they brought before the apostles, who after praying laid their hands upon them.

And the message of the Lord continued to spread, and the number of disciples in Jerusalem was greatly increased. A large number of the priests also accepted the faith.

Stephen, who had personal charm and power, did great wonders and miracles among the people. Some belonging to the Synagogue of the Libyans, and Jews from Cyrene, Alexandria, Cilicia, and the province of Asia began to argue with Stephen; but they were unable to get the better of him because of the wisdom and spirit with which he spoke.

Then secretly they bribed certain men to say, "We have heard him speaking blasphemous words against Moses and God." In this way they stirred up the people, the elders and the scribes, so that they seized Stephen and took him before the council. They also brought in false witnesses who said, "This man is always talking against this holy place and the law. We have heard him say that this Jesus of Nazareth will destroy this place and change the customs which Moses handed down to us!"

Then all who were sitting in the council fixed their eyes on Stephen and saw that his face shone like the face of an angel. But the high priest said, "Are these charges true?" Stephen answered, "Brothers and fathers, listen. The Most High God does not live in houses made by men.

"You stubborn and evil-minded people! you always resist the Holy Spirit, as did your fathers before you. Which of the prophets did they not persecute? They also killed those who foretold the coming of the Just One, whose betrayers and murderers you have become—you who received the law given through angels, and have not kept it!"

When they heard these words, they were furious and gnashed their teeth at him. But Stephen, filled with the Holy Spirit, looked up into heaven and saw the glory of God, and Jesus standing at the right hand of God. "Look, I see heaven open," he said, "and the Son of Man standing at the right hand of God." But they stopped their ears and with a howl rushed at him all together. Then they threw him out of the city and stoned him. The witnesses who threw the first stones, laid their clothes at the feet of a young man named Saul. As they stoned Stephen, he prayed, "Lord, Jesus, receive my spirit!" Then he knelt down and cried aloud, "Lord, do not lay this sin to their charge!" When he had said this, he fell asleep. Certain devout men buried Stephen, mourning deeply for him.

But Saul consented to his murder. He also tried to destroy the church, entering into every house, and dragging out men and women, put them in prison.

PHILIP AND THE ETHIOPIAN

When Stephen was stoned to death a great persecution broke out against the church in Jerusalem, and all except the apostles were scattered throughout Judea and Samaria. Those who were scattered went in different directions telling the good news about Jesus.

Philip went down to the city of Samaria, where he told the people about Jesus, the Christ. And the crowds, when they saw the miracles he performed, paid attention to what he said. Many who could not walk or were lame were healed. So there was great joy in that city. Both the men and women who believed Philip, as he told the good news about the Kingdom of God and the name of Jesus, were baptized.

When the apostles at Jerusalem heard that the Samaritans had believed God's message, they sent Peter and John to them, who, when they came, prayed that the Samaritans might receive the Holy Spirit, for it had not yet come upon any of them; they had only been baptized in the name of the Lord Jesus. Then Peter and John laid their hands on them, and they received the Holy Spirit.

When the apostles had told the people about Jesus and preached the word of the Lord, they went back to Jerusalem; and as they went, they told the good news in many villages of the Samaritans. But an angel of the Lord said to Philip, "Rise, and go south along the desert road from Jerusalem to Gaza." As he went on his way he met an Ethiopian who had charge of the treasures of Candace, the queen of the Ethiopians. He had gone to Jerusalem to worship and was on his way home. As the Ethiopian sat in his chariot reading from the prophet Isaiah, the Spirit said to Philip, "Go up and speak to the man in the chariot." As Philip ran up and heard him reading from the prophet Isaiah, he asked, "Do you understand what you are reading?" "How can I," said the Ethiopian, "unless there is some one to tell me what it means?" So he begged Philip to come up and sit beside him.

Now the passage of scripture that he was reading was this:

> "He was led like a sheep to the slaughter,
> And as a lamb is dumb before the shearer,
> So he opened not his mouth."

The Ethiopian said to Philip, "I beg of you, tell me of whom is the prophet speaking? Of himself or of some one else?" Then Philip, taking this verse as his text, told him the good news about Jesus. As they went along, they came to some water, and the Ethiopian said, "Here is water. What prevents my being baptized?" So he ordered the chariot to stop, and both went down into the water, and Philip baptized the man. After they had come up from the water, the Spirit of the Lord sent Philip on his way, and the Ethiopian did not see him again, but went away happy. But Philip told the good news in every town until he reached Cæsarea.

PETER AND THE ROMAN OFFICER

While Peter was going through the whole country, he stayed for a long time at Joppa, in the house of Simon, a tanner.

Cornelius, the captain of the Italian guard, lived in Cæsarea. He was a righteous man and he and all his household worshipped God. He gave many gifts to the poor people, and prayed to God at all times.

One day, about three o'clock in the afternoon, Cornelius had a vision; and he saw an angel of God coming and saying to him, "Cornelius." Looking straight at him, although he was afraid, Cornelius said, "What is it, Lord?" The angel said to him, "Your prayers and your gifts to the poor are pleasing to God. Now send men to Joppa, and bring a certain Simon, whose other name is Peter. He is staying with Simon, a tanner, whose house is by the seaside." When the angel who spoke to him had gone away, Cornelius called two of his household servants, and a trusted soldier who constantly waited on him. After he had explained everything to them, he sent them to Joppa.

On the next day, about noon, as they were on their way, and were coming near to Joppa, Peter went up to the housetop to pray. While he was praying, the men who were sent by Cornelius, having found the way to Simon's house, stood before the gate, and called out to ask whether Simon, whose other name was Peter, was staying there. The Spirit said to

Peter, "See, three men are looking for you. Rise and go down, and do not hesitate to go with them; for I have sent them." So Peter went down to the men and said, "I am the man you are looking for; what do you want?" They said, "Cornelius, a captain of the guard, a righteous man and one who worships God and is well spoken of by all the Jews, was told by a holy angel to send for you and ask you to come to his house, that he may hear what you have to say." So Peter invited them in and they stayed all night.

The next day he rose and went with them, and some of the disciples from Joppa went with him. The next day after that, they reached Cæsarea. Cornelius was waiting for them, having called together his relatives and his near friends. When Peter came in, Cornelius met him and fell down at his feet and worshipped him. But Peter said, "Stand up, I am only a man, like you." After he had talked with him, he went in, and found many people there. Then Cornelius said, "Just four days ago, in the afternoon, I was praying in my house, when a man stood before me in bright clothing, and said, 'Cornelius, your prayer is heard, and your gifts to the poor are pleasing to God. Send therefore to Joppa, and call for Simon, whose other name is Peter; he is staying in the house of Simon, a tanner, by the seaside.' So I sent to you at once; and you have done well in coming. Now therefore we are all here in the presence of God, to listen to whatever the Lord has commanded you to say."

Peter said, "I see, truly, that God shows no partiality; but in every nation, the man who reveres him, and does what is right, is pleasing to him."

While Peter was still speaking, the Holy Spirit filled all those who heard the word. And the Jewish disciples who came with Peter were amazed, because the gift of the Holy Spirit was poured out on those who were not Jews. For the Jews heard them shout and praise God. Then Peter said, "Can any one refuse to baptize those who, as well as we, have received the Holy Spirit?" And he commanded that they be baptized in the name of Jesus Christ. Then they begged him to stay with them several days.

When Peter came up to Jerusalem, the Jewish followers of Jesus found fault with him for preaching to those who were not Jews. But Peter explained the matter to them, saying, "I was in the city of Joppa praying; and while I was praying, three men stood before the house in which we were staying, having been sent to me from Cæsarea. And the Spirit told me to go with them, even though they were not Jews. These six brothers here went with me also; and we went into the man's house. He told us how he had seen the angel standing in his house, and saying, 'Send to Joppa, and bring Simon, whose other name is Peter, who shall tell you certain things through which you and your whole family shall be saved.' As I began to speak, the Holy Spirit came upon them, even as on us at the beginning. And I remembered the word of the Lord, how he said, 'John indeed baptized with water, but you shall be baptized with the Holy Spirit.' If then God gave to them the like gift as he gave also to us, when we believed on the Lord Jesus Christ, who was I, that I could stand against God?" When they heard these things, they stopped finding fault, and praised God, saying, "Then also to those who are not Jews, God has given, that they may turn from their wicked deeds and live."

PETER'S ESCAPE FROM PRISON

Now about that time Herod, the king, began to persecute the members of the church; and he killed James, the brother of John, with the sword. When Herod saw that it pleased the Jews, he seized Peter also. This was during the feast of the unleavened bread. Therefore when he arrested Peter, he put him in prison, and gave him into the keeping of four bands of four soldiers each. And he planned to bring him out to the people after the Passover.

So Peter was kept in prison; but the members of the church prayed earnestly to God for him. On the very night before the day on which Herod meant to bring him up for trial, Peter was sleeping between two soldiers, fastened to them with two chains. Watchmen were also on guard at the doors. All at once an angel of the Lord stood by him and a light shone in the cell. And he struck Peter on the side and awoke him, saying, "Get up quickly." And his chains fell off his hands. The angel said to him, "Put on your belt and your sandals." And Peter did so. The angel said to him, "Throw your coat around you, and follow me." So Peter went out with him; and he did not know that what had been done by the angel was really true, but he thought he was dreaming. They went past the first and the second guards, and came to the iron gate that leads into the city; and it opened to them of itself. They went out, and passed on through one street; and all at once the angel left him. When Peter found himself alone, he said, "Now I know for certain that the Lord has sent his angel, and saved me from the hand of Herod and from all that the Jews were expecting he would do to me." And after he had thought what to do, he went to the house of Mary, the mother of John Mark. Now many people had gathered together there for prayer. When he knocked at the door a girl named Rhoda came to answer. And hearing Peter's voice, she was so glad that she forgot to open the door, but ran in, and told that Peter was standing outside. They said to her, "You are out of your mind." But she insisted that it was so. They said, "It is his angel." But Peter kept on knocking: and when they opened the door and saw him, they were amazed. But he motioned to them with the hand to be silent, and told them how the Lord had brought him out of prison. And he said, "Go and tell James and the other brothers." Then he left the house and went to another place. Now as soon as it was morning, there was great excitement among the soldiers, as to what had become of Peter. After Herod had searched for him, and had failed to find him, he questioned the guards, and commanded that they should be executed.

PAUL'S ACCOUNT OF WHAT HE SAW AND HEARD ON HIS WAY TO DAMASCUS

I am a Jew, born at Tarsus in Cilicia, but I was brought up in Jerusalem, educated as a disciple of Gamaliel in the strict way laid down in the laws received from our fathers, and devoted to God, as you all are.

You know what I did in the past among the Jews. You know how bitterly I persecuted the church of God and tried to destroy it and how in my zeal for the laws and customs handed down from my forefathers I did more than any of my fellow countrymen. I indeed believed that it was my duty to do all in my power to oppose the cause of Jesus of Nazareth. This I did in Jerusalem. With authority from the high priests, I put many of Jesus' followers in prison. When they were put to death, I voted against them. In all the synagogues I often punished them and tried to make them speak against the name of Jesus, and in my insane fury I followed them even to distant cities.

When I was travelling to Damascus on this business, with written authority from the high priests, I saw, on the road in the middle of the day, a light from heaven, more dazzling than the glare of the sun, shining around me and those who were travelling with me. We fell to the ground, and I heard a voice say to me in Hebrew, "Saul, Saul, why do you persecute me? It is hard for you to kick against the goads." I asked, "Who art thou, Lord?" and the Lord answered, "I am Jesus whom you are persecuting. Rise and stand on your feet, for I have appeared to you to appoint you to be my servant and a witness to what you have seen and to the things that I will show you. I chose you from the Jews and the other peoples to whom I am sending you to open their eyes, that they may turn from darkness to light, from the power of Satan to God, so that they may receive forgiveness of their sins and a place among those who have given themselves to me because they believe in me."

When the God, who had set me apart even from my birth and called me by his love, chose to reveal his Son in me that I might tell to other races the good news about him, I at once went into Arabia instead of talking with any one else or going up to Jerusalem to see those who had been apostles before me. When I came back I preached first to those at Damascus. There the governor, appointed by King Aretas, put guards in the city to arrest me, but I was lowered in a basket through a window in the wall and so escaped from their hands.

After three years I went up to Jerusalem to visit Peter and stayed with him fifteen days. I saw no other apostle except James the brother of Jesus.

THE CHRISTIAN CHURCH AT ANTIOCH

The disciples who had been scattered by the persecution which came after the killing of Stephen went to Phœnicia and Cyprus and Antioch, but told about Jesus only to Jews. Some of them, citizens of Cyprus and Cyrene, when they reached Antioch also told the good news about the Lord Jesus to the Greeks. The power of the Lord was with them, and a large number believed and turned to him.

When the news of this reached the church in Jerusalem, they sent Barnabas to Antioch. After he saw the proofs of God's goodness, he was very glad and urged all to remain loyal to the Lord; and many more believed.

Then Barnabas went to Tarsus to look for Paul, whose name had been Saul. When he had found him, he brought him to Antioch, and for a whole year they were with the church there and taught a large number of people. It was at Antioch also that the disciples were first called Christians.

During these days some prophets came to Antioch from Jerusalem. One of them, Agabus, under the influence of the Spirit, told that a severe famine would come all through that part of the world, and this famine came when Claudius was emperor. Therefore, the disciples, each as he was able, sent something to help the brothers living in Judea. They sent their gifts to the elders by Barnabas and Paul. After Barnabas and Paul had done that for which they were sent, they returned from Jerusalem, bringing with them John, who was also called Mark.

Now in the church at Antioch there were prophets and preachers: Barnabas, Symeon (called Niger), and Lucius the Cyrenean, besides Manean (a childhood friend of Herod the ruler), and Paul. As they were worshipping the Lord and fasting, the Holy Spirit said, "Set apart for me Barnabas and Paul for the work to which I have called them." Then when they had fasted and prayed, they gave them their blessing and sent them on their way.

PAUL AND BARNABAS IN FOREIGN LANDS

Paul and Barnabas, sent by the Holy Spirit, went to Seleucia and from there sailed to Cyprus. When they came to Salamis, they, with Mark as their helper, told God's message in the Jewish synagogue.

When they had gone over the whole island as far as Paphos, they set sail, and Paul and his companions came to Perga in Pamphylia. There Mark left them to return to Jerusalem, but they went on to Antioch. On the Sabbath they went into the synagogue and sat down. After the reading of the law and the prophets the men in charge of the synagogue service sent word to them, "Brothers, if you have any word of encouragement for the people, say it." So Paul stood up and motioning with his hand said, "Listen, men of Israel and you who worship God. The God of this people Israel chose our fathers. While they were in Egypt he made them a great people, and then with wonderful signs of his power he led them out of that land. After destroying seven nations in the land of Canaan, he gave them that land to have as their own and later made David their king. From David's family God brought to Israel, as he had promised, a Saviour, Jesus.

"Brothers, sons of Abraham's race, and all among you who worship God, to us has been sent this saving message. The people of Jerusalem and their rulers did not believe Jesus, and though they could find no reason why he should be killed, they asked Pilate to put him to death. But God raised him from the dead, and for many days he was seen by those who had come with him from Galilee to Jerusalem. They are now his witnesses to the people. So we bring you the good news that God, by raising Jesus from the dead, has fulfilled for our children the promise made to our fathers."

As Paul and Barnabas were going out, the people begged that this be repeated to them on the following Sabbath. After the congregation broke up, many of the Jews and religious Greeks followed Paul and Barnabas, who spoke to them, urging them through God's help to remain loyal.

On the next Sabbath nearly all the people of the city came to hear the message of the Lord. But when the Jews saw the crowd, they were jealous and began to contradict what Paul said, and to insult him. But Paul and Barnabas spoke out fearlessly and said, "It was necessary that God's message should be spoken first to you; but since you will not hear it and prove yourselves unworthy of eternal life, here and now we turn to those who are not Jews. For this is the Lord's command to us: 'I have set you as a light to other races, to bring salvation to the ends of the earth.'"

When those who were not Jews heard this, they were glad and gave thanks for God's message; and as many as were ordained to receive eternal life believed, and God's message was carried far and wide throughout the country. But the Jews, with the help of women of high rank and the leading men in the city, started a persecution against Paul and Barnabas and drove them from the city. So the apostles shook the dust from their feet as a protest against them, and went on to Iconium. The new disciples, however, were filled with joy and the Holy Spirit.

At Iconium, Paul and Barnabas went into the Jewish synagogue and spoke, so that a great number of both Jews and Greeks believed. But the Jews who did not believe stirred up the other races and poisoned their minds against the apostles. The people of the town were divided, some being on the side of the Jews and others on the side of the apostles. An attempt was made both by the other races and by the Jews, with the help of their rulers, to attack and stone the apostles; but they learned of it and escaped to the towns of Lystra and Derbe, and there they continued to preach the good news.

At Lystra there was a man who could not move his feet, who had been lame from his birth and had never walked. As this man listened to Paul's preaching, the apostle fixed his eyes on him and, seeing that he had faith enough to make him well, said in a loud voice, "Stand up on your feet." And the man sprang up and began to walk. When the crowds saw what Paul had done, they shouted in their language, "The gods have come down to us in the form of men!" Barnabas they called "Zeus," and Paul "Hermes," because he was the chief speaker. The priests of the temple of Zeus, which stood in front of the town, brought oxen and wreaths to the gates, so as to join the crowds in offering sacrifice to them.

But when Barnabas and Paul heard this, they tore their clothes and rushed into the crowd, shouting, "Men, why are you doing this? We are but men like yourselves, and are bringing you the good news so that you may turn from these idols and worship the living God who made the heaven, the earth, the sea, and all that is in them. In past ages he allowed all nations to worship as they pleased; yet as the bountiful Giver he did not leave himself without a witness, for he gives you rain from heaven and fruitful seasons and makes your hearts happy with food and good cheer." Yet even with these words they could hardly keep the crowd from sacrificing to them.

But Jews came from Antioch and Iconium and won over the crowds, who stoned Paul, and then, believing him dead, dragged him out of the city. However, when the disciples had gathered about him, he got up and went into the city.

The next day he went with Barnabas to Derbe. After they had preached the good news to that city and had won many disciples, they returned to Lystra, Iconium, and Antioch, and encouraged the disciples urging them to be true to the faith. Then they passed through Pisidia and came to

Pamphylia, and after preaching in Perga, they went down to Attaleia. From there they set sail for Antioch.

When they reached Antioch, they called together the members of the church and told everything that God had done with them, and how he had opened the door of faith to those who were not Jews. And they stayed there a long time with the disciples.

WHY PAUL WENT TO MACEDONIA

After they had stayed at Antioch for some time, Paul said to Barnabas, "Let us return and visit the brothers in all the cities where we have told the good news from the Lord, and see how they are getting on." Barnabas wished to take Mark with them, but Paul did not think it wise to take with them one who had deserted them in Pamphylia instead of going on with them to work in Pisidia. So they parted company, and Barnabas took Mark with him to Cyprus. Paul chose Silas and went away, commended by the brothers to the gracious care of the Lord. He went through Syria and Cilicia, encouraging the churches.

He also went to Derbe and Lystra. At Lystra there was a disciple, called Timothy, the son of a Christian Jewess and a Greek father. As he had a good reputation among the brothers at Lystra and Iconium, Paul wished to have him go with him. And the churches were strengthened in the faith and increased in numbers daily.

Then Paul and his companions crossed the Phrygian and Galatian country, but were prevented by the Holy Spirit from preaching in the province of Asia. When they reached Mysia they tried to enter Bithynia, but the Spirit of Jesus did not permit them; so passing by Mysia they went down to Troas.

One night Paul had a vision: a man of Macedonia was standing and begging him, "Come over into Macedonia and help us." As soon as Paul saw the vision, we were eager to start at once for Macedonia, believing that God had called us to tell the good news to them. So, setting sail from

Troas, we ran straight to Samothrace, and on the next day to Neapolis. From there we went to Philippi, which is the principal city in that part of Macedonia. In that city we spent some days.

On the Sabbath we went outside the city gate by the river, where we believed there was a place of prayer. And we sat down and talked to the women who had gathered. Among them was a woman named Lydia, a dealer in purple cloth from the city of Thyatira, who was already a worshipper of God. The Lord opened her mind, so that she listened to what Paul was saying; and when she and her household had been baptized, she urged us, saying, "If you are sure that I am a true believer in the Lord, come and stay at my house." And she made us do so.

PAUL AND SILAS IN MACEDONIA

One day as we were going to the place of prayer, a slave girl met us who was under the control of a spirit that made her clairvoyant, so that she brought great gain to her owners by fortune-telling. She kept following Paul and the rest of us, crying, "These men are servants of the Most High God; they proclaim to you the way of salvation." This she did for many days until Paul, unable to stand it longer, turned and said to the spirit, "In the name of Jesus Christ I command you to come out of her." And it left her at once.

But when her owners saw that their hope of gain was gone, they seized Paul and Silas and dragged them into the public square before the city officials. Bringing them before the military rulers, they said, "These are Jews who are making a disturbance in our city; they proclaim customs which it is not lawful for us as Romans to adopt or follow." The mob also joined in the attack upon them, so the military rulers tore their garments off them and ordered them to be beaten with rods. After beating them severely, they threw them in prison and ordered the jailer to be sure to keep them safely. On receiving this strict order, he put them into the inner prison and fastened their feet in the stocks.

About midnight, as Paul and Silas were praying and singing hymns to God, and while the prisoners were listening to them, there was suddenly such a great earthquake that the very foundations of the prison were shaken. Immediately all the doors were opened and the chains that bound all the prisoners were loosened.

When the jailer suddenly awoke and saw the prison doors wide open, he drew his sword and was about to kill himself, thinking the prisoners had escaped. But Paul shouted, "Do no harm to yourself, for we are all here!" So calling for lights, the jailer rushed in, and trembling with fear, fell down before Paul and Silas. Then bringing them out of the prison he said, "Sirs, what must I do to be saved?" They answered, "Believe in the Lord Jesus Christ and you and your household will be saved." So Paul and Silas preached the word of the Lord to him and to all his family. Then the jailer took them at that very hour of the night and washed their wounds, and he and all his family were at once baptized. He then brought them to his house and gave them food to eat, and greatly rejoiced with all his family that they had come to believe in God.

The next morning the city officials sent the police with the order, "Release these men." So the jailer told Paul, "The police have brought an order to have you released; now you may come out and go in peace." But Paul answered, "They have beaten us publicly without trial, although we are Roman citizens, and they put us in prison! Now they are going to send us out secretly! No, indeed. Let them come here themselves and take us out."

The police reported this to the military rulers, who, when they heard that they were Roman citizens, were afraid and came to make peace with them, and when they had brought them out of prison, they begged them to leave the city. So Paul and Silas left the prison, and went to Lydia's house; and after they had seen the brothers and encouraged them, they left the city.

After they had passed through Amphipolis and Apollonia, they came to Thessalonica, where the Jews had a synagogue. As usual, Paul went in, and for three weeks he argued with them, to prove to them from the scriptures that the Christ had to suffer and rise from the dead, and Paul said that "this Jesus I proclaim to you is the Christ." Some of the Jews and a large number of God-fearing Greeks and many of the leading women believed and threw in their lot with Paul and Silas.

But the Jews were jealous and got hold of the loafers in the market-place, and raised a mob and started a riot in the city. They attacked Jason's house, so as to bring Paul and Silas out before the people, and when they did not find them, they dragged Jason and some of the brothers before the city officials, shouting, "These men who have upset the whole world have come here too! Jason has welcomed them. They do not keep the laws of Cæsar and declare that some one else called Jesus is king." On hearing this the crowd and the city officials were greatly troubled; but after Jason and the others had pledged to keep the peace, they let them go.

Then the brothers at once sent Paul and Silas away by night to Berœa. When they arrived there, they went to the Jewish synagogue, where the people were of a nobler spirit than at Thessalonica, for they were very ready to hear the teaching about Jesus, and studied their scriptures daily to see if what Paul said was true. Many of the Jews believed and also prominent Greek women and many men.

As soon as the Jews at Thessalonica learned that God's message was being proclaimed by Paul at Berœa, they came there also to stir up the people to riot. Then the brothers at once sent Paul on his way to the sea-coast, but Silas and Timothy stayed at Berœa. The friends who escorted Paul went with him as far as Athens, and left him there, after receiving instructions that Silas and Timothy were to come to him as soon as possible.

PAUL'S GREAT SPEECH AT ATHENS

St. Paul Preaching at Athens
Painted by Raphael

While Paul was waiting at Athens for Silas and Timothy, his anger was aroused when he saw that the city was filled with idols. So he argued in the synagogue with the Jews and with the Greeks who joined in their worship, and every day with those whom he happened to meet in the market-place. A few of the philosophers also met him. Some of them said, "What has this picker-up of scraps of learning to say?" Others said, "He seems to be a herald of some new deities." This was because he had been telling the good news about Jesus and how he rose from the dead. And they took him to the Court of Areopagus and said, "May we hear what this new teaching of yours is? For the things you are saying sound strange to us; so we want to know what they mean." (For all the Athenians and the foreign visitors spent their time doing nothing but telling or hearing something new.)

So Paul stood in the middle of the Court and said, "Men of Athens, I see wherever I go that you are very religious, for as I passed along and looked at your objects of worship, I found an altar with the inscription,

TO AN UNKNOWN GOD

Whom, therefore, you worship without knowing, him I proclaim to you. The God who made the world and all things in it is Lord of heaven and earth and does not live in temples made by men. He is not served by men's hands, as though he needed anything, for he it is who gives to all men life and breath and all things. He has made all nations from one family that they may live over the whole earth. He has also fixed for them when and where they are to live, that they should seek God in the hope that, as they feel after him, they may find him, for he is not far from each one of us; for it is in him that we live, and move, and have our being, as in fact, some of your own poets have said, 'We also are his children.'

"Therefore, as the children of God, we ought not to think of the divine nature as being like gold or silver or stone, carved by man's art and invention. God overlooked the ages of ignorance, but now he commands all men everywhere to repent, for he has fixed a day on which he will judge the world justly by the one whom he has appointed, and he has given proof of this to all mankind by raising him from the dead."

When they heard of raising one from the dead, some sneered, but others said, "We will hear what you have to say about that some other time." So Paul went out from among them. Some men, however, joined him and believed, among whom were Dionysius, a member of the Court of the Areopagus, a woman named Damaris, and several others. After this Paul left Athens and went to Corinth.

PAUL WRITES TO HIS FRIENDS AT THESSALONICA

Paul and Silas and Timothy to the church of the Thessalonians which lives in God the Father and the Lord Jesus Christ.

May good-will and peace be granted to you.

We thank God always for you all and mention you in our prayers, for we constantly remember before our God and Father your active faith and loving service and firm hope in our Lord Jesus Christ.

You yourselves know, brothers, that our visit to you was not without results. At Philippi, as you remember, we had the courage through divine help to tell you the good news of God even though we had been ill treated and insulted. We loved you so much and you had become so dear to us that we would gladly have given to you not only God's good news, but also our very lives.

Brothers, you remember our hard labor and toil, how we worked at our trade night and day so as not to be a burden to any of you, while we told you God's good news. You are witnesses, and so is God, that our dealings with you who believe in Christ were pure, just, and beyond reproach, and that we treated each of you as a father treats his own children, persuading and encouraging you, and appealing to you to live so that you would be worthy of the God who calls you to his own Kingdom and glory.

We thank God constantly for this also, that when you received God's message from us you accepted it not as a mere word of man but for what it really is, the message of God, which even now is doing its work in the hearts of you who believe. You have begun to follow the example of the churches of God in Judea which are united with Jesus Christ, for you have suffered the same things from your own countrymen as they have suffered from the Jews who killed the Lord Jesus.

Brothers, when we were torn away from you for a little time (out of sight but not out of mind!), we were exceedingly eager to see you face to face. We did want to come to you—I, Paul, did more than once, but Satan put difficulties in our way. For who is "our hope, our joy, our crown" of which we have a right to be proud? Is it not you? For you are our glory and our joy!

So when I could stand it no longer, I decided that it was best to remain alone at Athens and send Timothy, our brother and God's servant in telling the good news about Christ, to strengthen your faith and so to encourage you that none of you might be disturbed by the troubles through which you are passing, for you know that we must have them.

But now that Timothy has just come back and brought me the good news of your faith and love and how you always remember me lovingly, longing to see me as I long to see you, I have been comforted, brothers, in all my distress and trouble by your faith.

How can we thank God enough for all the joy that comes to us through you? Night and day we pray most earnestly that we may see your faces and supply whatever is lacking in your faith. May our God and Father himself and our Lord Jesus direct our way to you, and may the Lord make your love for one another and for all men grow ever greater, even as does our love for you, so as to make your hearts strong and your characters without fault in the sight of our God and Father.

I solemnly charge you in the name of the Lord to have this letter read aloud to all the brothers. The love of our Lord Jesus Christ be with you.

PAUL'S WORK AT CORINTH

And Paul left the place and went to the home of Titius Justus, who worshipped God, whose house was next to the synagogue. Crispus, the president of the synagogue, and all his family, believed in the Lord; and many of the Corinthians when they heard Paul, believed and were baptized. One night the Lord said to Paul in a vision, "Do not be afraid, but speak and do not stop, for I am with you and no one shall harm you; I have many followers in this city." So Paul lived there a year and a half and taught them the word of God.

But when Gallio was governor of Greece, the Jews joined in an attack on Paul and brought him before the court on the charge that he led people to worship God contrary to the law. But just as Paul was about to speak, Gallio said to the Jews, "If it were something about wrong-doing or a serious crime, there would be some reason for my listening to you, O Jews; but if these are only questions about names and your own law, take care of them yourselves. I do not wish to be a judge of matters like these." And he drove them out of the court. Then all the people caught hold of Sosthenes, the president of the synagogue, and beat him in front of the court; but Gallio paid no attention to these things. Paul, after staying some time longer in Corinth, said good-by to the brothers and with Priscilla and Aquila, sailed for Syria.

PAUL WRITES TO HIS FRIENDS IN CORINTH

Paul, called to be an apostle of Christ Jesus by the will of God, and brother Sosthenes to the church of God at Corinth.

I thank God continually for the blessing which he has given you through Jesus Christ. Through him you have been so richly and fully gifted with every kind of speech and knowledge that you have proved the truth of the testimony which I bore to Christ when I was with you.

Brothers, in the name of our Lord Jesus Christ I beg of you all to agree in your statement of faith. There must be no quarrels among you, but you must be one both in your way of thinking and in your purpose. For I have been told, brothers, by the members of Chloe's household, that there are quarrels among you.

Avoid all impurity! Every other sin that a man commits is outside the body, but the impure man sins against his own body. Do you not know that your body is the temple of the Holy Spirit that is within you, which you have received from God? You do not belong to yourselves, for you were bought for a price. Be sure to honor God with your bodies.

No temptation has come to you that is beyond your power to resist. God is faithful and will not let you be tempted beyond what you can stand; but when the temptation comes, he will provide the way of escape, so that you will have strength to endure.

In all things I can do as I like, but they are not all good for me. In all things I can do as I like, but they do not all make me a better man. Each of us must seek not only his own good but that of his neighbor.

Do you not know that in a race, though all run, only one wins the prize? So run that you may win the prize. Every athlete exercises self-restraint in every way; but while they do this to win a crown that perishes, we do it to secure one that is eternal. So then I run as one who is sure of his goal. I do not plant my blows as a boxer who beats the air; rather I constantly train my body and keep it under control for fear that I, who told others of the contest, might myself be disqualified.

Now brothers, I wish you to understand about spiritual gifts. There are different kinds of gifts, but all are given by the same Spirit. There are different ways of serving, but all are for the same Master. There are different ways in which God's power is shown, but the same God is working in all of you in all these ways. Each is given his own gift of the Spirit for the common good.

Just as a man's body has many parts, and these parts, although many, form only one body, so it is with Christ. For we have all been baptized by the one Spirit so as to form one body. Whether we were Jews or Greeks, slaves or freemen, we have all been given the same Spirit. For the body consists not of one part but of many. If the foot were to say, "Because I am not the hand I do not belong to the body," that would not make it any less a part of the body. If the ear were to say, "Because I am not an eye, I do not belong to the body," it would be, for all that, a part of the body. If the whole body were an eye, where would the hearing be? If the whole body were an ear, where would the sense of smell be? But as it is, God gave each part of the body its proper place, exactly as he wished. If they were all only one part, where would the body be? As it is, while there are many parts, there is only one body.

The eye cannot say to the hand, "I have no need of you," nor can the head say to the feet, "I have no need of you." On the contrary, even those parts of the body which seem weaker are necessary. If one part suffers, all parts suffer with it. If one part is honored, all the parts share its honor.

Now you are one body—the body of Christ, and each of you are parts of it. And God gave each his proper place in the church: apostles first, prophets next, teachers third, then workers of miracles, healers, helpers, and directors.

Are all apostles? Are all prophets? Are all teachers? Are all able to work miracles? Are all healers? Are all able to tell what their words mean? But always seek to attain the highest gifts.

Yet I will show you a far better way. Though I speak with the tongues of men and of angels but have not love, I am only sounding brass or a clanging cymbal. Even though I have the gift of prophecy, and can understand all mysteries and all knowledge, and have faith enough to remove mountains, but have not love, I am nothing. And if I give all I have to feed the poor and my body to be burned, but have not love, I gain nothing.

Love is patient and kind; love is not envious; love is not boastful, is not conceited, does not act rudely, is not selfish, is never provoked, does not resent wrong; rejoices not in evil, but rejoices in the truth. Love forgives all things, believes all things, hopes for all things, endures all things.

Love never fails. As for prophecies they shall come to an end. As for tongues they shall cease. As for knowledge it also shall come to an end;

for we know in part, and we prophesy in part. But when that which is perfect has come, that which is imperfect shall come to an end.

When I was a child, I spoke as a child, I felt as a child, I thought as a child; but now that I am a man I have put away childish ways. For now we see only the dim reflection in a mirror, but then face to face. Now I know only in part, but then I shall know fully, even as also I am fully known.

And now abide faith, hope, and love, these three; but the greatest of these is love.

THE NEW LIFE AFTER DEATH

Now, brothers, remember the good news I preached to you, that Christ died for our sins, and that he was buried and rose again the third day.

Now if we preach that Christ rose from the dead, why do some of you say that there is no resurrection of the dead? If there is no such thing as a resurrection of the dead, then Christ did not rise; and if Christ did not rise then our preaching is of no value and your faith also is of no value.

But some one will say, "How do the dead rise and what kind of body will they have when they come back?" Foolish one! The seed you sow does not come to life again unless it dies. What you sow is not the body that will be, but a mere grain, perhaps of wheat or of some other seed. God gives it the kind of body that he sees fit, to each kind of seed a body of its own.

All flesh is not the same; there is human flesh, another flesh of beasts, another flesh of birds, and another of fishes. There are heavenly bodies and also earthly bodies, but the splendor of the heavenly is one thing and that of the earthly is another. There is one splendor of the sun, another splendor of the moon, and another splendor of the stars; for one star differs from another in splendor.

So it is with a man's body when he rises from the dead. It is sown a perishable thing, it is raised imperishable; it is sown without honor, it is raised in glory; it is sown in weakness, it is raised in power; it is sown a natural body, it is raised a spiritual body. If there is a natural body, there is also a spiritual body.

In a moment, in the twinkling of an eye, we shall be changed and this perishable body must put on the imperishable and this mortal body put on immortality. Then shall come true what is written in Scripture "Death is swallowed up by victory. O grave, where is your victory? O death, where is your sting?" Thanks be to God who gives us the victory through our Lord Jesus Christ.

WAYS OF SHOWING LOVE

Now about the collection for God's people in Jerusalem, you must carry out the same directions that I gave to the churches in Galatia. On the first day of every week let each one put aside a certain part of what he has gained, so that the money will not have to be collected when I come. When I arrive I will send those whom you select, with letters, to carry your gift to Jerusalem, and if it is worth while for me to go too, they shall go with me.

I will come to you after I have passed through Macedonia, for I am going there. Perhaps I shall spend some time, or even pass the winter with you, that you may start me on my way, wherever I may be going. I do not wish to see you merely in passing, for my hope is to stay some time with you, if the Lord permits. But I will stay in Ephesus until the Feast of Pentecost, for I have a great opportunity here for work, and there are many foes.

If Timothy comes, see that he has nothing to fear while among you, for he is carrying on the Lord's work even as I am. So let no one slight him, but see him safely on his way that he may come to me, for I am waiting for him along with the other brothers.

Be watchful, stand firm in the faith, be men, be strong! Let all that you do be done in love.

The churches of the province in Asia send you greetings. Aquila and Prisca, with the church that meets in their home, also send you greetings, and so do all the brothers.

I, Paul, add this greeting with my own hand: "The Love of the Lord Jesus Christ be with you. My love be with you all in Christ Jesus."

PAUL'S TRIALS AND VICTORIES AT EPHESUS

After spending some time at Antioch Paul went off on a trip to Galatia and Phrygia to strengthen the faith of all the disciples; then he returned to Ephesus. There Paul entered the synagogue, and spoke out fearlessly for three months, arguing and trying to convince people about the Kingdom of God. But as some were stubborn and refused to be convinced and publicly slandered the Christian way of thinking and living, Paul, taking the disciples with him, left the synagogue and continued his teaching every day in the lecture-room of Tyrannus. This continued for two years, so that all the people who lived in the province of Asia, both Jews and Greeks, heard the message of the Lord.

And God did wonderful miracles through Paul, and the name of the Lord Jesus was held in high honor. Many who believed in him came to confess and to tell all the wicked things they had done.

About that time a great disturbance arose over the Christian way of teaching and living. A silversmith, by the name of Demetrius, made silver models of the temple of Artemis which brought much profit to his workmen. He gathered the workmen together, and others who were in the same kind of business, and said to them, "Men, you know that we get our wealth from this business of ours. You also see and hear that, not only at Ephesus but throughout the whole province of Asia, this Paul has drawn away many people by telling them that gods made by human hands are not gods at all. There is danger not only that this business will be hurt, but also that the temple of the great goddess Artemis will be neglected, and that she will even lose her importance in all the province of Asia and throughout the world."

When they heard this they were greatly enraged, and shouted, "Great is Artemis of the Ephesians!" The uproar spread throughout the whole city until the people all rushed into the theatre, dragging along Gaius and Aristarchus, men of Macedonia, who were Paul's travelling companions. Paul wanted to enter the assembly, but the disciples would not let him. Some of the leading religious officers of the province of Asia, who were friends of his, also sent messages begging him not to risk going into the theatre.

Some of the people shouted one thing and some another, for the assembly was all in confusion, and most of those present did not know why they had come together. For about two hours they shouted, "Great is Artemis of the Ephesians!" When the city recorder had quieted the mob, he said: "Men of Ephesus, what man is there who does not know that this city is the guardian of the temple of the great Artemis and of the statue that fell from heaven? As these facts cannot be denied, you should keep calm and do nothing reckless. You have brought these men here who are neither robbers of temples nor blasphemers of our goddess. If Demetrius and his fellow workers have a complaint against anybody, there are the courts and the Roman officials; let both sides state their charges. But if there is anything else you want, it must be settled in the regular assembly. We are indeed in danger of being charged with riot because of what we have done to-day, for there is no good reason that we can give for this gathering." With these words he dismissed the assembly.

When the uproar had ceased, Paul sent for the disciples and encouraged them. Then, after bidding them good-by, he started for Macedonia.

PAUL WRITES TO THE CHRISTIANS AT ROME

Paul, a servant of Jesus Christ, called to be an apostle, set apart to tell God's good news about Jesus Christ our Lord, to all God's loved ones who are in Rome and have been called to be his people: Love to you, and peace from God our Father and the Lord Jesus Christ.

First of all I thank my God through Jesus Christ for you all, because your faith is reported throughout the whole world. The God whom I serve with my spirit, as I tell the good news about his Son, is my witness how often I speak of you in my prayers, asking that at last the way may be opened for me to come to you, if it is God's will. For I long to see you that I may give you some spiritual gift, that you may be strengthened; or rather that we may each be encouraged by the other's faith, I by yours, and you by mine.

Brothers, I also wish you to know that many times I planned to come to you (but thus far was prevented) that I might gather some fruit from my labors among you, as I have already in the other nations. I have a duty to perform both to Greeks and to barbarians; both to the wise and to the ignorant; so I am eager to tell the good news to you also who are in Rome. I am not ashamed of the good news, for it is the power of God that is able to save every one who believes it, the Jew first and the Greek as well.

Do not follow the example of those who have not heard the good news, but be made different by a complete change of mind, so that you may be able to know what is the will of God, even what is good and perfect and acceptable to him.

Let your love be sincere; abhor that which is evil, cling to that which is good. In your love for your brothers, feel genuine devotion for one another. Be eager to honor one another. Never let your zeal grow less; keep alive your enthusiasm; serve the Lord; rejoice in your hope. Be patient in trouble, persevering in prayer; share with fellow Christians in need, be friendly and generous.

Bless those who persecute you, bless and curse not. Rejoice with those who rejoice, and weep with those who weep. Be sympathetic with one another. Set not your heart on high things but be ready to do humble tasks. Do not be conceited.

Do not pay back evil for evil; aim to do what is honorable in the eyes of all men. If possible, as far as it depends on you, live at peace with all men. Never seek revenge, dear friends, but let God punish those who wrong you. Therefore, if your enemy is hungry, feed him; if he is thirsty, give him drink, for in so doing you will heap coals of fire upon his head. Do not let evil overcome you, but overcome evil with good.

Owe no man anything, except to love one another, for he who loves his neighbor has done what the law demands. For all the commandments are summed up in this one command: "You shall love your neighbor as yourself." Love never wrongs a fellow man; that is why love meets all the demands of the law.

I have, for several years, been longing to visit you when I go to Spain. I am hoping to see you on my way there, and to be sent on my journey by you after I have first enjoyed being with you for a time. But now I am on my way to Jerusalem to do a service for God's people; for the Christians in Macedonia and Greece have been good enough to make a contribution for the poor Christians at Jerusalem.

Now I beg of you, brothers, in the name of our Lord Jesus Christ and by the love which his Spirit inspires, that you join me in earnest prayer to God in my behalf. Pray that I may be delivered from those in Judea who refuse to believe in Jesus, that my mission to Jerusalem may prove acceptable to God's people, and that I may through the will of God come to you joyfully and find rest with you.

May the God who gives peace be with you all. Amen.

PAUL'S LAST JOURNEY TO JERUSALEM

After we had said good-by to the elders of Ephesus we sailed to Syria and landed at Tyre, where the ship was to unload her cargo. There we found certain Christian disciples and stayed a week with them. Speaking under the influence of the Spirit, they told Paul not to set foot in Jerusalem; but when it was time for us to go, we went on our way, and they all, with their wives and children, came with us until we were out of the city. Then kneeling on the beach, we prayed and said good-by to one another; we went on board and they returned home.

Sailing from Tyre to Ptolemais, we completed our voyage. After greeting the Christian brothers who lived there, we spent a day with them. The next morning we set out and reached Cæsarea, where we went to the house of Philip the evangelist, who was one of the Seven, and stayed with him. He had four daughters who had the gift of prophecy.

During our stay there, which lasted a number of days, a prophet named Agabus came down from Judea. Coming up to us, he took Paul's belt, bound his own feet and hands with it, and said: "This is what the Holy Spirit says, 'In the same way the Jews will bind the owner of this belt at Jerusalem and will turn him over to the Romans.'" When we and the brothers who lived there heard this, we begged Paul not to go up to Jerusalem, but Paul answered, "What do you mean by weeping and breaking my heart? For I am ready not only to be bound but to die in Jerusalem for the cause of the Lord Jesus." So when he could not be kept from going, we stopped pleading and said: "The Lord's will be done."

After some days we started for Jerusalem. Some of the disciples from Cæsarea went with us and brought us to the house of Mnason of Cyprus, one of the early disciples, with whom we were to stay. When we reached Jerusalem the brothers welcomed us gladly.

The next day Paul went with us to see James, and all the elders of the church were present. After Paul had greeted them, he told, one by one, all the things that God had done among the foreign peoples through his ministry. When they heard it they praised God and said to him, "Brother, you see how many thousands of Christian believers there are among the Jews and that they are all eager to have men keep the law. They have been told that you teach all Jews living in foreign lands not to keep the law of Moses. Now what is to be done? They will certainly hear that you have come; therefore do this: we have here four men who have solemnly promised to make certain offerings at the Temple. Join with them, pay their expenses, and all will know that there is no truth in the stories told about you, but that you live as the law of Moses commands."

So Paul joined the men the next day and went with them into the Temple to give notice of the time when sacrifice was to be offered for every one of them.

PAUL'S NARROW ESCAPE FROM DEATH

The seven days during which the men had promised to make special offerings were almost over when some Jews from Asia, who saw Paul in the Temple, stirred up the whole crowd and laid hands on him, shouting, "Men of Israel, help! This is the man who teaches all men, everywhere, to despise the Jewish people, the Jewish law, and this sacred place." So the whole city was aroused. The people rushed together, seized Paul, and dragged him outside the Temple; and at once the doors were closed.

The people were trying to kill Paul when it was reported to the commander of the soldiers that all Jerusalem was in an uproar. He at once took some soldiers and officers and rushed down among them. When they saw the commander and the soldiers, they stopped beating Paul. Then the commander came up and arrested him and ordered him to be bound with two chains, and inquired, "Who is he and what has he done?" Some of the crowd shouted one thing, some another; and as the commander could not learn the real truth on account of the uproar, he ordered Paul to be taken to the castle. When Paul reached the steps, he had to be carried by the soldiers on account of the violence of the crowd, for all the people followed, shouting, "Kill him!"

Just as Paul was being taken into the castle, he said to the commander, "May I say something to you?" The commander said: "Do you speak Greek? Then you are not the Egyptian who some time ago started a rebellion and led four thousand outlaws into the desert?" Paul answered, "I am a Jew, of Tarsus in Cilicia, a citizen of a great city. I beg of you, let me speak to the people."

So when the commander had given him permission, Paul stood on the steps and motioned with his hand to the people, and when there was a great silence, he spoke to them in Hebrew: "Brothers, and fathers, listen to the defense I now make before you." When they heard him speaking to them in Hebrew they were all the more quiet; so he went on to say, "I am a Jew, born in Tarsus in Cilicia, but brought up in this city, educated under Gamaliel in all the strictness of our law. I was as eager to serve God as you all are to-day. I persecuted and even killed the followers of Jesus. I bound and put in prison both men and women, as the high priest himself and all the elders can testify.

"It was also from them that I had letters to our fellow Jews in Damascus, and I was on my way to bring the Christians who were there back to Jerusalem in chains for punishment. While I was on my way not far from Damascus, suddenly, about noon, a bright light from heaven shone around me. I fell to the ground and heard a voice saying to me, 'Saul, Saul, why do you persecute me?' 'Who art thou, Lord?' I asked. He answered, 'I am Jesus of Nazareth, the one whom you are persecuting.' And I said, 'What shall I do, Lord?' And the Lord said to me, 'Rise, and go to Damascus, and there it shall be told you what you are to do.' And when I could not see because of the bright light, I went to Damascus, led by the hand of those who were with me. And one Ananias, a religious man, well thought of by the Jews, came and, standing beside me, said, 'Brother Saul, receive your sight,' and that very minute I received my sight and saw him. And he said to me, 'The God of our fathers has chosen you to know his will and to see the Righteous One. For you shall be his witness to all men of what you have seen and heard.' And the Lord said to me, 'Go, for I will send you far away to those who are not Jews.'"

Up to this time the people had listened to him, but when they heard these words they shouted, "Away with such a fellow from the earth, for he is not fit to live," and they threw off their clothes and flung dust into the air until the commander ordered Paul to be taken into the castle and examined, by flogging, to find out why the people had shouted so against him. When they had tied him up with straps, Paul said to the officer who was standing by, "Is it lawful for you to flog a Roman citizen without trial?" When the officer heard this he reported it to the commander and said: "Take care what you do, for this man is a Roman citizen." Then the commander came to Paul and said, "Tell me, are you a Roman citizen?" He said, "Yes." The commander answered, "I paid a large sum for this citizenship"; and Paul said, "But I was born a Roman citizen." The men who were to have examined him, at once left him. And the commander, when he learned that Paul was a Roman citizen, was also afraid because he had bound him.

The next day the commander, so as to find out just what charge the Jews had made against Paul, unbound him and ordered the high priests and all the members of the council to come together. Then they brought Paul down and placed him before them. Paul, looking straight at the members of the council, said: "Brothers, I have done my duty, with a clear conscience before God, up to the present moment."

When Paul saw that some of the council were Sadducees and some Pharisees, he cried out, "Brothers, I am a Pharisee, a son of Pharisees. It is because of my hope that the dead will live again that I am on trial!" When he said this a quarrel arose between the Pharisees and the Sadducees, and there was a great difference of opinion among them. For the Sadducees say that there is no life after death, nor angel, nor spirit; but the Pharisees believe in all these; so there was a great uproar. Some of the scribes who belonged to the party of the Pharisees sprang to their feet and protested,

"We find this man guilty of no crime. What if some spirit or an angel has spoken to him?" When the uproar became so great that the commander was afraid that Paul would be torn in pieces by them, he ordered the troops to go down and take him from among them by force and bring him into the castle.

The next night the Lord stood beside Paul and said, "Be of good cheer, for as you have spoken for me at Jerusalem, so you must speak also at Rome."

Early the next morning the Jews plotted together and solemnly promised not to eat or drink until they had killed Paul, and there were more than forty who made this promise. They went to the high priests and elders and said, "We have made a solemn promise to taste no food until we have killed Paul. Now you and the council must tell the commander that you wish him to bring Paul down to you, as though you wanted to examine more carefully the charges brought against him. We shall be ready to kill him before he comes here."

But Paul's sister's son heard of their plot and went to the castle and told Paul. And Paul called one of the officers and said, "Take this young man to the commander, for he has something to tell him." So the officer took him to the commander and said, "Paul the prisoner asked me to bring this young man to you, for he has something to tell you." The commander then took him by the hand, and after he had led him aside, asked him privately, "What is it that you have to tell me?" He said, "The Jews have agreed to ask you to bring Paul down to-morrow to the council pretending that they wish to examine his case more carefully. Now do not grant their request, for more than forty are lying in wait for him and have solemnly promised not to eat or drink until they have killed him. Even now they are ready, only waiting for your consent."

The commander let the young man go, bidding him, "Tell no one that you have informed me of this." Then he called two officers and said, "Get ready two hundred soldiers, seventy horsemen, and two hundred spearmen by nine o'clock to-night to go as far as Cæsarea." He also told them to provide horses for Paul to ride on so as to bring him safely to Felix the governor. So the soldiers, as they had been commanded, took Paul and brought him by night to Antipatris. The next day the soldiers returned to the castle, leaving the horsemen to go on with him. When they reached Cæsarea they brought Paul to the governor.

A PRISONER WHO PREACHED TO HIS JUDGES

Some days later Felix came with his wife, Drusilla, who was a Jewess, and sent for Paul and heard what he had to say about the faith in Christ Jesus. But when he talked about upright living, self-control, and the future judgment, Felix became alarmed and said, "You may go for the present; when I can find a convenient time I will send for you." All the time Felix was hoping that Paul would give him money, and for this reason he sent for him often and talked with him. But after two years had passed Felix was succeeded by Porcius Festus, who, wishing to win the favor of the Jews, left Paul in prison.

After Festus had been governor three days, he went up from Cæsarea to Jerusalem. Then the high priests and the leading Jews made charges to him against Paul and begged Festus as a favor to send and have him brought to Jerusalem, for they were plotting to kill him on the way. But Festus answered that Paul would be kept in Cæsarea and that he himself was going there in a short time. "Therefore," he said, "let your leading men go down with me and let them charge the man with whatever crime he has committed." After staying eight or ten days in Jerusalem, Festus went back to Cæsarea.

The next day Festus took his place on the judgment seat and ordered Paul to be brought in. When he came, the Jews who had come down from Jerusalem surrounded him and brought many and serious charges against him which they were unable to prove. In answer to them Paul said, "I have committed no crime against the Jewish law or the Temple or the Emperor."

But as Festus wished to win the favor of the Jews, he interrupted Paul with the question, "Are you willing to go up to Jerusalem and be tried before me there on these charges?" Paul said, "I am standing before the Emperor's judgment seat, where I ought to be tried. I have done no wrong to the Jews, as you yourself very well know. If, however, I have broken the law or have committed any crime that deserves death, I am willing to die. But if there is no truth in any of their charges against me, then no man has the right to give me up to them. I appeal to the Emperor!" After talking with the council, Festus answered, "You have appealed to the Emperor, to the Emperor you shall go."

After some days had passed, King Agrippa and Bernice arrived at Cæsarea to visit Festus. As they remained there for many days, Festus laid Paul's case before the King. Agrippa said to Festus, "I should like to hear the man myself." "You shall hear him to-morrow," said Festus. So the next day Agrippa and Bernice came with much pomp to the court-room, along with the commanders and the leading citizens; and at the command of Festus Paul was brought in. And Agrippa said to Paul, "You have permission to speak for yourself." At this Paul stretched out his hand and began his defense: "I am happy, King Agrippa, that I am permitted this day to defend myself before you against all the charges which the Jews have brought against me, for you know all about the Jewish customs and questions. So I beg of you to hear me patiently. All the Jews know the kind of life I lived from my youth, among the men of my own nation and in Jerusalem. As a Pharisee I lived according to the standards of the strictest party in our religion. I indeed believed that it was my duty to do all in my power to oppose the cause of Jesus of Nazareth. This I did in Jerusalem. With authority from the high priests, I put many of Jesus' followers in prison. When they were put to death, I voted against them. In all the synagogues I often punished them and tried to make them speak against the name of Jesus, and in my insane fury I followed them even to distant cities.

"When I was travelling to Damascus on this business, with written authority from the high priests, I saw, on the road in the middle of the day, a light from heaven, more dazzling than the glare of the sun, shining around me and those who were travelling with me. We fell to the ground, and I heard a voice say to me in Hebrew, 'Saul, Saul, why do you persecute me? It is hard for you to kick against the goads.' I asked, 'Who art thou, Lord?' and the Lord answered, 'I am Jesus whom you are persecuting. Rise and stand on your feet, for I have appeared to you so as to appoint you my servant and a witness to what you have seen and to the things that I will show you. I chose you from the Jews and the other peoples to whom I am sending you to open their eyes, that they may turn from darkness to light, from the power of Satan to God, so that they may receive forgiveness of their sins and a place among those who have given themselves to me because they believe in me.' O, King Agrippa, I have not disobeyed the heavenly vision. To this day I have had the help of God and have stood firm and, without adding a single word beyond what the prophets and Moses said would take place, I have testified to small and great how the Christ was to suffer and to be the first to rise from the dead and to proclaim the message of light not only to the Jews but to all peoples."

When Paul said these words in his defense, Festus cried, "Paul, you are mad! Your great learning is driving you insane!" But Paul said, "I am not insane, most noble Festus, but I am speaking the sober truth. For the King, to whom I can speak freely, knows about these things, for I am sure that nothing escaped his notice, since this has not been done in a corner. King Agrippa, do you believe the prophets? I know that you do." But Agrippa said to Paul, "With but little persuasion you would make me a Christian!" Paul replied, "I pray to God that whether with little or much not only you but also every one who hears me this day may become a Christian as I am."

Then the King, together with the governor and Bernice and those who had been sitting with them, rose and, when they were alone, they said to one another, "This man has done nothing deserving of death or of imprisonment." And Agrippa said to Festus, "This man might have been set free if he had not appealed to the Emperor."

PAUL'S SHIPWRECK

When it was decided that we were to sail for Italy, Paul and certain other prisoners were placed in charge of Julius, an officer of the Emperor's regiment. We went on board a ship which was bound for the seaports of Asia Minor. The next day we stopped at Sidon, where Julius very kindly allowed Paul to visit his friends and be entertained by them. Putting to sea again, we sailed under the lee of Cyprus, for the wind was against us. Then after sailing past Cilicia and Pamphylia, we came to Myra in Lycia. There the officer found a ship from Alexandria bound for Italy and put us on board. For many days we made slow progress and it was only with great difficulty that we arrived off Cnidus. Then as the wind was against us we sailed under the lee of Crete, opposite Cape Salmone, and after coasting along with great difficulty came to a place called Fair Havens, near the city of Lasea.

As our voyage had taken some time and sailing had become dangerous (for it was already late in October) Paul warned them, saying, "Men, I see that the voyage will mean serious injury and loss, not only to the cargo and the ship but also to our own lives." But the officer paid more attention to the captain and to the owner of the ship than to what Paul said. As the harbor was not a good one in which to winter, most of them advised putting to sea from there, hoping that they could get to Phœnix (a safe harbor) so as to winter there.

When a light breeze from the south sprang up, they thought that they could reach Phœnix. So, after lifting up the anchor, they ran close along the coast of Crete: but in a short time a tempestuous wind called a "Northeaster" beat down upon them. The ship was caught in it and was unable to keep her head to the wind. So we had to give up and run before it. Running under the lee of a little island called Cauda, we managed with difficulty to haul in the ship's boat. After lifting it on board, the men used ropes to bind together the lower part of the ship. As they were afraid that they might run ashore on the African quicksands, they lowered the sail and drifted. But as we were being terribly battered by the storm, the next day the men began to throw out the ship's cargo. On the third day, with their own hands, they threw overboard the ship's tackle. For many days neither sun nor stars were seen and the heavy gale continued, so at last all hope that we would be saved was given up.

When the men had gone a long time without food, Paul stood up among them and said, "Men, you should have listened to me and not have sailed from Crete, then you would have escaped this hardship and loss. But now I urge you to cheer up, for there will be no loss of life, but only of the ship. For last night, an angel of the God, to whom I belong and whom I serve, stood beside me and said, 'Paul, have no fear, for you must stand before the Emperor. God also has granted you the lives of all of those who sail with you.' Therefore, men, cheer up! For I believe God and am sure that it will be just as I have been told; but we will be wrecked on a certain island."

When the fourteenth night came and we were drifting about in the Adriatic Sea, the sailors about midnight thought that they were nearing land. So they took soundings and found one hundred and twenty feet of water; and when they had gone a little farther they found ninety feet. Fearing that we might be wrecked on the rocks, they threw out four anchors from the stern and prayed for daylight. The sailors wanted to escape from the ship and had even lowered the boat into the sea, pretending that they were going to lay out anchors from the bow, when Paul said to the officer and to the soldiers, "Unless these men stay on board, we cannot be saved." Then the soldiers cut the ropes which held the boat and let her drift away.

Just before daybreak Paul begged them all to take some food, and said, "This is the fourteenth day that you have been constantly on the watch, taking little or no food. Take some food, then, I beg of you, because this will keep you alive, for not one of you will lose even a hair from his head." When he had said this, he took bread, and gave thanks to God before them all, and he broke the bread and began to eat it. Then they were all cheered up and they also took food. There were about seventy-six of us on board. When they had eaten enough, they lightened the ship by throwing the wheat into the sea.

When it was day they could not make out what land it was; but they saw an inlet with a sandy beach on which they planned, if possible, to run the ship ashore. So cutting away the anchors they left them in the sea. At the same time unloosing the ropes which tied the rudders and hoisting the foresail to the wind, they made for the beach; but coming to a place where two seas met they ran the ship aground. The prow stuck fast and could not be moved, but the stern began to break up under the beating of the waves. Then the soldiers wanted to kill the prisoners for fear some of them might swim ashore and escape. But as the officer wished to save Paul, he kept them from carrying out their plan, and ordered those who could swim to jump overboard and get first to the land; the rest followed, some on planks and some on other things from the ship. In this way they all got safely to land. After we had escaped we found that the island was called Malta.

THE END OF PAUL'S LONG JOURNEY

The natives of the island showed us unusual kindness, for they kindled a fire and welcomed us all, because of the pouring rain and the cold. Now Paul had gathered a bundle of sticks and was laying it on the fire when a poisonous snake, driven out by the heat, fastened itself on his hand. When the natives saw the creature hanging from his hand, they said to one another, "Surely this man is a murderer; although he has been saved from the sea, justice will not let him live." But he shook the creature off into the fire and was unhurt. They expected that he would at once swell up or fall down dead; but after they had waited a long time and saw that no harm had come to him, they changed their minds and said that he was a god.

On the part of the island where we landed there was an estate belonging to Publius the governor. He welcomed us and entertained us most generously for three days. Now it happened that the father of Publius was lying ill from fever and dysentery. So Paul went to see him and prayed, and, laying his hands on him, cured him. After this the other sick people in the island came and were cured. They also presented us with many gifts, and when we sailed, they put on board everything we needed.

After three months we set sail on a ship from Alexandria called "The Twin Brothers," which had wintered at the island. We put in at Syracuse, and remained there three days. Then we tacked around and came to Rhegium. The next day a south wind sprang up, and we arrived on the following day at Puteoli, where we found Christian brothers who asked us to spend a week with them, and so we reached Rome.

The brothers there, when they heard about us, came as far as the Market of Appius and the Three Taverns to meet us. When Paul saw them, he thanked God and took courage.

When we reached Rome, Paul received permission to live by himself with the soldier who guarded him. Three days after our arrival, Paul invited the leading Jews to meet him and said to them, "Brothers, although I have done nothing against the Jewish law or the customs of our fathers, I was handed over as a prisoner from Jerusalem to the Romans, who, when they had examined me, were willing to set me free, for I was innocent of any crime deserving of death. But the Jews objected; so I was forced to appeal to the Emperor—not that I had any charge to bring against my nation. This is the reason why I have asked to see you and speak with you, for it is on account of Israel's hope that I am bound."

They replied, "We have received no letters about you from Judea nor has any brother come here with any bad report or statement about you;

but we wish to hear from you what you teach, for we know that the Christian sect is everywhere attacked." So they fixed a day and many of them came to him to the place where he was staying. Then from morning until evening he explained his teachings and told them about the Kingdom of God, and tried to lead them to believe in Jesus by proofs from the law of Moses and from the prophets. Some believed what he taught and others would not believe. When they could not agree among themselves they departed after Paul had said to them: "Well did the Holy Spirit say to your fathers through the prophet Isaiah:

"'Go to this people and say to them,
You will hear and hear but never understand,
You will look and look but never see;
For this people's mind is stupid,
And their ears are too dull to hear,
And they have closed their eyes,
To keep them from seeing with their eyes,
Or hearing with their ears,
Or understanding with their minds,
And turning back that I may heal them.'

"Remember, therefore, that this opportunity to be saved, that God has given you, is given to other peoples, and they will listen to it."

For two whole years Paul lived in his own hired house. He welcomed all who came to him, and preached the Kingdom of God, and taught about the Lord Jesus Christ openly, no one stopping him.

PAUL'S LAST WORDS TO HIS FRIENDS

Paul and Timothy, servants of Jesus Christ, to all of Christ's followers in Philippi, as well as to the ministers and their helpers. May love and peace be granted you from God our Father and the Lord Jesus Christ.

I hope, if the Lord permits, to send Timothy to you before long, that I too may be cheered by news about you. I have no other like him who will take a genuine interest in you, for every one is looking out for his own interests, not those of Christ Jesus. But you know how Timothy has stood the test, how like a son working with his father he has served with me in spreading the good news. So I hope to send him shortly, as soon as I see how it will go with me; though I am confident, if the Lord permits, that I myself will come to you before long.

Rejoice in the Lord always. Again, I say, rejoice. Let all know that you are patient. Do not be anxious, but always make your requests known to God in earnest prayer and thanksgiving; so shall the peace of God, which is beyond all human understanding, keep guard over your hearts and your minds in union with Christ Jesus.

Finally, brothers, whatever is true, whatever is honorable, whatever is just, whatever is pure, whatever is lovely, whatever is of good report, if there be any virtue or anything worthy of praise, consider the value of these things. Practise also what you have learned and received and heard and seen in me, and then the God of peace will be with you.

It is a great joy to me as a Christian brother to know that you are again thoughtful of me. Indeed, you have always been thoughtful, but you did not have an opportunity to show it. Not that I speak of want, for I have learned, wherever I am, to be content. I know how to live simply; I know, too, how to live in prosperity. I have learned in all things the secret of being content, both when I have plenty and when I am hungry, when I am in prosperity and when I am in want. I can do everything through Christ who strengthens me.

But you acted nobly in sharing my affliction. Even when I was in Thessalonica, more than once you sent money for my needs. It is not the gift I am seeking, but the growing reward that is to your credit! I have enough of everything, and more than enough. I am fully supplied by what I received from you through Epaphroditus. It is like fragrant incense, a sacrifice acceptable and well pleasing to God. My God will supply your every need out of his glorious wealth in Christ Jesus. Now to God our Father be glory forever and ever.

Already my life-blood is poured out and the time for me to go has come. I have fought the good fight. I have finished the course, I have kept the faith. Now the crown for right-doing awaits me which the Lord, the righteous judge, will give to me on that day, and not to me only but to all who have loved and longed for his appearing.

THE MEANING OF FAITH

Now faith is the confidence that we shall receive the things for which we hope, the proof of the reality of things we do not see. It was because of their faith that the men of old were approved by God. Through faith we know that the universe was made perfect by God's command and that what is seen was made out of what is not seen.

Through faith Abel offered God a better sacrifice than Cain, and so received the assurance that he was an upright man, for God approved of his gifts. Though dead, yet because of his faith he still speaks.

Through faith Noah, having been told by God about things still unseen, in reverent obedience built an ark to save his household; and in doing so he condemned the world and became heir to the righteousness that comes through faith.

Through faith Abraham obeyed, when he was called to go to the place which he was to receive as an inheritance, and he set out, not knowing where he was going. Through faith he made his home in the land that had been promised to him as in a foreign country, living in tents with Isaac and Jacob, who shared the same promise with him.

Through faith Abraham, when put to the test, sacrificed Isaac, yes, was ready to sacrifice his only son, although he had received the divine promises and had been told, "It is through Isaac that your family name will be carried on," for he believed that God was able to raise men even from the dead. In a sense, he did receive his son back from the dead.

Through faith, also, Isaac blessed Jacob and Esau, even telling them of things to come. Through faith Joseph, as he was dying, thought of the time when the Israelites would go out of Egypt and gave orders about his own bones.

Through faith Moses was hidden by his parents for three months after birth because they saw that the child was beautiful, and because they did not fear the King's command.

Through faith Moses, when he had grown up, refused to be called the son of Pharaoh's daughter, choosing rather to share ill treatment with God's people than to enjoy for a short time the pleasures of sin.

Through faith he left Egypt, not because he feared the King's wrath, but like one who saw the Unseen King he never faltered.

Through faith the Israelites crossed the Red Sea as through dry land, and when the Egyptians tried to cross they were drowned.

What more shall I say? For time would fail me if I tried to tell of Gideon and Barak and Samson and Jephthah, of David and Samuel and the prophets—they who through faith conquered kingdoms, did righteous acts, received promises from God, closed the mouths of lions, quenched the power of fire, escaped the edge of the sword, in the hour of weakness were made strong, who proved mighty in war and put to flight foreign armies!

Women received back their dead restored to life. Others were tortured, refusing release, that they might be raised to a better life. Others stood the test of taunts and blows, yes, even chains and imprisonment. They were stoned, they were burned, they were sawn in two, they were killed by the sword. They went about in skins of sheep and goats, lacking everything, persecuted, ill treated (men of whom the world was unworthy), wandering in lonely places and among the hills, in caves and in holes in the ground. Through faith they all won God's approval, but they did not receive the promised blessing, for God had planned something better for us, that apart from us they should not be made perfect.

Therefore, surrounded as we are by such a host of witnesses, let us also lay aside every handicap and the sin which clings so closely to us, and let us run with patience the race that is set before us, fixing our eyes on Jesus, the Author and Perfecter of faith, who for the joy which lay before him, patiently endured the cross, thinking nothing of the shame, and is now seated at the right hand of the throne of God.

THE IMPORTANCE OF DOING WHAT IS RIGHT

James, a servant of God and of the Lord Jesus Christ, to the true Israelites scattered among the nations, greeting.

My brothers, regard it as only a cause for joy, when you fall into all kinds of trials. Know that the testing of your faith develops patience; but let your patience do its perfect work, that you may be perfect and complete, lacking nothing.

If any of you lacks wisdom, let him ask God who gives to all men liberally and without reproach, and it will be given him. Only let him ask with faith, with never a doubt, for the man who doubts is like the waves of the sea, driven and tossed by the winds. Let not such a man think, that a half-hearted man, unstable in all his ways, will receive anything from God.

Blessed is the man who endures temptation; for when he has stood the test, he will receive the crown of life which is promised to all who love God. Let no man say when he is being tempted: "I am tempted of God," for God cannot be tempted to do wrong, and he himself tempts no one. Each man is tempted when he is drawn away and enticed by his own evil desire. Then the evil desire gives birth to sin, and sin, when it is full grown, brings death.

Do not be deceived, my beloved brothers. Every good gift and every perfect blessing comes from above, from the Father who is the source of all light, with whom there is no variation nor shadow made by turning.

Know this, my beloved brothers: let every one be quick to hear, slow to speak, slow to be angry, for a man's anger does not promote the righteousness that God approves. So putting away all that is vile and wicked, receive with humility the message of truth that is deeply rooted in you which is able to save your soul.

Do what that message commands, and do not merely hear it and deceive yourselves. For if any one hears that message but does not do as it commands, he is like a man who looks at his own face in the mirror, for he looks at himself, goes off, and at once forgets what he is like. But he who looks into the perfect law of freedom and continues to do so, not merely listening to it and then forgetting, but does real work, will be blessed in what he does.

If any one thinks he is religious and does not bridle his tongue but deceives himself, his religion is worthless. Religion that is pure and stainless, such as God our Father approves is this: to visit the orphans and widows in their trouble and to keep oneself clean from the evil of the world.

THE LOVE THAT MAKES MEN BROTHERS

We know what love is by this, that Christ laid down his life for us; so we ought to lay down our lives for the brothers. But if any one has this world's wealth and looks on while his brother is in need and shows no sympathy for him, how can the love of God remain in him? My dear children, let us show our love not with words nor with our lips only, but by deeds and sincerity.

Beloved, let us love one another, for love comes from God and every one who loves is a child of God and knows God. He who loves not man does not know God, for God is love. God showed his love for us, for he sent his only Son into the world that through him we might have life. His love is shown in this, not that we loved God, but that he loved us and sent his Son to be the sacrifice that made possible the forgiveness of our sins.

Beloved, if God so loved us, then we ought also to love one another. No one has ever seen God; but if we love one another, then God lives in us, and the love which is his is made perfect in us. By this we know that we shall live in him and he in us, because he has given us a portion of his own Spirit, and we have seen and bear witness that the Father has sent the Son to be the Saviour of the world.

We ourselves know and believe in the love that God has for us. God is love, and he whose life is full of love lives in God and God lives in him. In love there is no fear, but perfect love drives out all fear, for fear means punishment, and he who fears has not become perfect in love. We love him because he first loved us.

If any one says, "I love God," and yet hates his brother, he is a liar; for he who does not love his brother whom he has seen, cannot love God whom he has not seen. And we have this command from him, that he who loves God is to love his brother also.

Every one who believes that Jesus is the Christ, is a child of God; and every one who loves the Father, loves every child of his. We know that we are his children when we love him and obey his commands, for love for God means obeying his commands. And his commands are not hard to follow, for whatever is born of God conquers the world. And our faith is the power that conquers the world. Who is the conqueror of the world but he who believes that Jesus is the Son of God?

Now the confidence that we have in God is this, that he listens to us whenever we ask anything in accordance with his will. And if we know that he listens to whatever we ask, we know that we have the things which we have asked from him.

THE GLORY AND HONOR THAT JESUS HAS WON

John, to the seven churches in the province of Asia. May a blessing be granted you and peace from him who is and was and ever shall be, and from the seven spirits before his throne, and from Jesus Christ who is the faithful witness, the first of the dead to be restored to life and the ruler of the kings of the earth.

I, John, your brother who shares with you the distress, the dominion, and the patient endurance which we have through our faith in Jesus, found myself in the island called Patmos because of my loyalty to God's message and to the testimony of Jesus. On the Lord's Day I was under the influence of the Spirit, and I heard behind me a loud voice like a trumpet calling, "Write what you see in a book and send it to the seven churches."

Then I turned to see whose voice it was that spoke to me; and on turning around I saw seven golden lamps and in the midst of the lamps One, like a Son of man, clothed in a long robe and with a belt of gold around his breast. His head and hair were white as wool, white as snow; his eyes were like a flame of fire, his feet were like burnished bronze melted in the furnace, his voice was like the sound of many waters. In his right hand he held seven stars; a sharp, two-edged sword came out from his mouth, and his face shone like the sun in its full strength.

When I saw him, I fell at his feet as if I were dead; but he laid his hand on me and said: "Do not be afraid; I am the First and the Last, I was dead but now I am alive for evermore. Therefore write down what you see and what is now and shall be hereafter. As for the secret meaning of the seven stars which you have seen in my right hand and of the seven golden lamps—the seven stars represent the angels of the seven churches, and the seven lamps represent the seven churches."

After this I saw a door opening into heaven. And the voice like a trumpet which I had previously heard talking with me, said: "Come up here, and I will show you what must take place in the future." At once I found myself under the influence of the Spirit, and there stood a throne in heaven whose appearance was like a diamond or ruby and One was sitting on the throne. Encircling the throne was a rainbow which looked like an emerald; also around the throne were twenty-four other thrones, and on these thrones were seated twenty-four elders, clothed in white robes with golden crowns upon their heads. From the throne came flashes of lightning and voices and peals of thunder, while in front of the throne were seven flaming torches, which were the seven spirits of God.

In front of the throne there appeared to be a sea of glass which looked like crystal. In the space about the throne and encircling it were four living creatures, and day and night they never ceased chanting:

> "Holy, holy, holy is the Lord God Almighty,
> Who was and is and ever shall be."

Then I saw, lying at the right hand of him who was seated on the throne, a book sealed with seven seals. And I saw a mighty angel saying in a loud voice: "Who is worthy to open the book and to break its seals?" But no one was worthy, either in heaven or on the earth or under the earth to open the book or look into it. So I began to weep bitterly because no one was found worthy to open the book or look into it; but one of the elders said to me: "Weep not; behold the Lion of Judah's tribe, the Scion of David—he has won the right to open the book and its seven seals."

Then in the space between the throne and the four living creatures I saw a Lamb standing among the elders. He seemed to have been slain, but he had seven horns and seven eyes. And he came and took the book out of the right hand of him who was seated on the throne. And when he took the book, the four living creatures and the twenty-four elders fell down before the Lamb, each with his harp, and with his golden bowls full of incense which represent the prayers of the saints. They were singing this new song: "Thou art worthy to take the book and open its seals, for thou wast slain and by thy blood thou hast ransomed for God, men from every tribe and language and people and nation; thou hast made them a kingdom and priests for our God, and they shall reign on the earth."

And I looked and I heard the voice of many angels around the throne and of the living creatures and of the elders, numbering ten thousand times ten thousand and thousands of thousands, crying aloud, "Worthy is the Lamb that has been slain to receive power and wealth and wisdom and might and honor and glory and blessing." And I heard every creature in heaven and on earth and under the earth and in the sea and all things that are in them crying, "To him who is seated on the throne and to the Lamb, be blessing and honor and praise and dominion forever and ever!" Then the four living creatures said, "Amen," and the elders fell down and worshipped.

THE REWARD OF THE FAITHFUL

After that I saw a vast host, which no one could count, from every nation and tribe and people and language, standing before the throne and before the Lamb, dressed in white robes, with palm branches in their hands. They cried aloud, "It is to our God who is seated on the throne and to the Lamb that we owe our salvation!"

Then one of the elders turned to me and said: "Who are these dressed in white robes, and from where have they come?" I said to him, "You know, my lord." So he told me, "These are the people who have come through the great persecution and have washed their robes and made them white in the blood of the Lamb. For this reason they are now before the throne of God and serve him day and night within his temple. He who is sitting on the throne will shelter them; never again will they be hungry or thirsty; never again will the sun or any scorching heat smite them, for the Lamb that stands in the space before the throne will be their shepherd and will guide them to fountains of living water; and God will wipe away all tears from their eyes."

Then I saw another angel flying in mid-heaven with an eternal message of good news for the inhabitants of the earth, for every nation, tribe, language, and people. He cried aloud, "Revere God, praise him, for the hour of his judgment has come. Worship him who made heaven and earth, the sea and the flowing springs."

And I saw a great white throne and One seated upon it from whose presence earth and sky fled away, and were no more to be found. And I saw the dead, the great and the lowly, standing before the throne. Then books were opened; also another book, the Book of Life, was opened, and the dead were judged by what was written in the books according to what they had done. The sea gave up its dead, and Death and the Abode of the Departed also gave up their dead, and all were judged according to what they had done.

THE NEW HEAVEN ON EARTH

Then I saw a new heaven and a new earth, for the first heaven and the first earth had passed away and the sea was no more. And I saw the Holy City, the New Jerusalem, coming down from God out of heaven, all ready like a bride attired to meet her husband. I also heard a loud voice from the throne which said: "Behold, God's dwelling-place is with men, and he shall dwell among men, and they shall be his people, and God himself will be with them. He shall wipe away every tear from their eyes, and death shall be no more; neither shall there be mourning nor wailing, nor pain, for the first things have passed away." The One who is seated on the throne said: "Behold, I make all things new!" And he added, "Write this: 'These words are faithful and true.'"

And he said to me, "All is over! I am the Alpha and the Omega, the First and the Last. I will let the thirsty drink freely of the fountain of life. He who conquers shall obtain this, and I will be his God and he shall be my son."

The city has no need of the sun nor of the moon to give it light, for the glory of God illumines it and its light is the Lamb. Its gates shall never be shut by day and there shall be no night there. Nothing unclean nor any one who does what is shameful or deceitful shall enter it, but only those whose names are written in the Lamb's book of life.

Then he showed me the river of the water of life, clear as crystal, flowing through the streets of the city from the throne of God and the Lamb. On both sides of the river grew the tree that gives life, which bore twelve kinds of fruit and yielded its fruit each month; and the leaves of the tree were for the healing of the nations.

And the throne of God and the Lamb will be in that city; and his servants will serve and worship him; they will see his face and his name will be on their foreheads. There will be no more night there, and they will have no need of the light of lamp or sun, for the Lord God will be their light, and they will reign forever and ever.

And he said to me: "Do not keep secret the prophetic words contained in this book, for the time of their fulfilment is near. He who does wrong, let him still do wrong, and he who is filthy, let him still be filthy, and he who is righteous, let him still do right, and he who is pure, let him still be pure. Know that I am coming quickly and I will bring my rewards to repay each for what he has done. I am the Alpha and the Omega, the First and the Last, the Beginning and the End. Blessed are those who wash their robes, that they may have a right to the tree of life and to go through the gates into the city.

"I, Jesus, have sent my angel to testify to you for the churches. I am the Scion and Offspring of David, the bright, the Morning Star. Both the Spirit and the Bride say, 'Come.' Let him who hears say, 'Come,' let him who is thirsty come, and whoever will, let him take of the water of life freely."

"For God so loved the world, that he gave his only begotten Son, that whosoever believeth in him, should not perish, but have everlasting life."

Lightning Source UK Ltd.
Milton Keynes UK
UKHW021826160223
417092UK00004B/366

9 781015 818811